THE GREAT BRITISH
BAKE OFF

THE GREAT BRITISH
BAKE OFF

HOW TO TURN EVERYDAY BAKES INTO
SHOWSTOPPERS

Linda Collister

TECHNICAL CHALLENGE & SIGNATURE BAKE RECIPES BY
MARY BERRY AND PAUL HOLLYWOOD

BBC
BOOKS

This book is published to accompany the television series entitled *The Great British Bake Off*, first broadcast on BBC TWO in 2012.

Executive Producers: Anna Beattie, Kieran Smith
Series Editor: Amanda Westwood
Series Director: Scott Tankard
Producers: Tallulah Radulah-Scott, Samantha Beddoes
Production Manager: Nina Richards
Head of Production: Letty Kavanagh
BBC Commissioning Executive: Emma Willis

10 9 8 7 6 5 4
Published in 2012 by BBC Books, an imprint of Ebury Publishing. A Random House Group Company

Technical Challenges by Mary Berry and Paul Hollywood
Text by Linda Collister
Text and recipes © Love Productions 2012
Photography and design © Woodlands Books Ltd 2012
Love Productions has asserted its right to be identified as the author of this Work in accordance with the Copyright, Designs and Patents Act 1988

The Random House Group Limited Reg. No. 954009

Addresses for companies within the Random House Group can be found at www.randomhouse.co.uk

A CIP catalogue record for this book is available from the British Library.

ISBN 978 1 849 90463 6

The Random House Group Limited supports the Forest Stewardship Council® (FSC®), the leading international forest certification organisation. All our titles that are printed on Greenpeace approved FSC® certified paper carry the FSC® logo. Our paper procurement policy can be found at www.randomhouse.co.uk/environment

Commissioning Editor: Muna Reyal
Project Editor: Laura Higginson
Editor: Norma MacMillan
Designer: Smith & Gilmour
Photographer: Dan Jones
Food Stylist: Kim Morphew
Food Styling Ideas: Lucy Knox
Props Stylist: Polly Webb-Wilson
Production: Helen Everson

Colour origination by Altaimage, London
Printed and bound in the UK by Butler Tanner and Dennis Ltd

To buy books by your favourite authors and register for offers, visit www.randomhouse.co.uk

CONTENTS

INTRODUCTION

Food is part of the joy of life and *The Great British Bake Off* celebrates this in every aspect of baking. Baking evokes many happy emotions. We bake for our friends and family as well as for ourselves and we feel an enormous sense of pride in our achievements. Secretly we also want to show off, to earn praise and make people happy.

So this time, we have devoted our book to the Showstopper Challenge – the part of the show where the bakers endeavour to create beautiful tasting, but also beautiful-looking bakes.

LOOKING GOOD

You don't have to be an experienced baker to create culinary masterpieces. We have plenty of ideas for you, including familiar recipes for a sponge cake or shortbread that are transformed into Showstopping creations with the use of layering, a simple stencil, clever pastry finish or an easy chocolate ribbon.

You will also find Mary and Paul's own foolproof recipes, and the best (and most imaginative) ones made by the bakers during the competition – we guarantee you'll be amazed! Never have bakes been so closely examined. This year the judges devoted as much attention to the inside as to the outside. You could feel the anticipation building as they first cut open the bake and then check the slice for taste, texture and appearance. It certainly galvanized the bakers into perfecting their techniques and devising even more new ideas so as not to disappoint Mary and Paul.

OUR SHOWSTOPPING CHALLENGES

Each chapter begins with a Showstopping Challenge that takes its inspiration from the competition, but we've designed three stages for each of our Challenges. First we give a basic recipe. This can be made into three recipes from easy to a real culinary work out. We will show you how the simplest ingredients and straightforward recipes can be baked into memorable creations, tasting and looking truly fabulous, whatever your budget, skill level or time constraints.

Throughout each chapter are lots of tips to add a touch of magic to your recipe as well as some Showstopping Techniques to add a professional-style finish. Please do feel free to mix and match these with different recipes as your own creative muse takes you – we've added suggestions at the end of many recipes.

THE RECIPES

This year's bakers certainly got into the spirit of celebration from the very first round, producing some jaw-dropping cakes with hidden depths that tasted as spectacular as they appeared; you can see them in the first chapter where you can try your hand at making a hidden-picture cake too.

Our biscuits are simple recipes, but with standout design, whether in the shaping or decorating. You can decide what goes into them – your favourite chocolate, loads of nuts or nut-free – and what decoration, from the elaborate to a simple dusting of icing sugar or cocoa. Our Showstopping Challenge is gingerbread – easy enough for children to melt, mix, roll out and cut shapes, but also fun to build a gingerbread cottage as the centrepiece for a party.

Paul's technical challenge in chapter three is sure to raise many a cheer – doughnuts! The perfect jam-filled doughnut is one of life's simple pleasures so do have a go, you won't be disappointed. The Showstopping Challenge is brioche, an egg and butter-rich yeast dough that may take longer to make than a simple plain loaf, but bakes to a delicate and rich-tasting (almost cake-like) crumb. But there are easy recipes too: sandwiches made out of real home-made bread are so much better than anything out of a plastic bag so there's a range of loaves for slicing, rolls for filling, flatbreads for dipping; breads for every occasion.

There's an old saying: what you eat every day is a meal, but what you eat when you celebrate is a feast. Chapter Four is all about pies, from Paul's perfectly filled and beautifully layered hand-raised pies and luxurious beef wellington to the best of American pies. They form our Showstopping Challenge – a combination of excellent pastry (and no soggy bottoms!), a perfectly judged filling and appealing finish.

There's a large chapter devoted to Desserts with some real show-off recipes for special occasions as well as some pretty twists on old favourites. Meringues are centre-stage throughout – they make the perfect basis for so many desserts and

they're cheap! Mary's challenge was Crème Caramel, tricky to make perfectly, still much-loved. Of course we haven't forgotten the chocoholics with the Best of the Bake Off – an impressive flourless torte – and a great-looking striped cheesecake. These aren't difficult recipes, but just require a little time to make – and are well worth it.

Like most good meals we're ending with a pudding. We thought it would be fun to see how the bakers tackled strudel, so that's our Showstopping Challenge. The winning Sticky Toffee Sponge Pudding is also here, along with Mary's version of the Queen of Puddings. Paul has chosen a Rum Babas as his Challenge and, as you might expect, he shared his views on this most classic of French pudding-cakes.

It's been a great competition with so much for the judges to laugh (and cry about)! So, let's celebrate our love of baking with the three Graces associated with festivals – splendour, mirth and cheerfulness.

Happy Baking!

Cakes

THE MOMENT WHEN YOU REVEAL your cake is always accompanied by joy and excitement. It doesn't matter if your cake is simply or extravagantly decorated, it will make an impression. But as Mary and Paul emphasize as Bake Off judges, the cake must also taste as good as it looks.

This chapter will give you some mouth-watering recipes, but also lots of presentation and styling ideas. Some add an instant, easy touch of magic to a familiar or simple bake; others need a bit more skill or time – perfect for special occasions, when you really want to show off, celebrate and impress.

We begin this chapter with a basic Sponge Cake Mix that can be transformed into three very different and striking cakes. The bakers from this year's series were asked to create a Hidden Picture Cake as their first Showstopper Challenge. Not only did the decoration have to be delicious and the sponge perfectly baked, but when cut open, a picture was revealed. So we have created a showstopping Champagne Heart Cake for you to try. This recipe is not for beginners, so there is also a much simpler challenge – a beautiful Mocha Marbled Loaf Cake. Using the same basic sponge mix, there is also a Chess Cake, which though not technically difficult, does require a bit more time.

Two of the bakers' amazing creations are also included here. One reveals a Union flag when cut open, perfect for a summer of British celebrations (see page 24). The other takes inspiration from a well-known nursery rhyme and reveals a blackbird nipping the nose off an unfortunate maid (see page 28)!

Decorations have evolved too – who would have thought that you could find edible gold leaf, spray-on shimmer and glitter-dust in a supermarket along with the huge range of ready-made sugar paste and chocolate decorations available online? It's never been easier to transform a simple cake into a stunning showpiece.

Since there are no set rules, and even the most arcane ingredients are easy to find, you can be as creative as your imagination and skills will allow.

Use the recipes in this chapter as foundations to develop your own ideas. Mix and match the toppings, icings, frostings and decorations, and experiment with shape, colour scheme and presentation. There are also showstopping (but surprisingly simple) techniques to help you ice cupcakes, cover and stack cakes, create chocolate ribbons and make edible bunting, plus lots of helpful tips in the recipes themselves.

Basic principles and techniques don't change. There is no doubt that the best ingredients give the best results. The flavour of good butter will always be unbeatable, and the same goes for proper vanilla extract and good-quality cooking chocolate.

The right equipment is important, too. A large free-standing mixer is needed for big quantities, but a hand-held mixer will be fine for small, light mixtures and for whisking cream and egg whites. Using the right tin or tins is crucial: if you don't have, or can't borrow, the right shape or size, you can usually hire tins from local cookware shops. (Do remember, though, that they need to fit into your oven.)

Cake-decorating equipment can be found everywhere these days – even supermarkets sell disposable piping bags, tubes, spatulas and off-set palette knives, wire racks, icings, food colouring pastes and ready-made decorations. If you're contemplating a large decorating project, you might find it useful to have a turntable.

DON'T FORGET

To make a creamed cake mixture really light, all the ingredients should be at room temperature, so take butter and eggs from the fridge well ahead of time.

Always use the type of sugar specified in the recipe. Caster sugar is the best for creamed sponges – it has finer grains than granulated sugar and quickly breaks down as it is beaten with butter; granulated takes much longer to dissolve and often gives a speckled finish to the tops of cakes. Brown muscovado sugars (light and dark) add a slight toffee flavour and colour to cake mixes, but they also make them slightly more moist and heavy. Icing sugar – very finely powdered white or light golden unrefined sugar – dissolves readily and can be used for piped or spreadable icings, frostings and toppings like glacé icing, royal icing, buttercream and butter icing.

Ready-made sugar mixes are very useful and make good storecupboard standbys. Fondant Icing sugar is a combination of icing sugar and dried glucose syrup that you mix with water or juice to make a glossy, satiny icing that's slightly more substantial than glacé icing, or a dough-like modelling paste for edible decorations. Royal Icing sugar is a combination of icing sugar and dried egg white. Mixed with water, it makes a thick icing that can be left white or coloured and then spread, swirled, 'peaked' or piped. It dries hard, but adding a drop of glycerine prevents it from becoming brittle.

Prepare your baking tins well by brushing them inside with melted butter and lining with baking paper (or according to the recipe instructions). This will prevent sticking and scorching.

Make sure you use chocolate suitable for baking and that it contains the right cocoa content required by the recipe.

Presentation really counts. A cake set on a large decorative platter, a wooden board (well scrubbed and lightly oiled), a piece of slate or a glass tray can look dramatic against the right background.

For a really quick but dramatic effect a simple dusting of icing sugar or cocoa powder, or cocoa mixed with edible gold powder (see page 310), will look stunning.

Fabric or ribbons and fresh flowers (see page 310 for information on edible flowers) will immediately add glamour to any bake.

Sponge Mix

250g unsalted butter, softened
250g caster sugar
1 teaspoon vanilla extract
4 large free-range eggs, at room
   temperature, beaten
250g self-raising flour
good pinch of salt
2–3 tablespoons milk (optional)

1 Put the butter into a large mixing bowl or the bowl of a large free-standing electric mixer. Beat with a wooden spoon or electric mixer until very creamy. Gradually beat in the sugar, then the vanilla. Keep beating (scrape down the sides of the bowl from time to time) until the mixture is much lighter in colour and very fluffy in texture.

2 Gradually add the eggs, a tablespoon at a time, beating well after each addition. Add 1 tablespoon of the weighed flour with each of the last 2 portions of egg, to prevent the mixture from curdling.

3 Sift the remaining flour and the salt into the bowl and gently fold in using a large metal spoon until you can no longer see any streaks or specks of flour. At this point the sponge mixture can be flavoured and/or coloured. If leaving plain, without additions, fold in enough milk so the mixture is just soft enough to drop off a wooden spoon when lightly shaken. The sponge mixture is now ready to use.

In the first episode of series 3, the bakers were challenged to create showstopping hidden picture cakes – beautifully decorated sponges that, once sliced, revealed pictures sculpted out of coloured sponge and butter icing! The following three recipes, made using this creamed sponge mixture, draw inspiration from the Showstopper Challenge. Keep it simple and finish with butter icing, ganache or jam and cream (see below), or use the mixture to make a marbled loaf cake, a chess-inspired layer cake or a summery, Champagne-iced cake with a hidden surprise. This sponge recipe makes enough mixture for a large loaf cake OR a large round cake OR a 3-layer sandwich cake.

TO MAKE A SIMPLE ROUND CAKE OR LOAF CAKE

Preheat the oven to 180°C/350°F/gas 4. Transfer the sponge mixture to a greased and lined 26 × 7.5cm loaf tin or 20.5cm round deep cake tin. Bake for 60–70 minutes until golden brown and springy when lightly pressed in the centre. Turn out onto a wire rack and leave to cool. When cold, turn out and cover with Butter Icing (see page 305) or Ganache (see page 306).

Alternatively, divide among 3 × 20.5cm tins that have been greased and lined on the base with baking paper. Bake for 20–25 minutes and then sandwich the layers together with jam and whipped cream.

Mocha Marbled Loaf Cake

MAKES 1 quantity Sponge Mix
(see page 15)

CAKE **FOR THE CHOCOLATE MIXTURE**
30g cocoa powder
2 tablespoons milk

FOR THE COFFEE MIXTURE
1 tablespoon instant coffee powder
or granules, dissolved in
1 tablespoon boiling water
2 tablespoons dark chocolate chips

TO FINISH
1 quantity White Chocolate Ganache
(see page 306)
cocoa powder

1 x 900g loaf tin, about 26 x 12.5 x 7.5cm,
greased and lined with a long strip of
greaseproof paper

In this first Showstopping Challenge every slice of this cake looks and tastes slightly different. The rich chocolate and coffee sponge mixture is studded with chocolate chips and topped with a rich, creamy white chocolate ganache. Dust with cocoa powder for a cappuccino-style finish.

1 Preheat the oven to 180°C/350°F/gas 4. Make up the Sponge Mix using the method on page 15. Transfer half the sponge mixture to a second mixing bowl. Sift the cocoa powder onto one portion of sponge mixture, add the milk and fold in until completely mixed, with no streaks of cocoa.

2 Add the cooled coffee liquid to the other portion of sponge mixture and stir until thoroughly combined.

3 Spoon both mixtures into the prepared tin, adding a spoonful of each alternately and scattering the chocolate chips over the mixtures between each layer. Gently bang the tin on the worktop to eliminate any pockets of air, and gently smooth the surface. Marble the 2 mixtures by drawing a chopstick or round-bladed knife through them, swirling it.

4 Bake for 1–1 ¼ hours until the cake is well risen and a cocktail stick inserted into the centre comes out clean. Set the tin on a wire rack and cool for 20 minutes, then carefully turn out the cake and leave to cool completely. Store in an airtight container and eat within 5 days.

5 Spread the white chocolate ganache over the top of the cake and finish with a dusting of cocoa powder.

TIP
Keep it simple and finish the un-iced loaf cake with a dusting of icing sugar and then cocoa powder.

Chess Cake

MAKES **1 CAKE**

FOR THE SPONGE MIXTURE
350g unsalted butter, softened
350g caster sugar
1 teaspoon vanilla extract
6 large free-range eggs, at room
    temperature, beaten
350g self-raising flour
good pinch of salt
50g cocoa powder (for the chocolate
    mixture)
4 tablespoons milk

FOR THE WHITE CHOCOLATE GANACHE
175g good-quality white chocolate,
    finely chopped
125ml whipping cream
50g unsalted butter

FOR THE DARK CHOCOLATE GANACHE
300g dark chocolate (70% cocoa
    solids), finely chopped
300ml whipping cream

TO FINISH
100g dark chocolate
    (70% cocoa solids)

2 piping bags, each fitted with a
    1.5cm plain tube; 3 x 20.5cm
    sandwich tins, greased and the
    base lined with baking paper

This 3-layer cake is not as complicated to make as it might look. When cut, black and white squares (of vanilla and dark chocolate sponge) are revealed – just like a chessboard.

1 Preheat the oven to 180°C/350°F/gas 4. Make up the sponge mixture using the method on page 15 (the method is the same; the quantities are different). Transfer half to another mixing bowl. Sift the cocoa into one bowl and add 2 tablespoons of the milk; fold in until completely blended. Spoon into one of the piping bags. Fold the rest of the milk into the mixture in the second bowl, then spoon into the other piping bag.

2 Pipe a ring of chocolate mixture around the inside edge of one tin. Then pipe a ring of vanilla mixture inside the chocolate ring. Repeat with alternate dark and white rings until the tin is filled. Repeat with a second tin. For the third tin start with an outer ring of vanilla mixture, so this tin is filled in the reverse of the other 2 tins.

3 Bake for 22–25 minutes until well risen and springy when lightly pressed in the centre. Run a knife around the inside of each tin to loosen the sponge, then turn out onto a wire rack and leave to cool completely.

4 Make up the white chocolate and dark chocolate ganaches (see page 306 for the method). Set one sponge with a chocolate outer ring upside down on a cake board or platter. Spread with half of the white ganache, then set the sponge with the vanilla outer ring on top. Spread with the remaining white ganache. Top with the third sponge, browned top uppermost. Cover the top and sides of the cake with dark chocolate ganache. Leave in a cool spot (not the fridge) to set.

5 Temper the chocolate (see page 308), then use to make large chocolate curls (see page 309). Arrange on top of the cake, handling the chocolate as little as possible. Store in an airtight container and eat within 4 days.

TIP
You could also finish this cake with ready-made chocolate decorations, a sprinkling of edible glitter or edible gold shimmer spray (see page 310).

Champagne Heart Cake

MAKES

CAKE

FOR THE SPONGE

1 quantity Sponge Mix
    (see page 15), made with
    1 tablespoon milk

FOR THE FILLING AND TOPPING

220g marzipan
claret or dark pink edible food
    colouring paste
5 quantities Buttercream
    (see page 305), flavoured with
    5 tablespoons Champagne at
    room temperature

1 x 20cm Victoria Surprise loose-based
    cake set (2 sandwich tins with a
    raised base), greased, lined and
    floured (see below); a large piping
    bag fitted with a 6-point tube

The trickiest of the cake challenges, this recipe requires a steady hand to mould the marzipan hidden heart and pipe the buttercream roses over the cake, but the result is stunning. The sponges are baked in sandwich tins fitted with raised loose bases to allow for a deeper filling.

1 Preheat the oven to 180°C/350°F/gas 4. Use butter to grease the tins, then line the centre raised portion of each base with a disc of baking paper. Grease this, then dust the insides of the tins with a little flour so they have a fine coating (shake out the excess).

2 Make up the Sponge Mix following the method on page 15 – using less milk means it will be slighter stiffer than the basic sponge. Spoon into the prepared tins and spread evenly. Bake for 30–35 minutes until golden brown and springy when lightly pressed in the centre – the sponge will have risen right up to the top of each tin. Remove from the oven and allow to cool and firm up for 5 minutes, then carefully turn out onto a wire rack and leave to cool completely.

3 To make the heart-shaped marzipan decoration, knead the marzipan in your hands just to soften, then work in the colouring paste, one drop at a time (use a cocktail stick dipped in the tiny pot) until you get an even dark pink colour. Using your hands roll the marzipan to a sausage shape 36cm long and 2cm wide. Make a deep groove along the length of the sausage using a skewer. Gently open out the cut surfaces to make a V shape. Turn the sausage over and mould the upper side to a distinct point, so it looks like an upside-down V. Cut a sliver off one end of the sausage to check that the cross-section really does look heart-shaped. If not, mould and sculpt the marzipan a bit more. Form the sausage into a ring and press the ends firmly together. Set aside, uncovered, to firm up a bit while making the buttercream.

4 Make up the buttercream, gradually adding the Champagne with the butter (you may find it easier to make the mixture in 2 or 3 batches unless you are using a large free-standing electric mixer).

5 To assemble the cake, set one sponge layer on a cake board so the surface with the hollow is uppermost. Spread enough buttercream in the hollow so it almost fills it. Set the marzipan ring on the filling so the grooved side is uppermost, and gently press down a little way into the buttercream. Spoon a little more buttercream into the centre of the marzipan ring and around the outside of it so the filling is level with the rim of the sponge – the marzipan ring will be slightly taller.

6 Spread the hollow in the other sponge with buttercream to almost fill, then carefully invert it over the bottom sponge and gently press the 2 sponges together. Spread a thin layer of buttercream over the top and sides of the cake to cover completely. Chill the cake, uncovered, for 5 minutes so it just firms up.

7 Fill the piping bag with buttercream. Pipe large rose-like swirls all over the top and sides of the cake – the easiest way to pipe this type of swirl is to work from the centre of each rosette and pipe outwards so the ends are tucked under and are not visible. Pipe the swirls slightly overlapping – they don't have to be even in shape or size. If you make a mistake simply scrape off the swirl and start again.

8 Return the cake to the fridge, uncovered, to firm up for about 2 hours. Then place it in a cake box and keep in the fridge or at cool room temperature – the cake cuts best the day after it is assembled. Eat within 3 days and serve at room temperature.

TO MAKE THE CAKE USING 2 CONVENTIONAL SANDWICH TINS

Make up the sponge and bake as above using 2 conventional 20.5cm sandwich tins. Once the cake is completely cold you can 'carve' out the centre ready for the filling. The main problem with the carving technique is crumbs – it is hard to achieve complete neatness; for the best results wrap the cold sponges and leave overnight to firm up before starting work. Set a small plate 17cm across in the middle of the underside of one sponge. With the tip of a small sharp knife, score a deep line around the plate. Lift off the plate, then remove a disc of sponge 1cm deep (and 17cm across) – a serrated curved grapefruit knife is useful here. Don't worry if you can't remove the disc in one whole piece (you won't need it), but make sure the hollow has straight sides and is uniform in shape. Use your hand to press any loose crumbs back in place. Repeat with the second sponge, then assemble the cake and finish as before.

Jubilee Cake

MAKES

1 CAKE

FOR THE SPONGE
700g unsalted butter, softened
700g caster sugar
12 large free-range eggs, at room
    temperature, beaten
4 teaspoons vanilla extract
700g plain flour
3 tablespoons baking powder
about 125ml milk, at room
    temperature
navy and ruby edible food
    colouring gels

FOR THE BUTTER ICING
375g icing sugar, sifted
120g unsalted butter, at room
    temperature
2 ½ tablespoons milk
½ teaspoon vanilla extract

TO FINISH
1 x 370g jar apricot jam,
    sieved and warmed
1kg marzipan
1kg white ready-to-roll sugar
    paste icing
250g Royal Icing sugar

3 brownie pans or cake tins, 30 x 20 x
    5cm, greased and the base lined with
    baking paper; a piping bag fitted with
    a 2mm tube

A glorious sponge cake that cuts into slices revealing the Union flag. The pattern is assembled like a jig-saw and each section needs to be cut precisely so it all fits together neatly. It's much easier if the cakes are made a day or so before they are cut.

1 Preheat the oven to 180°C/350°F/gas 4. Unless you have a large free-standing electric mixer it will be easier to make the sponge mixture in 2–3 batches. Beat the butter and sugar together with an electric mixer until creamy. Gradually beat in the eggs, followed by the vanilla. Sift the flour and baking powder, then add to the mixture in 2 batches, beating on low speed. Add the milk and fold in using a large metal spoon.

2 Weigh 350g of the mixture and put into another bowl. Tint it a deep red. Transfer to one of the prepared tins and spread evenly – the mixture will be about 1cm deep. Bake for about 15 minutes until a cocktail stick inserted into the centre comes out clean. Leave in the tin for 5 minutes, then turn out onto a wire rack to cool completely.

Recipe continues overleaf

3 Colour the rest of the sponge mixture navy blue, then divide between the remaining 2 tins, spreading evenly; the mixture should be about 3cm deep. Bake for 30–40 minutes until a cocktail stick inserted into the centre of each sponge comes out clean, then cool as before. If possible, wrap the cooled sponges in foil or clingfilm and leave for a day before assembling the cake.

4 Make the butter icing by beating the ingredients together until very smooth and spreadable; add more milk if necessary. Cover and keep at room temperature.

5 Carefully trim the blue sponges so they are exactly 3.5cm high. From each blue sponge cut 2 strips exactly 6cm wide and 30cm long (you will have cake left over). Using an electric carving knife or a bread knife, cut each blue strip diagonally and lengthways to make 2 long triangular pieces of sponge 6cm wide × 3.5cm high: to make your diagonal cut, start from the top right-hand edge of the strip and slice down to the bottom left-hand edge.

6 Trim the red sponge, if necessary, so it is 1cm high. Cut the red sponge into 3 strips: 2 strips each 3.5cm wide and 30cm long, and the third piece 13cm wide and 30cm long.

7 Spread a thin layer of butter icing over the centre of a large rectangular cake board to anchor the sponge, then start to build – see the photo for guidance here (if in doubt do a dry run without the butter icing to make sure it all fits in place). Set a blue triangle on the board, 6cm side down, with the 3.5cm side close to the centre. Spread a thin layer of butter icing on the sloping top cut surface. Spread both sides of one of the thin strips of red sponge with butter icing and set it upright against the 3.5cm side of the blue triangle. Set another blue triangle against the red strip on the other side of it and spread its sloping side with butter icing. Invert 2 more blue triangles on top of the 2 already on the board and press them all gently together.

8 Spread the top surface of the assembled cake with a thin layer of butter icing, then set the wide strip of red sponge on top to cover it and press down gently. Spread this red sponge with butter icing, then repeat the pattern on top using the remaining blue triangles and red strip. Looked at from the end, you will see a Union flag design. Press everything together gently with your hands, then trim with a long knife to make sure the sides are straight. Brush off loose crumbs.

9 Brush the warm jam over the cake. Roll out the marzipan to a rectangle large enough to cover the cake, then carefully drape it over the cake and smooth it with the palm of your hand (see page 59 for help with covering a cake with marzipan and sugar paste icing). Trim off the excess marzipan.

10 Roll out the icing in the same way. Lightly brush the marzipan with cooled boiled water so it is just sticky, then cover with the white icing as you did for the marzipan. Press it on gently, then smooth and polish it with the palm of your hand. Trim off the excess.

11 Mark a cross of St George on the icing using a pin and a ruler to prick out straight lines. Mix the Royal Icing sugar with about 2 tablespoons water to make a smooth icing that can be piped. Tint it red. Spoon into the piping bag and pipe decorative swirls within the marked lines of the cross. Leave to set before cutting.

Chocolate & Praline Traybake

MAKES

20–24

PIECES

FOR THE SPONGE
200g blanched hazelnuts
6 large free-range egg whites,
   at room temperature
150g plain flour
good pinch of salt
50g cocoa powder
200g icing sugar
50g light brown muscovado sugar
175g unsalted butter, melted and cooled

FOR THE PRALINE
100g caster sugar
100g hazelnuts

FOR THE TOPPING
200g dark chocolate (70% cocoa
   solids), broken up
25g butter, diced

1 traybake tin or cake tin, 25.5 x 20.5 x
   5cm (or a shallow 23cm square tin),
   greased and the base lined with
   baking paper

1 Preheat the oven to 150°C/300°F/gas 2. To make the sponge, put the hazelnuts into a baking dish or small tin and toast in the oven for 12–14 minutes until lightly browned. Leave to cool, then grind in a food-processor to a fairly fine powder (not quite as fine as ground almonds). Set aside until needed. Turn up the oven to 180°C/350°F/gas 4.

2 Put the egg whites into a large bowl and whisk until they stand in soft peaks. Sift the flour, salt, cocoa powder, icing sugar and muscovado sugar into the bowl. Add the ground hazelnuts and the cool but still liquid butter. Using a large metal spoon,

The rich flavour of toasted hazelnuts in this easy sponge gets better and better as it matures, so plan to bake this a day or so in advance of eating. Each square is topped with chocolate and decorated with a chunk of praline (caramelized hazelnuts).

carefully fold all the ingredients together thoroughly.

3 Spoon into the prepared tin and spread evenly. Bake for 18–20 minutes until just firm to the touch. Transfer the tin to a wire rack and leave to cool before removing the sponge from the tin.

4 Make up the praline (see page 311). When firm, break into 20–24 chunks.

5 Melt the chocolate with the butter (see page 308). Cool, stirring every now and then, for 15–30 minutes until the chocolate is starting to thicken. Spread the chocolate over the sponge and swirl with the back of a metal kitchen spoon. Cut into squares. Stick a chunk of praline into each square, then leave to set. Store in an airtight container and eat within 5 days.

TIP
For a more colourful praline, sprinkle 1 ½ teaspoons each crystallized violet and rose fragments onto the well-oiled tray before pouring on the praline.

Sixpence Cake

MAKES

1 CAKE

FOR THE MAIN SPONGE CAKE
350g unsalted butter, softened
350g caster sugar
finely grated zest of 1 ½ lemons
6 large free-range eggs, at room
    temperature, beaten
350g self-raising flour

FOR THE COLOURED SPONGES
115g unsalted butter, softened
115g caster sugar
finely grated zest of ½ lemon
2 large free-range eggs, at room
    temperature, beaten
115g self-raising flour
black, yellow and flesh-pink edible
    food colouring gels

FOR THE BUTTER ICING
250g unsalted butter, softened
350g icing sugar, sifted
finely grated zest and juice of
    1 lemon

TO FINISH
1kg white ready-to-roll sugar
    paste icing
brown edible food colouring gel
gold lustre (optional, see page 310)

2–4 x 20.5cm sandwich tins, greased
    and the base lined with baking paper
    (see recipe); a small ovenproof bowl
    (base about 7cm, top about 10cm),
    greased; a muffin tray and 2 paper
    muffin cases; 5cm and 3cm round
    biscuit cutters

This witty cake, based on the nursery rhyme about blackbirds baked in a pie, is made from 4 sponge cakes sandwiched with butter icing. When cut you'll see the blackbird with the maid's nose in its beak. The 'pie' top and dish are actually painted sugar paste icing.

1 Preheat the oven to 180°C/350°F/gas 4. Make the main sponge layers first. Using an electric mixer, beat the butter with the sugar and lemon zest until light. Gradually add the eggs, beating well after each addition. Fold in the flour with a large spoon. Divide into 4 and use one portion for each sponge layer: spoon into the tins and spread evenly, then bake for 25 minutes until firm when gently pressed in the centre. Cool on a wire rack. (If you don't have 4 tins, bake in batches; use a cold, clean prepared tin for each sponge.)

2 Make the mixture for the coloured sponges in the same way. Transfer half to another mixing bowl and colour it black. Spoon into the prepared ovenproof bowl and bake for about 30 minutes until firm when gently pressed. Leave for 5 minutes, then carefully unmould onto a wire rack and cool.

3 Divide the rest of the cake mixture in half. Colour one portion yellow (for the bird's beak) and the other portion flesh-pink (for the maid's nose). Spoon each into a muffin case (set in the muffin tray). Bake for about 25 minutes until firm. Leave to cool, in the muffin cases, on a wire rack.

4 Make the butter icing by beating all the ingredients together until smooth, very soft and spreadable. Set aside, but do not chill.

5 To assemble the 'pie', set one sponge layer upside down on the worktop and spread butter icing over the top surface. Use the

Recipe continues overleaf

5cm cutter to cut a round hole from the centre of 2 of the other sponge layers, then sandwich them together with butter icing. Set on top of the first sponge layer.

6 Peel off the paper cases from the 2 small coloured sponges and turn them upside down on the worktop. With the 5cm cutter, cut a cylinder 5cm deep from the centre of the yellow sponge. Use the 3cm cutter to remove the centre of this cylinder – do not cut all the way through; the sponge should look like a bucket. With the 3cm cutter, cut a cylinder 5cm deep from the small pink sponge and gently press it into the hole in the yellow cylinder; trim level. Spread butter icing over the outside of this new cylinder, then press it upside down (yellow side up) into the hole in the 2 sponge layers so all you can see is a yellow disc in the middle. Spread with butter icing.

7 Trim the top of the black sponge to make it 3cm high and 10cm across the top (flat) surface. This will be the blackbird. Stand the ovenproof bowl in the centre of the fourth sponge layer and cut around it to remove a disc the size of the black sponge. Spread the curved, rounded surfaces of the black sponge with butter icing and press into the hole. Set on top of the other 3 sponge layers.

8 Trim the lower 2 layers of sponge so the sides slope in to resemble a pie dish. Trim the edges of the top sponge layer so the middle looks rounded like a well-filled pie. Spread butter icing over the whole cake.

9 Dust a spotlessly clean worktop with icing sugar, then roll out 250g of the sugar paste icing to a strip about 7 × 64cm. Measure the height of the 'pie dish' section of the cake,

and the circumference, then cut the strip to fit exactly. Gently press the strip around the lower part of the cake, moulding and smoothing it so it looks like a china pie dish.

10 Colour 120g of the sugar paste icing a creamy brown, then roll with your hands to a sausage about 1cm thick and 64cm long. Press this around the top edge of the cake – this is the 'pastry rim' – so it covers the top edge of the white icing strip.

11 Colour 500g of the remaining sugar paste icing a beige-brown colour – this will be the 'pastry lid' – then roll out to a large circle the thickness of a pound coin. Cut out a neat circle 25cm across and set on top of the cake. Press onto the rim to seal, then crimp or flute (see page 218 for details on crimping and fluting). Cut a cross in the centre of the 'pie crust' and lift back the 4 flaps.

12 Colour about 15g sugar paste icing black, then roll into 3 balls – these are the blackbirds' heads. Colour another 15g icing yellow and shape into 3 cones; attach one to each ball (use a dab of water if necessary). Snip the cones with scissors to make the beaks. Set in the exposed centre of the cake.

13 To finish the decoration, paint the edges of the pie with brown colouring to give a 'baked pie' effect, and add dots of colour as pattern for the 'pie dish'. Colour a little more icing black, roll out thinly and cut 5 leaf shapes (see page 311); slice the edges using a sharp knife or scalpel to resemble feathers, then add to the pie. Use the rest of the icing to make the king's moneybag, coins, the maid's clothes' peg and the queen's slice of bread and honey, colouring and painting them, if you like, to serve with the cake.

Chocolate Cake Pops

MAKES 10

125g un-iced chocolate cake
50g ground almonds
80g dark, milk or white chocolate,
  broken up

TO DECORATE

100g dark, milk or white chocolate,
  broken up
sprinkles or other edible
  decorations

10 x 15cm lolly (lollipop) sticks or
  cake pop sticks; a tray lined with
  baking paper; a block of polystyrene
  or an egg box

Use the chocolate sponge from Chocolate and Praline Traybake to make these little cakes, or any leftover sponge cake. Simply dip the cake pops in melted chocolate and decorate with sprinkles of your choice, choosing colours to match the occasion – such as white chocolate and multicoloured sprinkles for a children's party or dark chocolate plus edible gold leaf for a glam treat. Or see the Tip for a Christmas idea.

1 Break up the cake and put into the bowl of a food-processor with the ground almonds. Pulse a couple of times until the cake looks like coarse breadcrumbs, all about the same size. Tip into a mixing bowl.

2 Melt the chocolate (see page 308). Work all but 1 teaspoon of it into the cake crumbs until the mixture sticks together. Form into 10 walnut-sized balls.

3 Dip one end of a lolly stick into a little of the reserved melted chocolate and push it into the centre of a cake ball. Set upside down on the tray. Repeat with the rest of the cake balls.

4 When ready to decorate the pops, melt the chocolate as before. Have sprinkles ready in a small saucer. Spoon the melted chocolate over each cake pop, holding it upright and quickly turning it so that excess chocolate drips back into the bowl and not down the stick. Dip in sprinkles to coat all over (or add other decorations – see below), then push the base of the stick into the block of polystyrene and leave to set. Best eaten with 24 hours.

TIP

If making these at Christmas time, you can decorate milk chocolate-covered cake pops as Christmas puddings. Spoon a little melted white chocolate over the top of each pop to represent 'brandy sauce'. Colour a little marzipan green and red; roll out the green marzipan and cut into holly leaves using a fluted pastry cutter, and make tiny holly berries with the red marzipan. Set these on top of the white chocolate before it sets completely.

Chocolate Truffle Cake

MAKES

FOR THE SPONGE

170g dark chocolate (70% cocoa
   solids), broken up
125g unsalted butter, diced
6 large free-range eggs, at room
   temperature
150g caster sugar
1 teaspoon vanilla extract
150g self-raising flour
good pinch of salt

FOR THE GANACHE FILLING

100g dark chocolate (70% cocoa
   solids), finely chopped
100ml whipping cream

FOR THE GANACHE COVERING

150g dark chocolate (70% cocoa
   solids), finely chopped
150ml whipping cream

TO DECORATE

fresh rose petals

1 x 20cm round deep cake tin,
   greased and lined

This recipe makes one very rich 20cm round chocolate cake, but the sponge mixture is firm enough to make a 3-tiered cake, perfect for a celebration, as shown opposite. Turn to page 313 for quantities to make this 3-tiered cake and page 34 for how to stack your cakes. This cake keeps well and slices very neatly.

1 Preheat the oven to 160°C/325°F/gas 3. To make the sponge, melt the chocolate with the butter (see page 308). Leave to cool.

2 Break the eggs into a mixing bowl and whisk with an electric mixer until frothy. Add the sugar and vanilla and whisk at high speed for about 5 minutes until the mixture becomes very thick, pale and mousse-like, and the whisk leaves a ribbon-like trail.

3 Using a large metal spoon, fold in the melted chocolate mixture. Sift the flour and salt onto the mixture and carefully fold in. When you can no longer see any specks or streaks of flour, transfer the mixture to the prepared tin and spread evenly. Bake for about 1 hour until a skewer inserted into the centre of the cake comes out clean. Cool in the tin for 10 minutes, then carefully turn out onto a wire rack and leave to cool completely.

4 Make up the ganache filling with the dark chocolate and cream (see page 306 for the method). Split the cold sponge cake in half horizontally and sandwich the 2 layers back together with the ganache. Place the cake, upside down (the flat base of the cake is a smoother surface to ice), on a wire rack set over a plate to catch drips and leave until the filling is firm.

5 Make up the ganache for the covering and leave to thicken slightly before using. (Turn to page 34 for guidance on how to ice with ganache.)Decorate with rose petals just before serving, or with chocolate leaves or curls if you prefer (see pages 275 and 309).

6 Keep the cake in a cool place, not the fridge – the cake would become quite solid due to all the chocolate, and liable to condensation when removed. At its best 1–2 days after baking, the cake can be kept for up to 5 days.

Icing & Stacking a Cake

EQUIPMENT NEEDED
baking paper
medium palette knife
cake boards the same diameter as each
   cake tier (if making a stacked cake)
4 wooden dowels for each cake tier
   (if making a stacked cake)
sharp kitchen scissors or a small
   sharp knife

1 To ice a single-tiered cake with ganache (or similar thick icing), the ganache should be thick enough to hold its shape and have a spreading consistency. Set the cake on a sheet of baking paper.

2 Start by covering the top. Put a large dollop of ganache on the cake and spread it out thickly with the palette knife (photo 1).

3 Continue to add ganache, spreading it out gently to make a smooth, even layer over the surface and pushing the icing to the edges of the cake using a round, sweeping motion (photo 2).

4 Completely cover the sides of the cake with ganache, making sure there are no gaps around the base and that the top edge is straight (photo 3). Hold the palette knife vertically and smooth the icing, moving the knife left and right around the cake. Leave to set.

5 If you are making a stacked cake, first set each cake tier on a cake board of the exact same size. Then cover the cakes with ganache as explained above, but just with a thin layer at this stage, to contain the crumbs. Set aside to allow the ganache to firm up.

6 Set the largest cake tier on a large board, platter or cake stand. Make 4 evenly spaced marks about 6cm in from the edge of the cake. At each of the marks, push a wooden dowel gently down through the cake all the way to the cake board. Then carefully remove the dowels and cut to size so they are exactly the same height as the cake.

7 Replace the cut dowels into the cake – they will support the weight of the upper tier(s). Position the next cake tier, on its board, on top of the large cake, making sure it is centred (photo 4). Check the cake from several angles to be sure the tiers are straight.

8 If you are making a 3-tier cake, insert wooden dowels into the middle cake tier, as described in steps 6 and 7, before placing it on the bottom tier. Then put the top cake tier in position.

9 Ice the entire stacked cake with a final layer of ganache, covering the cake boards and smoothing any finger marks or dents.

Pear Upside-down Cake

MAKES

CAKE

FOR THE TOPPING
75g pecan nut halves
100g salted butter, thickly sliced
100g dark brown sugar
2–3 lumps stem ginger, finely
   chopped, plus 1 ½ tablespoons
   syrup from the jar
3–4 ripe but firm William's pears

FOR THE CAKE
115g unsalted butter, softened
170g caster sugar
2 large free-range eggs, at room
   temperature, beaten
175g plain flour
1 ½ teaspoons baking powder
¼ teaspoon salt
¼–½ teaspoon ground ginger
125ml milk
1 ½ teaspoons vanilla extract
2–3 lumps stem ginger, drained
   and finely chopped

FOR THE CREAM
225ml double cream, well chilled
25g icing sugar, sifted
1 tablespoon Poire William

1 x 22–23cm deep cake tin
   (not loose-based)

A very light and pretty sponge studded with chunks of fiery stem ginger and topped with a sticky fruit and nut mix. This is delicious served warm as a dessert, with double cream. The mix will look quite wet before it goes into the oven – this is how it should look so don't panic!

1 Preheat the oven to 180°C/350°F/gas 4. Toast the pecan nuts in the oven for 3–5 minutes until lightly browned. Cool, then chop fairly fine.

2 Spread the butter slices in the cake tin. Scatter the brown sugar on top and add the ginger syrup. Heat in the oven for 5 minutes. Stir the mixture, then return to the oven to heat for another 5 minutes until bubbling.

3 Meanwhile, peel 3 of the pears (you may not need the fourth), leaving them whole. Trim off the base and the stem ends, then cut across each pear to make circular slices about 1.25cm thick. Using an apple corer (or a small round cutter), cut out the cores to make neat circles in the centre of each slice. If necessary, slightly trim each slice of pear to make it circular (or use a round cutter).

4 Arrange large slices of pear over the bottom of the tin, on top of the sugar mixture (we used 11 slices). Then arrange halved (semi-circular) slices to fill in all the gaps. Fill all the centre holes with chopped pecan nuts. Scatter the stem ginger over the top.

5 To make the cake mixture, beat the butter and caster sugar together using a wooden spoon or electric mixer until light and fluffy. Gradually add the eggs, beating well after each addition. Sift the flour, baking powder, salt and ground ginger into another bowl. Add to the egg mixture in 3 batches alternately with the milk, beating on low speed if using a mixer. Add the vanilla and stem ginger and gently mix in.

6 Carefully spoon the cake mixture on top of the pears in the tin – try not to dislodge the nuts. Bake for about 50 minutes until golden brown and a skewer inserted into the centre of the cake comes out clean. Invert the tin onto a plate (take care as the topping can burn if it splashes your skin), then lift it off. Leave the cake to cool.

7 Whip the cream until soft peaks form. Add the icing sugar and Poire William and briefly whip to combine. Spoon into a bowl and serve with the cake.

Fondant Fancies

MAKES

16

FOR THE SPONGE
90g plain flour
10g cornflour
good pinch each of salt
    and ground cardamom
4 large free-range eggs
100g caster sugar
finely grated zest of 1 large
    unwaxed orange
50g unsalted butter, melted
    and cooled

TO FINISH
2 tablespoons no-peel marmalade
    or sieved marmalade
275g marzipan
icing sugar, for dusting
500g Fondant Icing sugar
about 6 tablespoons orange juice
edible sprinkles (optional)

1 x 20.5cm square cake tin, greased
    and the base lined with baking paper

TIP
If you don't fancy piping, top each
Fondant Fancy with a ready-made
sugar paste flower or similar edible
decoration. Mixing and matching
different decorations would look
good and can be themed for a
particular occasion.

A delicate, well-flavoured orange génoise sponge forms the base for these pretty little cakes, which are topped with marzipan and then flooded with a smooth, glossy orange icing. They can be simply finished with sprinkles or decorated with piped or feathered fondant, glacé or royal icing.

1 Preheat the oven to 180°C/350°F/gas 4. Sift the flour, cornflour, salt and cardamom onto a sheet of greaseproof paper; set aside.

2 Break the eggs into a large heatproof mixing bowl and whisk with an electric mixer until frothy. Set the bowl over a pan of simmering water (don't let the base of the bowl touch the water). Whisk in the sugar and orange zest, then whisk on high speed until the mixture is very thick, pale and mousse-like and leaves a ribbon-like trail when the whisk is lifted from the bowl. Remove the bowl from the pan, set on a damp cloth on a worktop (to prevent wobbling) and whisk for about 5 minutes until the mixture cools to room temperature.

3 Sift half of the flour mixture onto the egg mixture and dribble over half of the melted butter. Gently and carefully fold in using a large metal spoon. Repeat to add the rest of the flour and melted butter. As soon as you can no longer see any specks or streaks of flour, pour the mixture into the prepared tin and spread it evenly, easing it right into the corners.

4 Bake for 20–25 minutes until the sponge is a good golden brown and springy when lightly pressed in the centre. Run a round-bladed knife around the inside of the tin – the sponge will have started to shrink away from the sides – and leave for a minute to firm up, then turn out onto a wire rack and leave to cool.

5 Set the sponge upside down on a cutting board (the flat base makes a better surface for icing). Gently warm the marmalade, then brush over the top of the sponge.

6 Briefly knead the marzipan until pliable, then roll out on a worktop lightly dusted with icing sugar to a square to fit the sponge. Using the base of the cake tin as a guide, cut a neat square of marzipan and place on the sponge. Gently press the marzipan on with the palm of your hand, making the surface as smooth and even as possible. Leave to firm up for about 1 hour.

7 Cut the sponge into 16 even squares and set them, well apart, on a wire rack placed over a large plate or tray to catch the drips. Sift the Fondant Icing sugar into a bowl and stir in the orange juice to make a very smooth and glossy icing that will thickly coat the back of the spoon. Spoon the icing over each little cake so it floods over the surface and down the sides – use a palette knife to help the icing flow down the sides and completely coat them (use icing that drips onto the plate to fill in any gaps). If there are any air bubbles, prick them with a pin.

8 If decorating with sprinkles, add them while the icing is still wet; if adding piped decorations, wait until the icing sets. For piping, use any leftover fondant icing – or make up a little Glacé Icing (see page 306) or Royal Icing (see page 307), or use icing writing pens. Tint the icing with orange food colouring (to tie in with the orange cake), spoon into a small disposable piping bag and use to pipe zigzags on top of each cake. For feathering, pipe lines, or a spiral, on top of each cake, then quickly drag a cocktail stick through them (see page 69 for help with feathering). Once the icing is firm, set each cake in a pretty muffin case. Keep in an airtight container and eat within 24 hours.

TIP
You could also make 1 large cake instead of Fondant Fancies: set the whole marzipan-topped cake on the wire rack and flood with fondant icing (using 350g Fondant Icing sugar and about 4 tablespoons orange juice). To help the icing flow down the sides of the cake, lift up the rack and gently tap it down on the worktop.

Mini Mousse Cakes

MAKES

12

FOR THE SPONGE MIXTURE
75g plain flour
good pinch of salt
3 large free-range eggs
100g caster sugar
½ teaspoon vanilla extract
45g unsalted butter, melted
and cooled

FOR THE MOUSSE
5g leaf gelatine
250g hulled ripe strawberries
100g caster sugar
150ml whipping cream

TO FINISH
about 200g hulled ripe strawberries,
thinly sliced
12 tiny whole strawberries
50g white chocolate, melted (see
page 308)

1 x 12-cup loose-based mini sandwich
tin or non-stick muffin tray, greased;
a piping bag fitted with a star tube

You must use the most ripely sweet, perfumed berries for these little cakes, which are layered with strawberry mousse and topped with fresh berries dipped in white chocolate. The little cakes require a fair amount of work but are just sublime.

1 Preheat the oven to 180°C/350°F/gas 4. Make up the sponge mixture as given for Fondant Fancies on page 38, adding the flour and melted butter in one go. Spoon into the prepared cups so they are evenly filled.

2 Bake for about 15 minutes until golden brown, well risen and springy when lightly pressed. Cool for a couple of minutes, then carefully turn out onto a wire rack and leave to cool completely. When cold, split each cake horizontally in 3 using a serrated knife.

3 While the cakes are cooling make the mousse. Soak the leaves of gelatine in a bowl of cold water for about 5 minutes until softened. Put the strawberries and sugar into a food-processor and process to make a smooth purée. Measure 4 tablespoons of this purée into a small pan and heat until very hot but not boiling. Squeeze the gelatine to remove excess water, then stir into the hot purée until melted; cool, then stir into the rest of the strawberry purée.

4 Whip the cream until soft peaks will form. When the strawberry purée has thickened, but before it has started to set, fold in the whipped cream. Cover the bowl and chill for 5 minutes until the mousse is on the point of setting and can hold its own shape.

5 Spoon the mousse into the piping bag and pipe – or thickly spread – some mousse over the bottom layer of each little cake. Top with the middle layer and arrange a few slices of strawberry on this layer. Cover each cake with its top layer and add another layer of mousse. Chill until firm.

6 Meanwhile, make the decoration. Clean the small berries (don't wash if possible), leaving the green stalks intact. Dip the pointed ends of the berries in the melted chocolate, then leave to set on baking paper. Place one berry on the top of each tiny cake. Best eaten the same day.

MANISHA

Orange Praline Meringue Cake

FOR THE SPONGE
150g plain flour
15g cornflour
good pinch of salt
6 large free-range eggs
165g caster sugar
finely grated zest of 1 ½ large
    unwaxed oranges
75g unsalted butter, melted and cooled

FOR THE MERINGUE LAYERS
100g ground almonds
70g icing sugar
4 large free-range egg whites,
    at room temperature
70g caster sugar

FOR THE PRALINE
175g caster sugar
175g whole unblanched almonds

FOR THE BUTTER ICING
450g unsalted butter, softened
450g icing sugar, sifted
finely grated zest of 1 ½ unwaxed
    oranges
3 tablespoons Grand Marnier or
    orange juice

1 x 23cm round cake tin, greased and
    the base lined with baking paper;
    2 baking sheets; baking paper;
    a piping bag fitted with a star tube
    (optional)

A light génoise sponge, which is also used for Fondant Fancies and Mini Mousse Cakes, is perfect for more elaborate gâteaux. For this confection of beautifully contrasting textures and flavours, an orange sponge is layered with an orange and praline buttercream and crisp almond meringue discs.

1 Preheat the oven to 180°C/350°F/gas 4. Make up the sponge mixture as given for Fondant Fancies on page 38. Spread in the prepared tin and bake for 30–35 minutes until springy when pressed in the centre. Loosen in the tin and cool for 1 minute, then turn out onto a wire rack and leave to cool completely. Reduce the oven temperature to 150°C/300°F/gas 2.

2 Next make the meringue layers. Using the cake tin base, draw a circle on each of 2 sheets of baking paper; turn the paper over and lay on the baking sheets. Sift the ground almonds and icing sugar onto a sheet of greaseproof paper. Whisk the egg whites in a large bowl with an electric mixer until soft peaks will form. Whisk in the caster sugar, then continue whisking until the mixture stands in stiff peaks. Using a large metal spoon, fold in the almond mixture. Divide the meringue between the 2 prepared baking sheets and spread out to fill the drawn circles. Bake for about 1 ½ hours until crisp and dry. Leave to cool on a wire rack, then peel off the lining paper.

3 Make the praline (see page 311). When set, break up into pieces. Save a few of the best-looking pieces for the decoration, and put the rest into a food-processor. Process to make a coarse powder. Sieve the praline powder into a bowl; save the coarser, larger pieces of powder left in the sieve for coating the sides (about one-quarter) and use the fine powder for the butter icing.

4 To make the butter icing, beat the butter with an electric mixer until creamy. On slow speed, gradually beat in the icing sugar followed by the orange zest, orange liqueur or juice and the fine praline powder.

5 To assemble the cake, slice the sponge in half horizontally. Trim the meringue discs, if necessary, to the same size as the cake layers. Set one meringue disc on a serving plate and spread with a little butter icing. Place the top layer of sponge on top (save the base of the sponge, with its flat surface, for the top of the stacked cake). Spread the other meringue disc with butter icing and set it, icing side down, on the sponge layer. Spread the meringue with more butter icing, then top with the last sponge layer, cut side down.

6 Cover the top and sides of the cake with some of the remaining butter icing. Press the coarse praline powder onto the sides of the cake. Fill the piping bag with the remaining butter icing and pipe roses or rosettes on top of the cake (or make thick swirls of butter icing using a palette knife). Decorate with the reserved praline pieces. Leave the cake to stand for about 4 hours before cutting (the flavours will develop even more if the cake is left, carefully covered, at room temperature overnight). Best eaten within 2 days.

TIP

For even more glamour add a web of spun sugar to the cake right before serving – see how to make spun sugar on page 197.

Jewel Box Cake

MAKES

CAKE

FOR THE SPONGE
150g good-quality white chocolate,
   broken up
250g unsalted butter, softened
250g caster sugar
1 teaspoon vanilla extract
4 large free-range eggs, at room
   temperature, beaten
250g self-raising flour
good pinch of salt

FOR THE CHOCOLATE RIBBONS AND BOW
150g white chocolate, broken up
3 tablespoons liquid glucose

TO FINISH
about 4 tablespoons seedless
   raspberry jam, for brushing
500–600g small raspberries

1 x 20.5cm square deep cake tin,
   greased and lined

Looking as special as its name suggests, this is a square white chocolate sponge cake, completely covered with small raspberries and decorated with white chocolate ribbons, tied to look like a beautiful jewel box.

1 Preheat the oven to 180°C/350°F/gas 4. Melt the chocolate (see page 308). Leave to cool until needed.

2 Put the butter into a large mixing bowl and beat with an electric mixer until creamy. Gradually beat in the sugar, then add the vanilla and beat until the mixture is very light in colour and fluffy in texture, scraping down the bowl from time to time. Gradually add the eggs, beating well after each addition and adding a tablespoon of the weighed flour with the last portion of egg (to prevent curdling). Sift the rest of the flour and the salt into the bowl and fold in using a large metal spoon. Add the cooled white chocolate and fold in until all the ingredients are completely amalgamated.

3 Spoon the mixture into the prepared tin and spread evenly. Make a small hollow in the centre so the cake will rise evenly. Bake for about 1 hour until golden brown and just firm to the touch and a wooden cocktail stick inserted into the centre of the cake comes out clean. Leave to cool for about 15 minutes, then carefully remove from the tin and cool completely on a wire rack. Once cold the cake can be wrapped well and stored in an airtight container for a day before finishing.

4 When ready to finish, set the cake on a serving board or platter. Make the chocolate ribbons and bow (see page 46).

5 Gently warm the raspberry jam until melted. Brush over the top and sides of the cake, then gently press the ribbons onto the cake – across the top and down the sides – to resemble a parcel. Starting with the top of the cake, press the raspberries (pointed end up) onto the sponge in the squares between the ribbons, so the whole cake is covered, top and sides. Fix the chocolate bow in place with a dab of jam or chocolate. Serve the cake the same day.

Chocolate Ribbons & Bows

EQUIPMENT NEEDED
heatproof bowl and pan
rolling pin
ruler
large sharp knife
sharp kitchen scissors

1 Melt your chopped dark, milk or good-quality white chocolate (see page 308); remove the bowl from the pan and gently stir in liquid glucose (see recipe). Leave to thicken at room temperature. Once the mixture is firm and almost set, mould it into a ball with your hands. (Some types and brands of chocolate need to be chilled to firm up.)

2 Work and knead the mixture in your hands so it softens and becomes pliable and glossy (just like modelling clay or play-dough). As soon as it feels smooth, shape it into a sausage.

3 Set the sausage between 2 long pieces of baking paper and roll out into a long, flat sheet. Peel off the top piece of paper. To make the crossed ribbons for the Jewel Box Cake (see page 44), cut out 2 strips about 30 x 2.5cm, using a ruler and a long, sharp knife to get a straight, sharp edge.

If the ribbons feel very soft, firm up in the fridge for a few minutes. Attach the strips to your cake.

4 To make a bow, cut out 1 strip about 10 x 2.5cm, 2 strips 11 x 2.5cm and 2 strips about 14 x 2.5cm, cutting through the paper to leave the strips attached. Snip triangles out of one end of the 11cm strips using scissors, then rest the strips over a small paintbrush or similar implement to create a slight curve; these will be the bow ends.

5 With the paper side out, bend each 14cm strip into a bow loop and press the ends together. Then peel off the paper and position the ends of the loops so they are slightly overlapping; press gently together. Peel the paper from the 10cm strip, then wrap it around the centre of the loops in a ring to hide the join; press the ends of the bow ring to seal. Put all the shaped pieces in the fridge so they can firm up a bit.

6 Position the bow on top of the crossed ribbons on the cake, fixing in place with a dab of melted chocolate or jam if necessary. Reshape the loops and bow carefully until you are happy with the shape. Slot the bow ends under the loops and arrange over the cake.

English Summer Cupcakes

MAKES
12

FOR THE SPONGE MIXTURE
125g unsalted butter, softened
175g caster sugar
2 large free-range eggs, at room
    temperature
½ teaspoon vanilla extract
175g self-raising flour
good pinch of salt
3 tablespoons milk, at room
    temperature
100g hulled strawberries, cut into
    small pieces
1–2 tablespoons strawberry
    conserve

FOR THE FROSTING
125g unsalted butter, softened
250g full-fat cream cheese
½ teaspoon vanilla extract
275g icing sugar, sifted
strawberries, to decorate

1 x 12-hole muffin tray, lined with paper
    cupcake or muffin cases; a piping bag
    fitted with a star tube

Fresh strawberries are mixed into the vanilla sponge, then strawberry jam is added after baking these heavenly little cakes. They're finished with a piped swirl of sweet cream-cheese frosting and more lovely berries. The icing here was piped using a star nozzle. Turn to page 50 for some alternative ways of icing and help with piping a soft icing.

1 Preheat the oven to 180°C/350°F/gas 4. Put the butter into a large mixing bowl and beat with a wooden spoon or an electric mixer until creamy. Gradually beat in the sugar and keep beating for 4–5 minutes until very light and fluffy.

2 Beat the eggs with the vanilla, then add to the creamed mixture a tablespoon at a time, beating well after each addition and scraping down the sides of the bowl from time to time. Sift the flour and salt into the bowl, add the milk and gently fold together using a large metal spoon. Gently fold in the chopped strawberries.

3 Spoon the mixture into the paper cases, dividing it evenly. Bake for 20 minutes until risen, golden brown and firm to the touch. Remove the tray from the oven and cool for about 2 minutes, then carefully transfer the cupcakes to a wire rack and cool completely.

4 Using the tip of a small, sharp knife, remove a small cone of sponge from the middle of each cake. Add about ¼ teaspoon of strawberry conserve to each small hole, then replace the plug of sponge.

5 To make the frosting, beat together the butter, cream cheese and vanilla until soft and creamy, using an electric mixer or a wooden spoon. Gradually beat in the icing sugar (on low speed if using an electric mixer). Spoon the frosting into the piping bag and pipe a swirl on top of each cupcake. Decorate with a whole or halved strawberry. Eat the same day or the next.

Icing with Butter Icing

VARIATION 01

1 The butter icing, buttercream or frosting should be thick but spreadable. If icing a cupcake, hold it with one hand. For a bigger cake, a rotating cake stand will help. Use a round-bladed knife, such as a palette knife, to spread the icing.

2 For a cupcake, put a dollop of icing on top. Starting on one side, swirl the icing around the top in a continuous movement, pushing the icing almost to the edges. Turn the cupcake in your hand as you smooth the icing to create a gently peaked centre and swirled edge.

VARIATION 02

1 The butter icing, buttercream or frosting should be thick but spreadable. Spoon it into a piping bag fitted with a star tube (see page 312 for tips on how to fill a piping bag).

2 To ice a cupcake, hold it with one hand on a flat surface. With your other hand hold the piping bag, almost upright. Starting at the outside edge, with the tube about 1cm above the cupcake, gently squeeze the bag, moving it in a circular motion.

3 Work inwards and upwards to make a spiral, slightly overlapping the icing rings. To finish, press down very gently, then lift the piping bag up and away from the cake, leaving a peaked tip. Use the same technique for piping icing rosettes on a bigger cake.

VARIATION 03

1 The butter icing, buttercream or frosting should be thick but spreadable. Spoon it into a piping bag fitted with a star tube (see page 312 for tips on how to fill a piping bag).

2 If icing a cupcake, hold it with one hand on a flat surface; hold the piping bag with your other hand. With the bag almost upright, and the tube about 1cm above the centre of the cupcake, gently squeeze the bag, keeping the tube steady. Press down very slightly as you squeeze out the icing, then pull up to create a star peak.

3 Pipe a ring of small stars around the central star, and then a final ring around the edge of the cupcake to finish. Use the same technique for piping stars on bigger cakes.

Lemon Coconut Traybake

MAKES **20** **PIECES**

finely grated zest and juice
   of 2 unwaxed lemons
250g plain flour
60g desiccated coconut
3 large free-range eggs, at room
   temperature
300g caster sugar
125ml sunflower oil
250ml Greek-style yoghurt
1 teaspoon bicarbonate of soda

TO FINISH
100g caster sugar
200ml Greek-style yoghurt
135g desiccated coconut
100g icing sugar
toasted coconut shavings, to
   decorate (optional)

1 traybake tin or cake tin, 25.5 x 20.5
   x 5cm, greased and the base lined
   with baking paper

1 Preheat the oven to 180°C/350°F/gas 4.
Mix half of the lemon zest with the flour
and coconut in a bowl. Break the eggs into
another bowl and whisk with an electric
mixer until frothy. Add the sugar and whisk
until the mixture is very light and mousse-
like and the whisk leaves a ribbon trail when
lifted from the bowl. Slowly whisk in the oil
– the mixture will lose some volume.

2 Sprinkle half the flour mixture over the
egg mixture and gently fold in using a large
metal spoon. Combine the yoghurt and
bicarbonate of soda. Add to the bowl with
about a quarter of the lemon juice. Carefully
fold in, followed by the remaining flour
mixture. Spoon into the prepared tin and
spread evenly. Bake for about 35 minutes

Desiccated coconut adds distinct flavour
and texture to this easy-to-make sponge,
while thick and creamy yoghurt balances
the sweetness and gives a moist, soft crumb.
After baking, the cake is soaked in a lemon
syrup and then topped with a simple yoghurt
and coconut frosting.

until a wooden cocktail stick inserted into
the centre of the sponge comes out clean.

3 Meanwhile, make the lemon syrup. Mix
half of the remaining lemon zest with the
caster sugar. Add the rest of the lemon juice.

4 Remove the tin from the oven and set it
on a wire rack. Prick the sponge all over with
a cocktail stick, then spoon over the lemon
syrup. When the cake is cold, turn it out.

5 While the cake is cooling make up the
frosting. Mix the yoghurt with the coconut,
icing sugar and remaining lemon zest.
Chill for 30 minutes until thickened.

6 Spread the frosting over the cake,
then cut into squares. Keep in an airtight
container in the fridge. Just before serving
at room temperature, decorate with a
sprinkling of toasted coconut, if you like.

TIP

For a more richly iced cake, omit the
lemon syrup and spread or pipe the
white chocolate ganache used for the
Little London Stout Cakes (see page 55)
over the cold cake. Decorate with white
chocolate shavings or sprinkle with
lightly toasted coconut shreds.

JUDGE'S TECHNICAL CHALLENGE
Mary's Fraisier

MAKES
1
CAKE

FOR THE SPONGE
4 medium free-range eggs,
   at room temperature
125g caster sugar
finely grated zest of 2 unwaxed
   medium lemons
125g self-raising flour
50g unsalted butter, melted
   and cooled

FOR THE CRÈME MOUSSELINE
600ml milk
1 vanilla pod, split open
4 large free-range eggs plus
   2 egg yolks, at room temperature
180g caster sugar
1 tablespoon kirsch
100g cornflour
150g unsalted butter, at room
   temperature, diced

FOR THE SYRUP
75g caster sugar
juice of 2 medium lemons, strained

TO ASSEMBLE
about 600g medium strawberries
200g marzipan
200g dark chocolate, melted (see
   page 308)

1 x 23cm springclip cake tin or loose-
   based, deep round cake tin, greased,
   floured and the base lined with
   baking paper; a strip of acetate to
   fit inside the tin; a large piping bag
   fitted with a 2cm tube

Here, a whisked egg sponge cake is split and deeply filled with strawberries and a luxurious kirsch-flavoured crème mousseline – crème pâtissière (pastry cream) enriched with butter instead of whipped cream. The top is finished with a thin layer of marzipan and piped chocolate decorations.

1 Preheat the oven to 180°C/350°F/gas 4. To make the sponge, put the eggs, sugar and lemon zest into a large heatproof bowl set over a pan of simmering water. Whisk using a hand-held electric mixer until the mixture has more than doubled in volume and become very thick, pale and mousse-like. To check that the mixture is at the right stage, lift the beaters from the bowl – the mixture that falls off should leave a distinct ribbon-like trail on the surface.

2 Sift two-thirds of the flour onto the mixture, then gently fold in with a metal spoon. Add the remaining flour and fold in gently to retain as much air as possible, but make sure all the flour is incorporated. Gently fold in the melted butter.

3 Pour into the tin and bake for 25–30 minutes until pale golden brown and the sides of the cake shrink away from the tin. Cool the sponge in the tin for 5 minutes, to allow it to firm up a bit, then carefully turn out onto a wire rack (the sponge is delicate). Leave to cool while you wash the tin.

Recipe continues overleaf

4 To make the crème mousseline, bring the milk and vanilla pod just to the boil in a wide saucepan. Remove from the heat and leave to infuse for 10 minutes. Meanwhile, whisk together the eggs, egg yolks, sugar, kirsch and cornflour in a bowl just until smooth and creamy. Remove the vanilla pod from the milk, then pour through a sieve onto the egg mixture, whisking well. Pour the mixture into the washed saucepan, set over medium heat and stir constantly until the mixture boils and thickens; this will take about 4 minutes. It's important to keep stirring to avoid the custard going lumpy. Keep stirring for a minute over the heat to make sure the mixture will be thick enough to pipe, but take care that it doesn't catch on the bottom of the pan. Stir in the butter.

5 Allow to cool slightly, then pour into a shallow dish. Press a disc of dampened greaseproof paper onto the surface, to prevent a skin from forming, then chill for at least 1 hour until cold and set firm.

6 To make the syrup, put the sugar, lemon juice and 70ml water into a small pan and heat gently until the sugar has completely dissolved, then boil for 2 minutes. Remove from the heat and cool.

7 Roll out the marzipan on a worktop lightly dusted with icing sugar to make a thin disc 23cm across. Keep chilled until needed.

8 When ready to assemble the cake, slice the cold sponge in half horizontally to make 2 thin, even discs. Place the strip of acetate around the inside of the tin so it will fit snugly between the side of the tin and the sponge (or line the tin with clingfilm or parchment-lined foil). Set one sponge disc, cut side up, in the tin and brush liberally with the syrup. With the back of a spoon, gently squash the edges of the cake down so that they are pushed directly against the sides of the tin.

9 Choose 12 strawberries of the same height and cut them vertically in half. Arrange pointed end up on top of the sponge layer, cut side against the acetate, making sure the berries are fitting snugly next to each other.

10 Spoon about two-thirds of the crème mousseline into the piping bag to start off with. Pipe a spiral over the sponge base in the tin to cover completely; pipe between the strawberries to fill all the gaps. (Add the remaining crème mousseline to the piping bag when there is space.) Set 3–5 strawberries aside for the decoration, then quarter the rest. Spread these over the crème so it makes the filling about 2.5cm higher. Pipe another spiral of crème on top of the berries and smooth level with a palette knife.

11 Set the other disc of sponge on top, cut side up, and brush with the rest of the syrup. Gently press the top sponge layer down onto the crème so the assembled cake is firmly pressed against the acetate all round. Lay the marzipan disc on top, then chill well.

12 Make some decorations from the melted chocolate (see page 309). To serve, remove the acetate-wrapped cake from the tin, then gently remove the acetate. Set the cake on a plate and finish with the reserved strawberries and chocolate decorations.

Little London Stout Cakes

FOR THE SPONGE MIXTURE
65g cocoa powder
225ml London stout
225g unsalted butter, softened
350g caster sugar
2 large free-range eggs, at room
    temperature, beaten
85ml buttermilk, at room
    temperature
250g self-raising flour
good pinch of salt

FOR THE WHITE CHOCOLATE GANACHE
175g white chocolate, finely
    chopped
125ml whipping cream
50g unsalted butter
½ teaspoon vanilla extract

1 x 12-cup muffin tray, lined with paper
    cupcake or muffin cases; a piping
    bag fitted with a star tube (optional)

If you can find some, a chocolate-flavoured London stout will add extra richness to these malty chocolate cakes but it's not essential. The moist, dense sponge cakes are topped with a froth of sweet, creamy white chocolate ganache, reminiscent of the pint that gives them their distinct flavour. Make these and bring a bit of British pride to any occasion.

1 Preheat the oven to 180°C/350°F/gas 4. Put the cocoa and stout into a medium-sized pan and bring to the boil, whisking constantly to make a smooth liquid. Remove from the heat and leave to cool to room temperature.

2 Meanwhile, beat the butter with the sugar in a mixing bowl using a wooden spoon or an electric mixer until thoroughly combined and fluffy. Gradually add the beaten eggs, a tablespoon at a time, beating well after each addition. Beat in the buttermilk. Sift the flour and salt into the bowl and add the cooled cocoa liquid. Fold everything together until completely blended.

3 Divide the mixture evenly between the paper cases – you can either bake the cakes in 2 batches, or use doubled paper cases (one inside the other) set on a baking tray for the extra 4 cakes. Bake for 25–30 minutes until firm when gently pressed. Leave to cool for 5 minutes, then carefully remove the cakes from the tray and cool completely on a wire rack.

4 When ready to finish the cakes, make up the ganache (see page 306), adding the vanilla with the cream. Chill it for 5–10 minutes, then whisk until thick enough to hold a shape and to pipe. Spoon into the piping bag and pipe small swirls in the centre of each cake, or just spread the ganache thickly over the cakes using a palette knife (see page 50 for help with icing techniques). Store in an airtight container and eat within 5 days.

Lemon & Pecan Celebration Cake

MAKES 1 CAKE

FOR EACH SPONGE LAYER (MAKE 2)
85g pecan nuts
20g cornflour
225g unsalted butter, softened
225g caster sugar
grated zest and juice
   of 1 ½ unwaxed lemons
4 large free-range eggs, at room
   temperature, beaten
115g self-raising flour
good pinch of salt
½ teaspoon baking powder

TO ASSEMBLE AND FINISH
9 tablespoons lemon curd
   (for a home-made lemon curd
   recipe, see page 306)
1kg marzipan
icing sugar, for dusting
1kg ready-to-roll sugar paste

TO DECORATE
200g Royal Icing sugar
¼ teaspoon glycerine
fresh or silk rose petals

1 x 20.5cm round deep cake tin,
   greased and lined; a disposable
   piping bag fitted with a star tube

This is a rich and buttery lemon sponge, flavoured with finely ground pecans, and a good choice for a summer celebration. The 2 cakes are sandwiched with lemon curd, then covered in marzipan and sugar paste icing. You can finish with a piped edging and edible petals as shown here, or use ready-made decorations or even home-made sugar paste bunting (see page 60), as well as piped letters or numbers.

1 Preheat the oven to 160°C/325°F/gas 3. Make the sponges one at a time, following the method here. Put the pecan nuts and cornflour in a food-processor and grind to a fine powder. Set aside until needed.

2 Put the soft butter into a large mixing bowl and beat with an electric mixer until very creamy. Gradually beat in the sugar and lemon zest, then beat until the mixture looks very pale and fluffy. Gradually add the eggs, beating well after each addition – add a tablespoon of the weighed flour with the last portion of egg to prevent the mixture from curdling.

3 Sift the remaining flour, the salt and baking powder into the bowl. Add the ground pecan mixture and 3 tablespoons of the lemon juice and gently fold in using a large metal spoon. When the ingredients are completely amalgamated, spoon the mixture into the prepared tin and spread evenly. Make a slight hollow in the centre so the sponge will rise evenly.

4 Bake for about 1 hour until a skewer inserted into the centre comes out clean. Cool on a wire rack, then carefully turn out and remove the lining paper. Make the second sponge in the same way. (The cooled sponges can be wrapped and stored in an airtight container for a day before finishing.)

Recipe continues overleaf

5 When ready to assemble and cover the cake, set one sponge upside down on a cake board (the flatter underside will give a smoother finish). Spread over 5 tablespoons of the lemon curd, then cover with the second sponge, also upside down. Brush all over with the remaining lemon curd. Knead the marzipan until smooth and pliable. If there is a gap between the cake and the board, make a thin sausage of marzipan and press it around the base so the sides are completely flat and straight.

6 Lightly dust the worktop with icing sugar and roll out the marzipan to a round large enough to cover the top and sides of the cake (check with a tape measure). Carefully wrap the marzipan around the rolling pin and lift it over the cake so the edge just touches the cake board, then continue unrolling the marzipan over the cake so it covers it evenly and touches the board all around. (You may find it easier to do this if the cake is raised up on an upturned bowl or turntable; see opposite page.) Using the palms of your hands, smooth the marzipan on the top surface and down the sides of the cake to make sure it is securely fixed to the cake, and to push out any pockets of air. Using a sharp knife, trim off any excess marzipan flush with the board, and make sure there are no gaps or holes. If time allows, loosely cover the cake and leave to firm up overnight.

7 Brush the marzipan very lightly with warm water (or a little brandy). Roll out the sugar paste as for the marzipan and cover the cake in the same way. Use your hands to gently polish the surface of the sugar paste once it is in place – it should look slightly glossy and very smooth. If you like, keep the sugar paste trimmings, very tightly wrapped in clingfilm, to make decorations. Leave the sugar paste icing to firm up in a cool dry spot for 4–6 hours or overnight before adding piped decorations or edible icing ribbons or cake ribbons.

8 Mix the Royal Icing sugar with the glycerine and 2 tablespoons water using a wooden spoon, to make a thick icing that can be piped. If the icing is too soft to hold its shape, stir in more sugar a teaspoon at a time; if it's too stiff, add more water a few drops at a time. Spoon into the piping bag and pipe stars around the top edge of the cake (see opposite). Leave to set overnight before adding the rose petals. The finished cake, without petals, can be carefully stored in an airtight container in a cool spot (not the fridge) for up to 4 days.

CAKES

Icing with Sugar Paste

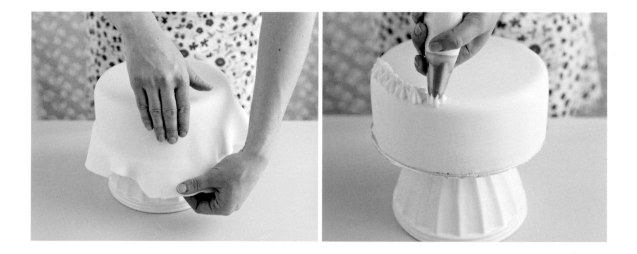

EQUIPMENT NEEDED

cake board or platter the same diameter
  as the cake
bowl
rolling pin (optional)
cake smoother (optional)
small sharp knife
piping bag fitted with a star tube

1 The technique here for icing a cake with sugar paste can also be used to cover a cake with marzipan. Use either ready-to-roll or ready-rolled sugar paste. Set the cake, on its cake board, on an upturned bowl so that the icing can hang below the board. This will make it easier to cover the cake with icing and then to trim off the excess.

2 It's best to remove all rings/bangles/watches first so the icing won't be dented or marked, and to make sure the worktop and your hands are spotlessly clean. Roll out the sugar paste, if necessary. Carefully lift it on the rolling pin and drape it over the cake. Use the palms of your hands to gently press it onto the top and sides of the cake, and to smooth and polish the surface. Take care not to dent the soft icing.

3 Stretch the icing very gently by pulling it down with your left hand while smoothing it with your right hand (photo 1). Take care not to press too heavily, otherwise finger marks will appear. Work your way around the cake. Go around the cake once more with your hands or using a cake smoother to buff the icing to a smooth finish.

4 Trim the excess icing from around the cake base using a small sharp knife. Smooth the icing again. Once you're happy with the icing finish, leave it to firm up. Then you can decorate with shapes cut from sugar paste, edible ribbons and bows, or piping.

5 For a decorative star edging, use royal icing containing glycerine (see page 307) to prevent it from setting too hard. Spoon the royal icing into the piping bag (see page 312). Holding the piping bag almost upright, about 1cm above the edge of the cake, gently squeeze the bag with your other hand, keeping the tube steady. Press down very slightly as you squeeze out the icing, then pull up to create a star peak. Repeat all around the edge of the cake (photo 2). Leave to set before moving the cake from the upturned bowl.

Making Edible Bunting

EQUIPMENT NEEDED
string
metal ruler
tape measure
rolling pin (optional)
small sharp knife
a little Royal Icing (see page 307)
edible food colouring
bowls
small paintbrushes

1 You can use ready-rolled, or ready-to-roll, sugar paste. First, work out how many ropes you need to encircle your cake. Cut a piece of string 12cm long and use this to decide the positioning and curve of your bunting rope. Measure the distance between the 2 ends of the string when it is curved into position along the side of your cake.

2 Measure the circumference of your iced cake, then divide this number by the distance you measured between the string ends. This will give you the number of bunting ropes you will need. For a 20cm cake with a 70cm circumference, we needed 7 ropes.

3 If necessary, roll out the sugar paste on a sheet of baking paper to a rectangle about the thickness of a pound coin. For the 20cm cake we used 200g sugar paste for the bunting.

4 You can make your bunting flags and ropes as large or as small as you like. Our flags are about 2.5cm wide and the ropes are 12cm long and 5mm wide. We needed 42 triangular flags (6 for each rope). Cut out the ropes and flags using a ruler and small sharp knife to ensure straight sides (photo 1).

5 Position your ropes around the side of your cake, using a little royal icing to glue them in place. Do this before you paint your bunting, otherwise the ropes will dry out before they can be curved into position. Use a pin to mark out the spacing of the ropes around the side of your cake.

6 Using small paintbrushes and as many colours as you want, decorate your flags – polka dots and stripes are simple but effective (photo 2).

7 Once they are dry, fix 6 flags underneath each rope, using a little more royal icing. You can finish by piping a rosette of icing over the rope joins.

Sticky Toffee Traybake

MAKES
20
PIECES

FOR THE SPONGE
200g stoned dates, chopped
1 teaspoon bicarbonate of soda
300ml boiling water
80g unsalted butter, softened
160g light brown muscovado sugar
2 large free-range eggs, at room
    temperature, beaten
1 teaspoon vanilla extract
175g self-raising flour
good pinch of salt
75g walnut pieces

FOR THE TOPPING
100g light brown muscovado sugar
75g unsalted butter
100ml double cream
4 tablespoons mascarpone
good pinch of sea salt flakes
walnut halves or pieces, to decorate

1 traybake tin or cake tin, 25.5 x 20.5
    x 5cm, greased and the base lined
    with baking paper

If you're a fan of steamed sticky toffee pudding you'll want to try this easy traybake, made using the same kind of mixture with cooked dates, and finished with a caramel cream topping.

1 Preheat the oven to 180°C/350°F/gas 4. To make the sponge mixture, put the dates into a saucepan, add the bicarbonate of soda and pour over the boiling water. Simmer over low heat for a minute, then remove from the heat and leave to cool and soften for 15 minutes.

2 Put the butter into a mixing bowl and beat with a wooden spoon or an electric mixer until creamy. Add the sugar and beat until fluffy, then gradually add the eggs, beating well after each addition. Beat in the vanilla. Sift the flour and salt into the bowl and fold in with a large metal spoon. Add the cooled date mixture and the walnuts, and fold in.

3 Transfer the mixture to the prepared tin and spread evenly. Bake for 25–30 minutes until the sponge feels springy when gently pressed in the centre. Cool for 15 minutes, then carefully turn out and leave to cool completely on a wire rack.

4 To make the caramel topping, put the sugar, butter and double cream into a saucepan and heat gently until melted, then bring to the boil and simmer for 3–4 minutes until sticky. Remove from the heat and leave to cool completely.

5 Beat the mascarpone until smooth, then fold in the caramel mixture and the salt. Swirl over the top of the cold cake. Decorate with walnuts. Leave in a cool spot to firm up a little before cutting into squares. Store in an airtight container and eat within 4 days.

White Winter Fruit Cake

MAKES

1 CAKE

FOR THE CAKE MIXTURE
100g glacé cherries
175g crimson jumbo raisins,
    golden raisins or sultanas
100g soft-dried apricots
2 tablespoons finely chopped
    mixed peel
100g walnut pieces
4 tablespoons brandy or
    apricot brandy
175g unsalted butter, softened
175g caster sugar
4 large free-range eggs,
    at room temperature, beaten
200g self-raising flour
good pinch of salt
60g ground almonds

FOR THE TOPPING
2 tablespoons sieved apricot jam
    or apricot glaze
250g marzipan
icing sugar, for dusting
450g Royal Icing sugar

TO FINISH (OPTIONAL)
coloured or edible ribbon,
    edible or piped decorations,
    edible glitter or shimmer spray
    (see pages 310–311)

1 x 20.5cm round deep cake tin,
    greased and lined

This is a white or 'blond' fruit cake, so-named because it is made without spices and dark sugars. Remember that the better the dried fruits you use, the richer and sweeter the flavour of the cake will be. It is topped with marzipan and then royal icing, which can be smoothed flat for piping, or swirled or peaked with a knife. Special Royal Icing sugar comes ready-mixed with dried egg white so you only have to add water. If you'd prefer to make your own royal icing with fresh egg whites, the recipe is on page 307.

1 Halve the cherries, rinse with warm water to remove the sticky syrup and pat dry with kitchen paper. Put into a bowl with the raisins. Using kitchen scissors, snip the apricots into chunks the same size as the cherry halves and add to the bowl with the mixed peel and walnuts. Add 3 tablespoons of the brandy and stir well, then cover the bowl tightly and leave to soak overnight.

2 Next day, preheat the oven to 150°C/300°F/ gas 2. Put the soft butter into a large mixing bowl and beat until creamy with a wooden spoon or an electric mixer. Gradually beat in the sugar, then beat until very light and fluffy. Add the eggs a tablespoon at a time, beating well after each addition. Scrape down the sides of the bowl from time to time, and add a tablespoon of the weighed flour with each of the last 2 additions of egg, to prevent the mixture from curdling.

Recipe continues overleaf

3 Sift the rest of the flour and the salt into the bowl and add the ground almonds and the last tablespoon of brandy. Gently fold in with a large metal spoon. Add the soaked fruit and nut mixture, with any remaining liquid, and stir in well. When thoroughly combined, spoon the mixture into the prepared tin and spread evenly. Make a shallow hollow in the centre so the cake will rise evenly.

4 Bake for 2–2 ½ hours until golden and firm and a skewer inserted into the centre of the cake comes out clean. Set the tin on a wire rack and leave to cool. When cold, remove the cake from the tin and peel off the lining paper. Wrap in greaseproof paper and foil, then store in an airtight container for at least 24 hours. (The cake will taste better if it's allowed to mature – it's at its best about a week after baking.)

5 To finish the cake set it upside down on a cake board (the flat underside will give a smoother surface for icing). Gently warm the apricot jam or glaze and brush over the top of the cake. Knead the marzipan until it is smooth and supple, then roll it out on a worktop lightly dusted with icing sugar to a circle big enough to cover the cake. Using the base of the cake tin as a guide, cut a neat circle of marzipan and set it on top of the cake. Press it down firmly, then smooth it with the palm of your hand. Cover loosely and leave to firm up overnight.

6 Next day make up the royal icing. Put 75ml cold water into a large mixing bowl and gradually beat in the Royal Icing sugar with an electric mixer, using low speed at first. Keep beating until the icing stands in soft peaks. If it becomes very stiff, work in a little more water; if it feels too soft or runny, work in more Royal Icing sugar. Cover the cake with the icing and finish the top with a fan pattern (see opposite). While the icing is still wet, add candles, sprinkles or sugar decorations; or leave overnight in an airy place until firm and dry before piping decorations. Store the cake in an airtight container in a cool place and eat within 3 weeks. Before serving, you could tie a ribbon around the cake, if you like.

TIP

Large whole or halved glacé fruits, or confit fruits such as pears, clementines, figs and pineapple, make a glamorous alternative to the marzipan and icing. After brushing the top of the cake with warm apricot jam, arrange a selection of fruits on top. Once you are happy with how it looks, brush the fruit very lightly with more warm apricot jam or glaze and leave to set.

Icing with Royal Icing

EQUIPMENT NEEDED
large palette knife
plastic cake spatula (optional)
icing ruler (optional)

1 Your royal icing should have a spreadable consistency. Set the cake, on its cake board, on a sheet of baking paper. Put a large dollop of icing in the centre of the cake and spread it out thickly with the palette knife.

2 Continue to add icing, using about half the quantity to cover the top, spreading it out gently to make a smooth, even layer over the surface and pushing the icing to the edges of the cake using a round, sweeping motion.

3 Next, completely cover the sides of the cake with icing, making sure there are no gaps around the top or base and that the top edge is straight. Hold the palette knife vertically and smooth the icing, moving the knife left and right around the cake. For neat, smooth sides use a plastic cake spatula held vertically and draw it around the sides at a 45 degree angle to the side of the cake.

4 Return to the top to finish it. Starting at the edge of the cake furthest away from you, drag the palette knife along the still-wet royal icing, halfway around the cake circumference, to create a 2.5cm wide arc.

5 Starting at the same beginning point, drag the palette knife across the icing again, creating another arc, slightly overlapping the first arc. Continue this motion, always starting at the same point but moving down the top of the cake towards you, creating a fan pattern in the icing. Alternatively, if you want a perfectly smooth surface, you could carefully draw an icing ruler (or a large clean ruler) across the iced top at a 45 degree angle.

6 While the icing is still wet, you can add candles, sprinkles and other decorations. For piped decorations, leave the cake overnight in an airy place until the icing is firm and dry.

Caramel Layer Cake

MAKES

CAKE

FOR THE SPONGE
300g self-raising flour
good pinch of salt
300g caster sugar
250g unsalted butter,
   very soft but not runny
4 large free-range eggs,
   at room temperature
4 tablespoons buttermilk,
   at room temperature
1 teaspoon vanilla extract

FOR THE FILLING
225g unsalted butter, softened
450g dark brown muscovado sugar
175ml double cream
300g icing sugar, sifted
¼ teaspoon sea salt flakes,
   or to taste
100g dark chocolate (70% cocoa
   solids), broken up

3 x 20.5cm sandwich tins, greased
   and the base lined with baking paper;
   a disposable piping bag

1 Preheat the oven to 180°C/350°F/gas 4. Sift the flour, salt and sugar into the bowl of a large free-standing electric mixer (or into a mixing bowl if you are going to use a hand-held electric mixer). Add the butter to the bowl, in pieces. Whisk the eggs with the buttermilk and vanilla using a fork, then add to the bowl. Beat on low speed until everything is thoroughly combined and very smooth, thick and light.

Standing proud, here is a fine 3-layer cake with a rich sea-salt caramel filling and icing plus a dark chocolate caramel layer. It's decorated with melted chocolate feathered through the still-soft caramel. The cake is made from a firm (all-in-one) sponge that slices neatly, without making a lot of crumbs. The flavours deepen as the cake matures, so plan to make this a day ahead. Turn to page 69 for help with feathering.

2 Divide the mixture evenly among the 3 tins and spread level. Bake for about 25 minutes until the sponges are springy when gently pressed in the centre and starting to shrink away from the sides of the tins. Set the tins on a wire rack and run a round-bladed knife around the insides to loosen the sponges, then cool for 2 minutes before turning out. Leave to cool completely.

3 Meanwhile, make the caramel filling. Put 175g of the weighed butter into a medium-sized pan with the muscovado sugar and cream. Heat gently until the butter has melted, then bring to the boil, stirring. Reduce the heat and simmer gently for 5 minutes, stirring frequently. Pour into a heatproof mixing bowl and gradually beat in the icing sugar, using an electric mixer. When all the sugar has been incorporated, continue beating until the mixture is fluffy and barely warm. Gradually beat in the rest of the butter followed by the salt. Taste and add a little more salt, if needed.

Recipe continues overleaf

4 Gently melt the chocolate (see page 308). Spoon about half the chocolate into another bowl, and stir in slightly less than a quarter of the caramel mixture.

5 To assemble the cake, set one sponge layer on a serving plate and spread over one-third of the caramel mixture. Spread a second sponge layer with the chocolate-caramel mixture and set on the first layer. Place the third sponge layer on top. Leave the filled cake to set, otherwise you might risk a landslide. When set, cover the top and then the sides of the assembled cake with the remaining caramel mixture. If the remaining icing has got too firm, gently reheat it until workable.

6 Spoon the remaining melted chocolate into the disposable piping bag and snip off the end. Starting in the centre, pipe a spiral of chocolate on top of the cake. Don't worry if it looks a bit wobbly. 'Feather' by drawing a cocktail stick through the chocolate and caramel icing (see opposite page). Leave to set. The cake can be kept, in an airtight container, for up to 4 days.

TIP
To 'marble' the icing, pipe random loops and circles of chocolate onto the caramel icing, then swirl the 2 together with a cocktail stick.

Feathering Icing

EQUIPMENT NEEDED
small disposable piping bag
1–2 cocktail sticks

1 The feathering technique works best on cakes and biscuits that are covered with wet icings, including fondant, glacé icing and the caramel icing on the Caramel Layer Cake (see page 66). For the feathered pattern you can use melted chocolate, or an icing with a soft, piping consistency, or melted jam.

2 Spoon the chocolate (or icing or jam) into the piping bag and fold down the top. Snip off the corner to give a writing tip 3–4mm across. Hold the bag vertically over the cake, without touching the surface. Starting in the centre of the cake, gently squeeze the bag and pipe an evenly spaced spiral on top of the icing on the cake.

3 Working quickly, before anything sets, gently draw the tip of a cocktail stick through both the piped spiral and the cake icing, from the centre to the edge at regular intervals, to make the first set of lines. We marked 6 outward lines but you could make more for a larger cake, or fewer for a smaller one. Then draw the tip of the cocktail stick back to the centre, from the edge, to make lines in between the first lines.

4 Alternatively, pipe parallel lines, diagonally or straight, on top of the cake, then draw the tip of the cocktail stick through them and the cake icing, at right angles to the piped lines.

5 Leave the feathered cake icing to dry and set before cutting the cake.

Biscuits

YOU CAN HAVE A LOT OF FUN MAKING AND DECORATING BISCUITS as the Bake Off bakers have shown. Simple to make, biscuits also offer the greatest scope to be creative and imaginative. But as Mary advises, good-quality ingredients are crucial because most biscuit recipes contain just a few ingredients, so the flavours really need to be outstanding.

This year, the Bake Off bakers were challenged to create a showstopping Gingerbread Structure. Our biscuit challenges are based on this. Using a basic Gingerbread Dough, we have given three different recipes – Gingerbread People are fun and easy, great for children to make too. The Iced Stars require a slightly more elaborate icing. And if you have an afternoon to spare, you could have a go at making a gingerbread house. The bakers' ideas were extraordinary and they do require patience, a steady hand and practice. We've included a simpler gingerbread house here with a white winter-wonderland look, but you could make one for Hallowe'en complete with scary spiders, cobwebs and witches' broomsticks, using black and orange icing. Or what about creating a pretty flower-covered cottage fit for Snow White?

Also included in this chapter is one of *The Great British Bake Off* bakers' best recipes for savoury crackers. Try these crunchy bites as an alternative to crisps and nuts with drinks.

For biscuit-making you don't need a lot of fancy equipment, but it is worth investing in at least one heavy-duty baking sheet that won't buckle in the heat of the oven or rapidly turn your dough to cinders. Non-stick baking paper for lining the sheets is helpful: the cooked biscuits lift off without damage. Although most biscuit doughs can be mixed with a wooden spoon, for some an electric mixer or food-processor will help. And you'll want to have a long rolling pin for cut-out biscuits.

Cutting rolled-out doughs into a variety of pretty shapes rather than just plain round circles makes them much more fun and interesting. Cookie and biscuit cutters come in a multitude of shapes and sizes, or you can make your own cardboard templates to cut around. You will also need a big wire cooling rack, although you can always use the rack from the grill pan; a flat metal spatula or fish slice for lifting biscuits; and an airtight storage container to prevent them from losing crispness.

Biscuits make lovely presents – pretty card or Perspex gift boxes tied with ribbons will make them look special.

You can leave your biscuits unadorned, but it's easy to add icing – spread or piped, white or coloured (see our Showstopping Technique) – or melted chocolate, plus decorations as simple or as elaborate as you like. Look out for disposable piping bags, piping tubes, edible food colours for icing, sparkles and sprinkles in large supermarkets and specialist shops.

To turn home-baked biscuits into beautiful edible decorations, hung with ribbon, is a lot of fun and something children can help with.

Biscuits can be turned into desserts, too. For a fast, imaginative sweet treat simply sandwich a couple of freshly baked biscuits or macaroons with a scoop of ice cream and watch the smiles appear!

DON'T FORGET

❤ Most biscuit recipes use only a few ingredients, so quality is important. For the best flavour, only butter will do.

❤ Ready-made icing in tubes or piping bags saves time, although you can easily make and colour your own glacé or royal icing.

❤ Use good-quality chocolate that contains the right cocoa content called for in the recipe, chopped into chunks or carefully melted (see page 308 for how to do this successfully), rather than a bag of 'chocolate chips' that are made with far less chocolate and therefore have less flavour.

❤ The oils in nuts can quickly stale, so buy in small amounts. When you open a new pack weigh what you need, then tightly wrap the remainder and freeze.

❤ Spices quickly lose their power and aroma, so don't use an ancient pack lurking at the back of a cupboard.

JAMES

Gingerbread Dough

350g plain flour
1 tablespoon ground ginger
1 teaspoon ground cinnamon
½ teaspoon ground mixed spice
good pinch of salt
1 teaspoon bicarbonate of soda
175g unsalted butter
150g dark muscovado sugar
4 tablespoons golden syrup

This easy dough for crisp, well-spiced, dark gingerbread biscuits is made by the melting method – the butter, golden syrup and sugar are gently melted together in a saucepan, then the flour and spices are stirred in with a wooden spoon. Use this dough to make any of the following Showstopping Challenges: 12 Gingerbread People, 12 Iced Stars or a Winter Woodland Cottage.

1 Sift the flour, ginger, cinnamon, mixed spice, salt and bicarbonate of soda into a mixing bowl.

2 Put the butter, sugar and golden syrup into a saucepan large enough to hold all the ingredients. Set over low heat and stir gently until everything is completely melted and smooth. Remove the pan from the heat and tip in the flour mixture. Mix well with a wooden spoon to make a firm dough.

3 Tip the dough out onto a lightly floured worktop and leave until cool enough to handle, then gently knead to make a neat ball. Leave until cold before rolling out. In warm weather, wrap the dough in clingfilm and chill for about 20 minutes until firm. The dough is now ready to use.

TIP
For a milder flavour, omit the cinnamon and mixed spice; for a paler colour use light brown muscovado sugar rather than dark.

Gingerbread People

MAKES
12

1 quantity Gingerbread Dough
(see page 75)

TO DECORATE
½ quantity Royal Icing (see page
307), with a piping consistency
edible silver balls, mini white
chocolate beans or white
chocolate stars (optional)
edible silver shimmer spray or white
rainbow dust (optional, see page 310)

gingerbread people cutter(s), about
13.5cm long; 2 baking sheets, lined
with baking paper; a piping bag fitted
with a No. 2 tube or white icing pens

You'll have a lot of fun decorating these
biscuits and they are a great bake for children
to make as well, with adult help. Keep the
decoration simple – use edible silver balls or
chocolate drops to create eyes and buttons,
fixed with a little royal icing, or have a go at
some simple piping (see page 110 for help).
When you've mastered the technique, you
can be as detailed as you like.

1 Preheat the oven to 180°C/350°F/gas 4.
Make up the Gingerbread Dough following
the method on page 75. Lightly dust the
worktop and rolling pin with flour, then roll
out the Gingerbread Dough to a rectangle
just slightly thicker than a pound coin.
Dip the cutter(s) in flour and cut out figures.
Carefully transfer them to the lined baking
sheets, setting them well apart to allow for
spreading. Don't worry if a limb or head
falls off; just press the dough together again.
Gather up all the trimmings into a ball, then
roll out again and cut more figures as before.

2 Bake for 8–10 minutes until just slightly
darker; if necessary, rotate the baking sheets
halfway through the baking time so the
biscuits cook evenly. Remove from the oven
and leave the biscuits to cool completely
on the baking sheets.

3 Spoon the icing into the piping bag or use
white icing pens to pipe eyes, nose, mouth
and hair onto each figure. Use the rest of the
icing to pipe on clothes such as a bow tie,
shorts, shirts, gloves, hats and then buttons
– whatever you like. Press edible silver balls,
chocolate beans or stars onto the piped
buttons, then top with a little silver shimmer
spray or rainbow dust for added sparkle, if
you wish. Store in an airtight container and
eat within a week.

Iced Stars

MAKES 12

1 quantity Gingerbread Dough (see page 75)
½ quantity Royal Icing (see page 307), with a piping consistency
edible food colouring (optional)
edible decorations, such as silver balls, mini white chocolate beans or white chocolate stars; hundreds and thousands; silver glitter dust or silver shimmer spray (see page 310)
thin ribbon or raffia, for threading

star-shaped cutter(s), 10cm or 7.5cm; 2 baking sheets, lined with baking paper; a piping bag and a No. 2 or writing tube

1 Preheat the oven to 180°C/350°F/gas 4. Make up the Gingerbread Dough following the method on page 75. Roll out, cut out 12 large star shapes (or 18 medium) and bake as for Gingerbread People (see page 76).

2 As soon as the shapes come out of the oven, make a small hole in one of the points of each star using a skewer or cocktail stick (for threading in ribbon), then leave to cool completely before carefully removing the stars from the baking sheets.

3 Put the icing (white or coloured) into the piping bag fitted with a No. 2 tube (or a writing tube or a small-shaped tube) and pipe dots, zigzags, swirls, snowflakes or other shapes on top of the stars. Decorate with edible silver balls or other edible decorations. Leave the icing to set before threading with fine ribbon or raffia.

These stars use the same basic dough as the Gingerbread People, but are decorated with a more elaborate piped icing design and then sprinkled with edible glitter for a festive sparkle. See Variations below and also page 110 for more ideas for decorating biscuits, using piping and flooding icing.

ALTERNATIVE DECORATIONS

Instead of piping icing decorations, make a star stencil and spray the stars with edible silver shimmer spray (see page 310).

For glossy iced stars, stir warm water, a teaspoon at a time, into the royal icing to make a smooth and runny icing 'glaze'. (You can stir in coloured hundreds and thousands or sprinkles at this point.) Dip the top side of each star into the icing to coat completely, leaving the underside un-iced. Leave to set on a wire rack lined with baking paper, adding silver balls or sprinkles before the icing sets.

Decorate the stars with sparkling 'snow': spread on the royal icing with a round-bladed knife, then swirl or 'peak' the icing so it is raised rather than smooth. Scatter over some silver balls or sprinkle with silver glitter or dust and leave to set.

Pipe an outline around the edge of each star and flood the centre with thinned royal icing, in the same or a contrasting colour (see page 110 for flooding and piping).

Winter Woodland Cottage

MAKES

HOUSE

2 quantities Gingerbread Dough
(see page 75)
about 4 clear, coloured, fruit-
flavoured boiled sweets,
for windows (optional)
2 quantities Royal Icing
(see page 307)

TO DECORATE
5 mini marshmallows, 1 left whole
for the chimney and 4 sliced into
6 pieces to decorate the wall joins
about 110 white chocolate buttons,
for the lower eaves
about 9 white chocolate Maltesers,
for the roof ridge
white and silver edible sprinkles
or edible glitter (see page 310)
miniature snowflake sprinkles,
to decorate the trees

cardboard templates (see pages
314–315); baking paper; small
round, square or circular cutter(s)
for windows; 2 or more baking
sheets; small Christmas tree or
gingerbread people cutters; a
piping bag fitted with a No. 2 tube

1 Preheat the oven to 180°C/350°F/gas 4.
Make up 2 quantities of the Gingerbread
Dough following the method on page 75.
While the dough is chilling, cut out the
templates for the 2 side walls, front and
back walls, and 2 roof sections.

2 Divide the dough into 5 equal portions and
work with one portion at a time (keep the

The Showstopper Biscuit Challenge this year
was to create a gingerbread structure. Hansel
and Gretel wouldn't be able to resist this
edible home. How you decorate your 'cottage'
is up to you – you can go as colourful or
minimal as you like. It helps to have at least
one extra pair of hands for assembling the
house, and there's plenty of work for small
helpers. Before you start sticking the pieces
together it's worth having a quick run-through
to work out which piece goes where.

others covered to prevent them from drying
out). Start with the 2 side walls, cutting
them from one portion. Roll out the dough
between 2 sheets of baking paper to the
thickness of 2 stacked one-pound coins.
Remove the top piece of paper, set the
templates on the dough and cut out the
shapes using a sharp knife. Lift the shapes,
on the baking paper, keeping them about
2cm apart to allow for spreading.

3 Cut out 1 or 2 windows from each side
wall, using a small round, square or circular
cutter. Crush the boiled sweets in a small
plastic bag using a rolling pin, then carefully
spoon into the window holes, filling evenly
up to the level of the dough.

4 Bake for 10 minutes until just beginning
to deepen in colour. Leave until completely
cold and set before removing from the
baking sheet.

Recipe continues overleaf

TIP
If the pieces break while you are assembling them, just glue them back together with icing and leave until firm before using – it will look like snow by the end!

1

2

5 Cut the front wall of the house from one portion of rolled-out dough. Cut out a window from the front and fill with crushed sweets as for the side windows. Also cut out a door, but don't discard it; place it next to the front shape on the baking sheet. Bake as for the side walls. Make the back wall of the house in the same way, but without a door; bake. Use a rolled-out portion of dough for each roof piece; bake and trim as above.

6 You will now have 6 gingerbread shapes with which to construct the house (see photo 1). Gather up all the dough trimmings into a ball and roll out on a lightly floured worktop. Cut out 2 Christmas trees, 1 gingerbread person and 3 square 'slabs' to make the path. Transfer to a baking sheet lined with baking paper and bake for 10 minutes. Leave to cool.

7 When ready to assemble, spoon some of the icing into the piping bag fitted with the No. 2 tube (if using a disposable bag cut off the tip). Pipe a thick rope of icing (it doesn't need to be neat) down a short side of one side wall. Set the front wall on a cake board and place the side wall at 90 degrees to the front (make sure the 'stained glass window' is facing the right way) so the icing mortar is between them. Press the walls gently together. Use more icing to fill in any gaps. Prop up the front and side walls with a jar so you don't have to hold them in place while the icing sets (see photo 2).

8 Attach the other side wall to the front in the same way. Pipe plenty of icing down both short sides of the back wall and set it in between the side walls to complete the base of the house. Again, gently press the walls together and fill in any gaps with icing. Hold the walls in place with small bowls.

9 While the icing mortar is setting, pipe around the windows and doorway. Press the sliced marshmallows carefully into the icing of the wall joins (use a little extra, if necessary, to make them stick). Use a little icing to attach the door to the front of the house.

10 Spread icing over each roof section, swirling it to resemble snow, and decorate with chocolate buttons. When the base of the house is completely firm, pipe icing along the top of each side wall and along the triangular tops of the front and back walls, then carefully lift the roof sections into place – they will overhang the walls. Pipe icing along the centre ridge to join the two roof sections (you will need to hold them in place until the icing starts to set or they will slip off). Cover the join with Maltesers. Add a marshallow chimney, fixed with a dab of icing.

11 Decorate the 'garden' with swirls of icing; ice the Christmas trees and gingerbread person; and add the paving slabs. Finish with a good sprinkling of edible glitter, if you like. Leave in a cool, dry spot until set and firm. At this point the house can be draped in clingfilm. Best eaten within a week.

Lebkuchen Lollipops

MAKES 16

30g dark chocolate (70% cocoa
  solids), broken up
100g unblanched almonds
½ teaspoon each ground ginger
  and cinnamon
¼ teaspoon each freshly grated
  nutmeg, ground cloves and
  ground allspice
⅛ teaspoon freshly ground black
  pepper
1 tablespoon chopped mixed peel
1 tablespoon chopped glacé ginger
2 large free-range egg whites, at
  room temperature
120g icing sugar, sifted

TO FINISH
200g dark chocolate (70% cocoa
  solids), broken up
coloured edible sprinkles (optional)

16 heatproof 15.2cm lollipop/cake pop
  sticks; 2 baking sheets, lined with
  baking paper

An essential Christmas treat in Germany,
lebkuchen are crisp and very spicy. The
original recipe dates back to medieval
monasteries; the thick chocolate topping
is a more modern tradition. For a professional
extra-smooth finish, use tempered chocolate
(see page 308).

1 Preheat the oven to 150°C/300°F/gas 2.
Put the 30g chocolate into the bowl of a
food-processor with the almonds, spices
and black pepper and process to make
fine crumbs. Tip into a mixing bowl.

2 Finely chop the mixed peel with the glacé
ginger. Add to the bowl and thoroughly
combine with the spicy crumbs.

3 Whisk the egg whites in a clean, grease-free
bowl using an electric mixer until the mixture
will stand in stiff peaks when the whisk is
lifted. Gradually whisk in the icing sugar to
make a stiff, glossy meringue. Using a large
metal spoon, fold in the spice mixture.

4 Arrange the lollipop sticks on the lined
baking sheets, placing them well apart.
Using a rounded tablespoon for each
lebkuchen, spoon the mixture onto the
sheets, spreading each spoonful gently
around a stick to make a neat, thick round
about 7cm across. Be sure at least 4cm of
the stick is covered thickly with mixture.

5 Bake for 15–20 minutes until pale golden
and firm to the touch; if necessary rotate
the sheets halfway through baking so the
lebkuchen cook evenly. Set the sheets on
a wire rack and leave the biscuits to cool
completely before removing them carefully
from the paper lining (don't lift the sticks
until the biscuits are cold and firm).

6 To finish, melt the chocolate (see
page 308). Dip the rounded side of each
lebkuchen into the melted chocolate to
coat, then place on a baking sheet lined
with baking paper and leave to set; decorate
with edible sprinkles or chocolate transfers
(see page 309) while the chocolate
is setting, if you wish. Store in an airtight
container and eat within 5 days.

Sour Cherry Biscotti

MAKES 24

115g unsalted butter, softened
125g caster sugar
1 teaspoon vanilla extract
2 large free-range eggs, at room
temperature, beaten
275g plain flour
good pinch of salt
½ teaspoon baking powder
100g soft-dried sour cherries
100g blanched almonds, roughly
chopped
100g good-quality white chocolate,
roughly chopped

2 baking sheets, lined with baking paper

The best biscotti are crisp (but never dry) and packed with contrasting tastes and textures. Here, large nuggets of white chocolate, sour cherries and crunchy almonds make these twice-baked sliced biscuits a welcome treat with coffee at any time.

1 Preheat the oven to 180°C/350°F/gas 4. Put the butter, sugar and vanilla into a mixing bowl and beat with a wooden spoon or an electric mixer until light in colour and fluffy. Gradually beat in the eggs, beating well after each addition.

2 Sift the flour, salt and baking powder into the bowl and mix in with a wooden spoon to make a soft dough. Add the dried cherries, chopped almonds and chocolate and work in until evenly combined.

3 Dust your hands with flour, then turn out the dough onto a lightly floured worktop. Divide into 2 equal pieces. Lift each piece onto a lined baking sheet. Flour your hands again, then pat out each piece to a neat rectangle about 8 × 25cm.

4 Bake for about 25 minutes until just firm to the touch and golden; if necessary, rotate the sheets halfway through baking so the biscotti dough cooks evenly. Remove from the oven (leave the oven on) and allow to cool for 10 minutes.

5 Slice each piece of baked dough – still on the baking sheets – on the diagonal into 12 thick slices. Gently tip the fragile slices over so they are cut-side down on the sheets. Bake for a further 10 minutes until just starting to colour.

6 Remove from the oven and set the baking sheets on a wire rack. The biscotti are still fragile at this point, so leave them to cool and firm up before removing from the sheets. Store in an airtight container and eat within 2 weeks.

TIP
The biscotti can be broken into chunks and used in a trifle in place of sponge fingers.

Ruby Jacks

MAKES

115g unsalted butter
70g light brown muscovado sugar
5 tablespoons golden syrup
1 rounded tablespoon chopped
    glacé ginger
1 teaspoon ground ginger
180g porridge oats

1 x 20.5cm square tin, greased

1 Preheat the oven to 150°C/300°F/gas 2.
Put the butter, sugar, golden syrup, glacé
ginger and ground ginger into a pan large
enough to hold all the ingredients. Stir with
a wooden spoon over low heat until melted.
Remove from the heat and stir in the oats
until thoroughly combined.

2 Tip the mixture into the prepared tin and
spread evenly. Lightly press the mixture
down with the back of the spoon to level the
surface. Bake for 20 minutes until turning
golden brown around the edges; or for a
crunchy flapjack bake for an extra 5 minutes.

Glacé ginger – stem ginger cut into small
chunks – plus ground ginger adds a touch
of spicy warmth to these oaty squares, as well
as a little ruby colour. Other flapjacks may
be homely and comforting, but these are
a cut above.

3 Set the tin on a wire rack. Carefully score
the mixture into 16 squares using an oiled
knife, then leave until cold before removing
from the tin. Store in an airtight container
and eat within a week.

TIP
Melt 100g good-quality white
chocolate and spread on top of
the cold squares. Decorate with
75g dried sour cherries and 75g
dried cranberries. Leave until
the fruit has set in the chocolate.
Eat within 2 days.

Honey Madeleines

MAKES 20

2 large free-range eggs,
  at room temperature
½ teaspoon vanilla extract
65g caster sugar
25g well-flavoured honey (see TIP)
100g plain flour
good pinch of salt
50g ground almonds
100g unsalted butter,
  melted and cooled
2 tablespoons flaked almonds
icing sugar, for dusting

1 madeleine tray, silicone or
  well-buttered (see recipe)

1 Preheat the oven to 190°C/375°F/gas 5.
If not using a silicone madeleine tray, lightly
and evenly brush your tray with a coating of
very soft butter. Pop the tray into the freezer
and leave for a couple of minutes to harden
the butter, then brush once more with butter.
Keep in the fridge or freezer until ready to use.

2 Whisk the eggs with the vanilla, sugar and
honey using an electric mixer until the
mixture has massively increased in volume
and is very light in colour and mousse-like
in texture – the whisk should leave a distinct
ribbon-like trail when lifted out of the bowl.

3 Sift the flour, salt and ground almonds
into the bowl (tip in any bits of almond left
in the sieve). Gently fold in using a large
metal spoon. Slowly drizzle the melted
butter over the mixture and fold in until
you can no longer see any buttery streaks.

Madeleines, the staple of every good French
bakery, are forever linked to Proust and his
memories. But they are too good to be
enjoyed only on holidays across the Channel
– the whisked sponge mixture is light, with
almonds adding moisture and a good
texture, and the wonderful taste of the
honey shines through.

4 Spoon the mixture into the madeleine
moulds, filling them just under three-
quarters full to allow space for rising.
(Don't worry if you have to bake the mixture
in batches; it won't spoil.) Scatter over the
flaked almonds. Bake for 10–12 minutes
until lightly golden and firm to the touch; if
necessary, rotate the tray halfway through
baking so the little cakes cook evenly.

5 Tip the madeleines out of the tray onto
a wire rack and leave to cool. Store in an
airtight container and eat within 5 days –
the flavour will develop thc longer they are
kept. Serve dusted with sifted icing sugar.

TIP
A mild lavender or Spanish
orange-blossom honey will
give a more delicate flavour
than a stronger Scottish
heather or Greek wild
thyme honey.

Paul's Tea Cakes

MAKES

FOR THE SHELLS
400g dark chocolate

FOR THE BISCUIT BASE
50g plain wholemeal flour
50g plain flour
good pinch of salt
½ teaspoon baking powder
25g caster sugar
25g unsalted butter, at room
    temperature, diced
1 tablespoon milk

FOR THE MARSHMALLOW
3 free-range egg whites, at room
    temperature
150g caster sugar
2 tablespoons golden syrup
½ teaspoon salt
seeds scraped from ½ vanilla pod

1 x 7.5cm plain round cutter; a baking
    sheet, lightly greased; a 6-hole
    (7.5cm) silicone semi-dome
    chocolate mould; baking paper;
    2 disposable piping bags

These crisp chocolate-covered biscuits topped with fluffy marshmallow were one of Paul's favourite treats when growing up. As chocolate is such an important part of these cakes, use your favourite type with a flavour you love. Take your time and the cakes will look stunning on the tea table!

1 Break up 300g of the dark chocolate and melt it (see page 308). Leave to cool and firm up slightly.

2 Meanwhile, make the biscuits. Combine the flours, salt, baking powder and sugar in a mixing bowl. Add the butter and rub in until the mixture resembles fine crumbs, then add the milk and work the mixture with your hands until it comes together to make a smooth ball of dough.

3 Turn out onto a lightly floured worktop and roll out about 5mm thick. Using the round cutter, cut out 6 discs, re-rolling the trimmings if necessary. Arrange slightly apart on the prepared baking sheet and prick each biscuit a couple of times with a fork. Chill for 10–15 minutes while you preheat the oven to 160°C/325°F/gas 3.

4 Bake the biscuits for 10–12 minutes until firm and just starting to colour around the edges – don't let them get too dark or they will taste bitter. Transfer to a wire rack and leave to cool.

5 Wipe out the semi-dome mould with kitchen paper, then pour about 1 tablespoon of chocolate into each hole. Spread with the back of the spoon, and tip and swirl the mould for several minutes, so the holes are completely coated – the domes need enough chocolate to be sturdy but should be thin enough to bite through easily. Take your time doing this, to allow the chocolate to thicken up so it doesn't settle in the base of the holes. Leave to set (not in the fridge).

Recipe continues overleaf

6 Dip the cooled biscuits in the remaining melted chocolate to cover completely and evenly (or brush the chocolate over them), then place them uneven side down on a sheet of baking paper. Leave to set.

7 To make the marshmallow, put all the ingredients into a large heatproof mixing bowl set over a pan of simmering water. Whisk with a hand-held electric mixer on full power for 6–8 minutes until you have a bowl of thick, glossy, silky-smooth and very stiff meringue (rather like Italian meringue – see page 250). It needs to be stiff enough to pipe. Remove the bowl from the heat and whisk for a few more minutes until the meringue has cooled. Leave it until it is completely cold, then spoon it into one of the piping bags.

8 Melt the remaining 100g chocolate as before. Spoon into the other piping bag and turn up the tip so the chocolate doesn't set hard; stand it in a glass until it has cooled and firmed up to piping consistency.

9 To assemble the tea cakes, peel the biscuits off the paper and lay them, flat side down, on a clean sheet of baking paper. Snip the end off the piping bag containing the marshmallow to make a 2cm opening, then pipe the marshmallow into each chocolate dome to fill it level with the rim.

10 Snip off a 2cm opening from the piping bag containing the chocolate, then carefully pipe some chocolate on the marshmallow and a ring of chocolate around the edge of each biscuit. Swiftly place a biscuit on each marshmallow-filled dome. Smooth the join with a knife, then leave to set until sealed together.

11 Very carefully remove the chocolate domes from the mould by turning the mould upside down and gently popping out the domes (as though you are removing fragile ice cubes from a tray). Avoid getting finger marks on the glossy domes. Store in an airtight container in a cool place, but not the fridge, and eat within 2 days.

Aztec Cookies

MAKES
8

140g espresso-flavoured dark
chocolate (70% cocoa solids),
broken into squares
65g unsalted butter, diced
2 large free-range eggs, at room
temperature
½ teaspoon vanilla extract
good pinch of salt
130g caster sugar
185g plain flour
1 teaspoon baking powder
100g good-quality white chocolate
edible gold dust or glitter, to finish
(optional, see page 310)

2 baking sheets, lined with
baking paper

1 Melt the dark chocolate with the butter
(see page 308). Remove the bowl from the
pan and leave the chocolate mixture to cool
for about 5 minutes until barely warm.

2 Meanwhile, put the eggs, vanilla, salt
and sugar in a large mixing bowl. Using
a wire whisk or hand-held electric mixer,
beat for a couple of minutes until thoroughly
combined. Stir in the chocolate mixture.

3 Sift the flour and baking powder into the
bowl and stir in using a wooden spoon.
Roughly chop or break up the white
chocolate into small chunks and mix in.
Leave the mixture to stand for 15 minutes
to firm up a bit. Meanwhile preheat the
oven to 160°C/325°F/gas 3.

While coffee-flavoured cakes are easy to
find, biscuits and cookies are another matter.
These irresistible cookies, made from good
dark chocolate flavoured with real espresso
coffee and full of white chocolate chunks,
are a very adult treat. They taste even better
the next day, if you can wait.

4 Using a heaped tablespoon of mixture
for each cookie, drop onto the lined baking
sheets, spacing the spoonfuls well apart
to allow for spreading. Don't flatten the
mixture. Bake for about 15 minutes until
just set – the cookies will continue cooking
for a few minutes after they come out of
the oven. Leave on the sheets for about
5 minutes, then transfer to a wire rack and
allow to cool completely. Store in an airtight
tin and eat within a week. Before serving,
dust lightly with edible gold dust or edible
gold glitter, if you want extra sparkle.

TIP
If you can't find espresso dark chocolate bars, use your favourite dark chocolate and add 2 teaspoons ground espresso coffee when melting the chocolate with the butter.

Double Death by Chocolate Cookies

150g self-raising flour
25g cocoa powder
good pinch of salt
good pinch of bicarbonate of soda
60g caster sugar
60g light brown muscovado sugar
115g unsalted butter, very soft but
    not runny
1 large free-range egg, at room
    temperature
½ teaspoon vanilla extract
75g walnut or pecan pieces
175g dark chocolate (70% cocoa
    solids), chopped or broken into
    nut-size chunks

TO DECORATE

100g good-quality white chocolate,
    broken into chunks

2 baking sheets, lined with baking
    paper; a disposable piping bag

1 Preheat the oven to 180°C/350°F/gas 4. Sift the flour, cocoa powder, salt, bicarbonate of soda and both sugars into a large mixing bowl. Add the soft butter. Beat the egg and vanilla together with a fork until frothy, then add to the bowl with the nuts and chocolate. Mix all the ingredients together with a wooden spoon until thoroughly combined.

These are very, very dark and rich cookies, perfect when you want a deeply chocolatey treat at tea or coffee time. The secret is to use really good chocolate – look out for bars with around 70 per cent cocoa solids. And avoid overcooking because the rich mixture can easily scorch.

2 Using a rounded tablespoon of mixture for each cookie, drop or spoon it onto the lined baking sheets, spacing the spoonfuls well apart to allow for spreading. Bake for about 10 minutes until just firm – the cookies will continue cooking for a short time after they come out of the oven. If necessary, rotate the sheets during baking so the cookies bake evenly.

3 Leave to cool on the baking sheets for 5 minutes, then transfer to a wire rack and cool completely. Store in an airtight tin (undecorated) and eat within a week.

4 To decorate, melt the white chocolate (see page 308). Spoon the chocolate into the piping bag and pipe zigzags across the top of the cookies, then leave to set.

Marbled Lemon Squares

MAKES 20

FOR THE BISCUIT BASE
200g ginger biscuits, crushed
50g unsalted butter, melted

FOR THE CHEESECAKE MIXTURE
500g full-fat cream cheese
1 teaspoon vanilla extract
100g caster sugar
2 large free-range eggs, at room
   temperature

FOR THE TOPPING
225g lemon curd (for a home-made
   lemon curd recipe, see page 306)

1 traybake tin or cake tin (not loose-
based), 25.5 x 20.5 x 5cm, greased

1 Preheat the oven to 160°C/325°F/gas 3. To make the base, mix the biscuit crumbs with the melted butter until thoroughly combined. Tip into the prepared tin and spread evenly, then press down with the back of a spoon to make an even layer. Bake for 10 minutes. Remove and leave to cool for 15 minutes; leave the oven on.

2 For the cheesecake mixture, put the cream cheese, vanilla, sugar and eggs into a large mixing bowl and beat with a wooden spoon until smooth and creamy (or mix in a food-processor). Pour or spoon the mixture over the biscuit base and spread evenly.

3 Stir the lemon curd just to loosen it, then gently place teaspoonfuls of it randomly on top of the cheesecake mixture (don't worry if the curd starts to sink in). Using the narrow end of a chopstick, or a skewer, carefully swirl the lemon curd

Tiny squares of vanilla cheesecake marbled with plenty of lemon curd on a crunchy ginger-biscuit base – very impressive but easy to assemble. Home-made lemon curd is a real treat; there's a recipe on page 306 if you want to try it.

through the cheesecake to give a marbled appearance. Don't overdo it: you want to be able to still see blobs of lemon curd.

4 Bake for 25 minutes until just set (the mixture will continue cooking a bit longer after it comes out of the oven). Gently run a round-bladed knife around the inside of the tin to loosen the cheesecake, then leave to cool completely on a wire rack. Cover and chill for at least an hour before cutting into squares. Store in an airtight container in the fridge and eat within 5 days.

TIP
You can use broken bits and pieces of gingerbread from the Winter Woodland Cottage (see page 80) for the biscuit base. Remove any scraps of decorations before crushing the gingerbread.

Love Heart Biscuits

MAKES 12

FOR THE BISCUIT DOUGH
100g unblanched almonds
200g plain flour
good pinch of salt
80g icing sugar
125g unsalted butter, chilled
   and diced
3 large free-range egg yolks

FOR THE FILLING
200g raspberries
2 teaspoons cornflour
3 tablespoons caster sugar
icing sugar, for dusting

1 x 8cm heart-shaped cutter plus
   a smaller one; 2 baking sheets,
   lined with baking paper

Here, crisp butter-rich almond biscuits are sandwiched with a fresh fruit filling — an extra-special version of jammy dodgers. The biscuit dough is easily made in a food-processor. Make romantic hearts or cut out flowers or other pretty shapes.

1 Put the almonds, flour and salt into the bowl of a food-processor and process until the almonds are finely ground. Add the icing sugar and 'pulse' the machine a few times until combined. Add the pieces of butter and process until the mixture looks like coarse sand. Add the egg yolks and process until the mixture comes together in a ball of firm dough. Slightly flatten the dough, then wrap in clingfilm and chill for 15 minutes.

2 Roll out the dough on a lightly floured worktop to the thickness of a pound coin. Cut out heart shapes using the floured 8cm cutter, then use the floured smaller cutter to stamp out the middle from half of the shapes. Gather up the trimmings, re-roll and cut more heart shapes. Arrange them well apart on the lined baking sheets and chill for about 15 minutes.

3 Meanwhile, preheat the oven to 180°C/350°F/gas 4. Bake the biscuits for about 12 minutes until lightly coloured; if necessary, rotate the sheets halfway through baking so the biscuits cook evenly. Leave the biscuits to cool and firm up on the sheets for about 10 minutes, then transfer to a wire rack to cool completely.

4 To make the filling, put the raspberries, cornflour and caster sugar into a medium-sized pan. Set over medium heat and stir gently until the juices start to run and the fruit softens. Bring to the boil and simmer for 2 minutes, stirring, until thick. Pour into a heatproof bowl and leave to cool.

5 To assemble, spread the cold raspberry filling over the uncut biscuits, then top each with a cut-out shape. Dust with icing sugar. Once filled, eat the biscuits the same day. The unfilled biscuits can be stored in an airtight tin for up to 4 days, and the filling can be kept, covered, in the fridge for 4 days.

TIP
Add a swirl of whipped cream to each filled biscuit, top with a tiny fresh raspberry and serve for dessert.

Almond Swirl Sandwiches

MAKES 26

200g plain flour
pinch of salt
175g unsalted butter,
    chilled and diced
200g ground almonds
200g caster sugar
2 large free-range eggs,
    at room temperature, beaten
2 tablespoons cocoa powder

TO FINISH
½ quantity Butter Icing (see
    page 305)
1 tablespoon cocoa powder
milk, if needed

2 piping bags plus a large star tube;
    2 baking sheets, lined with
    baking paper

1 Preheat the oven to 160°C/325°F/gas 3.
Sift the flour and salt into a mixing bowl and
rub in the diced butter with your fingertips
until it resembles a fine crumb texture.
Using a round-bladed knife, stir in the
ground almonds and sugar followed by
the eggs, to make a firm dough.

2 Divide the biscuit dough into 2 equal
portions. Put one half into a piping bag fitted
with the large star tube and pipe 26 small
swirls about 3.5cm in diameter onto the
lined baking sheets. Space the biscuits

Simply elegant, with a rich buttery taste and
crisp texture, these biscuits make excellent
presents at Christmas, packed into
cellophane gift bags tied with gold ribbon.

slightly apart to allow for spreading. Bake
for 20–25 minutes until light golden (if your
swirls are smaller, check after 15 minutes);
rotate the sheets halfway through the baking
time so the biscuits colour evenly. Leave to
cool completely on the baking sheets.

3 While the first batch is baking, sift the
cocoa powder onto the worktop and gently
work it into the remaining dough. Spoon
the chocolate dough into the other piping
bag fitted with the clean star tube. Pipe
swirls and bake as before. Leave the to cool
on the baking sheets.

4 Use half of the butter icing to sandwich
the chocolate swirls together. Add the sifted
cocoa powder to the rest of the butter icing,
plus a little extra milk, if the mixture is too
stiff to spread, and use to sandwich the plain
swirls together. Serve the biscuits within
3 hours of filling.

TIP
The easiest way to pipe the
swirls is to imagine you are
starting to pipe the letter
'e', or piping shells.

Hippy Macaroons

MAKES 10

50g desiccated coconut
(unsweetened)
50g ground almonds
50g flaked almonds
125g caster sugar
1 tablespoon cornflour
2 large free-range egg whites,
at room temperature
½ teaspoon vanilla extract

TO DECORATE
Glacé Icing (see page 306),
made with 250g icing sugar
liquid edible food colouring

1–2 baking sheets, lined with baking
paper; 3 disposable piping bags

These free-form macaroons are a world away from the elegant, tiny French-style macaroons or the large, flattish round ones beloved of tearooms and traditional bakeries. They are quick and easy to make, crunchy on the outside and slightly chewy in the centre. And they have a groovy tie-dye finish.

1 Preheat the oven to 160°C/325°F/gas 3. Mix the coconut with the ground and flaked almonds, caster sugar and cornflour in a large mixing bowl. In another bowl, use a fork to whisk the egg whites with the vanilla until frothy. Tip onto the coconut mixture. Stir with a wooden spoon until thoroughly combined to make a stiff mixture. Leave to stand for 10 minutes to allow the mixture to thicken up a bit.

2 Spoon the mixture onto the lined baking sheet to make 10 macaroons, spacing them well apart to allow for spreading. They should look rough and craggy and be about 6cm across. Bake for about 20 minutes until a good golden colour. Remove the sheet from the oven and set it on a wire rack. Leave the macaroons to cool completely before carefully removing them from the lining paper. Store (undecorated) in an airtight container and eat within a week.

3 To decorate, divide 6 tablespoons of the glacé icing among 3 bowls and colour each with a few drops of edible food colouring. Put each colour into a piping bag, but don't snip the ends off just yet.

4 Spoon the remaining white icing over the macaroons – either over the domed tops or flat bottoms – leaving a 5mm edge clear of icing. While the white icing is still wet, snip the ends off the piping bags and pipe spirals of colour over the white icing.

5 To create a tie-dye effect, drag a cocktail stick through the spirals to merge the colours together (see page 69 for help with this feathering technique). Wipe the end of the cocktail stick after each stroke. Leave the icing to set.

TIP
Instead of glacé icing, you can simply drizzle 50g melted dark chocolate over the top of the cooled macaroons; leave to set before serving.

Crown Jewel Biscuits

MAKES 48

225g unsalted butter, softened
200g caster sugar
1 large free-range egg, at room
    temperature
1 teaspoon vanilla extract
450g plain flour
good pinch of salt
about 8 clear, fruit-flavoured,
    coloured boiled sweets or
    lollipops

1 crown-shaped cutter(or other shape
    to suit the occasion); a selection
    of smaller cutters for cutting out
    holes or other shapes (such as hearts
    and diamonds); 2–3 baking sheets,
    lined with baking paper, a cocktail
    stick (optional)

Made from a simple vanilla dough, these are truly lovely biscuits. The middle of each is cut out and filled with crushed boiled sweets, which melt during baking to form a shiny window in the crisp, pale gold biscuit. Once cold, they can be threaded onto thin ribbon to use as edible decorations.

1 Beat the butter with a wooden spoon or electric mixer until creamy. Gradually beat in the sugar. In a small bowl beat the egg and vanilla together with a fork until frothy, then gradually beat into the butter mixture. Sift the flour and salt into the bowl and work them into the butter mixture with your hands to make a shortbread-like dough. Bring the dough together into a ball, then flatten to a thick disc. Wrap in clingfilm and chill for 20 minutes until firm enough to roll out.

2 Roll out the dough on a lightly floured worktop to the thickness of a pound coin. Cut out crowns with a well-floured cutter, then cut out the centre of each shape using a smaller cutter. Gather all the scraps and trimmings into a ball, re-roll and cut more shapes. Arrange the shapes well apart on the lined baking sheets and chill for 10–15

minutes or up to an hour. (The biscuits can be easily baked in batches; just leave the baking sheets to cool down before adding the next batch.) To turn the biscuits into edible decorations, make a small hole in each biscuit using a cocktail stick.

3 Preheat the oven to 180°C/350°F/gas 4. Put the sweets into plastic bags, keeping the colours separate, and crush with a rolling pin. Using a teaspoon, fill the centre of each biscuit shape with a little of the crushed sweets, not mixing the colours – fill just up to the level of the dough. Use a dry pastry brush to remove any specks of crushed sweetie from the dough itself. (It's worth assembling and baking a trial batch of 2 or 3 biscuits so you can judge just how much filling you need.)

4 Bake for about 12 minutes until a pale gold colour; if necessary, rotate the baking sheets halfway through baking so the biscuits colour evenly. Leave the biscuits to cool on the baking sheets, then carefully peel from the lining paper. (Use a cocktail stick to go over the holes, if making edible decorations.) Keep in an airtight tin and eat within 3 days. See TIP for an icing suggestion.

TIP
Make up some Royal Icing (see page 307), spoon it into a piping bag fitted with a No. 2 tube and pipe dots to decorate the crown edges, as shown here.

Multi-seed Savoury Crackers

MAKES **48**

230g wholemeal plain flour
115g semolina
¾ teaspoon crushed sea salt
55g sesame seeds
55g linseeds (flaxseeds)
55g pumpkin seeds
1 tablespoon runny honey
3 ½ tablespoons vegetable oil, plus
   extra for working
210ml lukewarm water
extra seeds for sprinkling (optional)

several baking sheets, lined with
   baking paper

Crisp and crunchy, and perfect with dips and cheese. If you can find smoked salt, or fleur de sel Guérande, use it instead of sea salt flakes for an extra special flavour. Cut these crackers into rectangles, as shown here, or diamonds as seen on the Bake Off.

1 Put the flour, semolina and salt into a large mixing bowl and mix together with your hand.

2 Roughly grind the seeds, one kind at a time, in a spice mill or nut grinder to give a mix of broken seeds and some more like a coarse meal – this will give the crackers an interesting texture and colour. Add to the bowl and mix well.

3 Whisk the honey and oil into the water, then pour into the dry ingredients and mix to a pastry-like dough with your hands. Knead the dough in the bowl for 5 minutes until it feels firmer and leaves the sides of the bowl clean. Cover the bowl with clingfilm and leave to rest for 20 minutes.

4 Meanwhile, preheat the oven to 180°C/350°F/gas 4. Rub the worktop with a little oil. Divide the dough into 3 equal pieces and keep 2 pieces covered. Roll out the third piece on the oiled worktop to a very thin – about the thickness of a credit card – rectangle a little larger than 16 × 28cm. Trim the sides to make them straight, using a ruler and a pizza cutter or large sharp knife, then cut the rectangle into 16 smaller rectangles each 4 × 7cm. Arrange slightly apart on a lined baking sheet. Roll and cut the other 2 pieces of dough in the same way.

5 Lightly spray or mist the crackers with water using a water-spray bottle and sprinkle with extra seeds, if using. Bake for 16–18 minutes until the edges of the crackers are turning golden. Turn off the oven; open the oven door for 30 seconds to let out heat and steam, then close it and leave the crackers in the cooling oven for 10–15 minutes until crisp. Transfer to a wire rack and leave to cool. Store in an airtight container and eat within a week.

Time for Tea

MAKES 18

FOR THE BISCUIT MIXTURE
115g unsalted butter, softened
100g caster sugar
finely grated zest of ½ unwaxed
    orange
1 large free-range egg yolk,
    at room temperature
85g ground almonds
225g plain flour
good pinch of salt
¼ teaspoon baking powder
½ teaspoon ground cinnamon
1 tablespoon orange juice
beaten egg, to glaze (optional)

TO DECORATE
2 quantities Royal Icing (see
    page 307)
liquid edible food colourings

shaped biscuit cutters, about 7–8 cm;
    2 baking sheets, lined with baking
    paper; piping bags plus No. 2
    piping tubes

These are really fun and you can be as creative as you like – try different shapes and add as little or as much decoration as you fancy. Leave plenty of time to allow the icing to dry. Ideally, make the biscuits the day before icing them.

1 Put the butter, sugar and orange zest in a large bowl and beat with an electric mixer or wooden spoon until creamy. Beat in the egg yolk followed by the almonds. Sift the flour, salt, baking powder and cinnamon into the bowl and add the orange juice. Work the ingredients together, using the wooden spoon at first and then your hands, to make a fairly firm dough.

2 Alternatively, put the butter, sugar and orange zest into the bowl of a food-processor and process until thoroughly combined, then work in the egg yolk followed by the almonds. Add the flour, salt, baking powder, cinnamon and orange juice and process until the mixture just comes together into a fairly firm dough.

3 Wrap the dough in clingfilm and chill for about 15 minutes until firm enough to roll out. (The dough can be kept, tightly wrapped, in the fridge for up to 5 days; if it gets very hard, leave at room temperature for 30 minutes or so before rolling out.)

4 Roll out the dough on a lightly floured worktop to the thickness of a pound coin and cut out shapes with the lightly floured cutters. Arrange the shapes, slightly apart, on the lined baking sheets and chill for about 15 minutes. Meanwhile, preheat the oven to 180°C/350°F/gas 4.

5 If you aren't going to ice the biscuits, brush them with beaten egg. Bake the biscuits for 10–12 minutes until lightly golden; if necessary rotate the baking sheets halfway through baking so the biscuits cook evenly. Remove from the oven and leave the biscuits to firm up for 5 minutes before carefully transferring them to a wire rack. When they are cold you can ice and decorate them (see page 110). Store in an airtight container and eat within a week.

Decorating Iced Biscuits

EQUIPMENT NEEDED

edible liquid food colourings

bowls, for mixing

6 piping bags plus 3 plain No. 2 tubes
  (if using 3 colours)

edible sprinkles (optional)

edible gold lustre
  (optional, see page 310)

a little vodka (optional)

small paintbrush (optional)

1 For piping and flooding, use royal icing with a fairly thick consistency (see page 307). Ideally bake your biscuits the day before so they are completely cold. Before you start decorating them, it is worth spending a little time planning your designs and what colour icings you are going to use. You will find it much easier if you start off with no more than 3 colours (we used lilac, blue and white to decorate the Time for Tea Biscuits on page 108).

2 Put half of the icing into a large bowl and cover with clingfilm to prevent it from drying out – this will be your flooding icing. Divide the remaining icing among 3 small bowls (we reserved a little icing in a fourth small bowl for the pink cherries in the Time for Tea Biscuits). Cover all but one bowl to prevent the icing from drying out.

3 Add a couple of drops of food colouring to the first bowl. Mix thoroughly before adding any more colour, a drop at a time, until you have the vibrancy you want. The icing should hold its shape and be thick enough for piping. If it is too thick, add water a few drops at a time; if it is too runny, simply add more icing sugar a teaspoon at a time.

4 Fit a No. 2 tube onto a piping bag. Spoon the icing into the bag and test the flow speed and shape (see page 312). Keeping the pressure consistent, squeeze the bag to start the icing flow. Slowly trace the outline of a biscuit with piped icing (photo 1). If you are going to use flooding icing as well, make sure there are no gaps between the lines. You can use one or more colours to outline the biscuits, depending on how much detail you want to add.

5 Once you have finished piping the outlines with this colour, make up the next piping colour. (There should be a little icing left over in each piping bag when you finish this first stage.) Put the second icing into a clean piping bag fitted with a No. 2 tube and pipe outlines as before. Repeat with your third piping colour (or white).

6 Leave the piped icing to dry while you make your flooding icing. Divide the remaining royal icing between the 3 icing bowls and add just enough water to each bowl to give the icing a pourable consistency. Add food colouring as before until you have reached the desired shade.

7 Fill one of the clean piping bags, without a tube, with your first colour. (Using flooding icing that matches the colour of the piping works best, but do try out your own designs.) Hold the bag above the area on the biscuit you want to flood and gently squeeze (photo 2). Be careful not to overfill the area: the icing will run to fill the space marked by your piping icing. Push the flooding icing gently with the edge of the piping bag anywhere it doesn't run easily to cover. When you have finished with this colour, repeat the process with the next colour, and then the third.

8 You can add a pattern to your flooding icing, creating a 'flood-on-flood' design (we added polka dots and hearts). Do this before the first flooding icing colour has set. For polka dots, add blobs of flooding icing in a contrasting colour

Technique continues overleaf

over the flooded area (photo 3). Do this randomly or in an ordered pattern. To create heart shapes, simply drag the tip of a cocktail stick gently through the wet polka dots and background icing.

9 At this point, while the flooding icing is still sticky, you can finish the biscuits by sprinkling them with edible sprinkles. Leave to dry.

10 If you want to do more piping, to add details to the biscuits, leave them to dry completely – about 4 hours. Use the remaining piping icing to decorate. (If the piping icing has dried in the tip you will need to scrape the icing into a clean piping bag). On the Time for Tea cupcake biscuits, we piped 'texture' on the cupcake cases and swirls of 'icing' (photo 4), and we added another piped outline, in the same or a contrasting colour, on the other biscuit shapes, to create a 3D effect. We finished the cupcake biscuits with piped pink cherries on top. Leave the icing decoration to set completely before moving the biscuits.

11 To add a little sparkle to your plain or iced biscuits, mix edible gold lustre with a little vodka to create a gold paint and brush delicately onto the icing once the biscuits are completely dry (see page 310). Leave to set.

Toffee Almond Shortbread

MAKES 24

FOR THE BASE
175g plain flour
good pinch of salt
3 tablespoons caster sugar
125g unsalted butter,
    chilled and diced
1 large free-range egg yolk

FOR THE TOPPING
100g unsalted butter
200g flaked almonds
3 tablespoons caster sugar
2 tablespoons honey
3 tablespoons single or
    whipping cream
icing sugar, to decorate (optional)

1 swiss roll tin, 20.5 x 30.5cm,
    well greased

Something slightly different for an afternoon tea party or to pack up for a picnic. For a bit of fun, the squares can be decorated with delicate icing sugar shapes.

1 To make the base, sift the flour, salt and sugar into a mixing bowl. Add the butter and rub in with your fingertips until the mixture resembles fine crumbs. Add the egg yolk and gently work and knead the mixture together with your hands to make a dough. (Alternatively, put the flour, salt and sugar into a food-processor bowl and 'pulse' to mix, then add the butter and egg yolk and process until the dough comes together.)

2 Crumble the dough into the tin and spread evenly, then flour your fingers and gently press the mixture onto the base of the tin in a smooth, even layer. Prick well with a fork and chill for 15 minutes.

3 Meanwhile, preheat the oven to 190°C/375°F/gas 5. Bake the shortbread base for 10–12 minutes until it is light golden. Remove from the oven; leave the oven on.

4 Melt the butter in a non-stick frying pan. Add the almonds, sugar and honey and cook over low heat, stirring gently, until bubbling and straw-coloured. Stir in the cream. Bring back to a simmer and cook for just 1 minute. Pour the mixture over the base and spread evenly (take care as it will be very hot).

5 Return to the oven and bake for 10–12 minutes until the topping has turned a glossy golden brown. Transfer the tin to a wire rack and leave until completely cold and set (preferably overnight) before cutting into squares. Store in an airtight container and eat within 4 days.

6 For an optional decoration, cut out small, simple shapes – butterflies, diamonds and hearts work well – from greaseproof paper to make stencils. Place a stencil on each square and sprinkle liberally with sifted icing sugar. Carefully lift off the stencil, with the help of a small knife, to reveal the shape.

Bread & Sweet Dough

PAUL WOULD BE THE FIRST TO SAY THAT A HAND-BAKED LOAF HAS A TASTE AND TEXTURE A WORLD AWAY FROM MASS-PRODUCED BREAD. That's what makes it such a marvellous treat. It can make the simplest meal special – fine-looking rolls can turn picnic salads into a great al fresco feast, while richly fragrant, warm brioche rolls or just-fried doughnuts with freshly brewed coffee make a memorable brunch.

To make a basic loaf of bread, all you need is flour, yeast, salt, water, a baking sheet, an oven and some time. It's not difficult – you need no special skills and it's not expensive. Yet the rewards are immensely satisfying.

Our chapter begins with recipes based on the Showstopper Sweet Dough Challenge – baking a celebratory brioche. We have given you a basic recipe and our Showstopping recipes will challenge you to make easy Sweet Brunch Rolls, a slightly more complicated Camembert Brioche and finally Herby Brioche Rolls.

Paul has included his recipe for jam doughnuts here as well as his favourite flatbread recipe flavoured with Camembert and quince jam. There is also a delicious bagel recipe and flatbread from the bakers. The basic ingredients needed for these recipes are easy to find. Most supermarkets and health shops stock a broad selection of flours – from white and wholemeal wheat flours to ryes, spelts, combinations with wholegrains and a range of stone-grounds.

Bread can also be surprisingly beautiful – see Paul's Plaited Loaf on page 130 and we also show you some techniques for shaping and finishing bread on page 142.

Be creative with shape and pick what works best for the occasion. Bread rolls are the default bake for large numbers, but by varying the shapes – oval, round, baton, square, plaited or knotted – as well as the toppings, the rolls will look and taste distinctive. A loaf baked in a tin is best for sandwiches because the neat regular shape slices well. But that doesn't mean the bread has to be plain – try adding a handful of fresh herbs, or make a well-flavoured, dark pumpernickel-style loaf that's perfect for open-faced sandwiches.

It's fun to experiment with flours and discover what you can make. Each loaf you bake will be different and you will learn from each one. Find out if there's a mill in your area – you may be lucky enough to bake bread from grain grown locally, which is bound to be a showstopper!

You can adapt and flavour a simple dough; add cubes of Manchego cheese and a handful of stuffed green olives for a free-form bread to serve with good-quality olive oil and balsamic vinegar; mix dried cranberries, raisins and pecans into the sweet dough for an attractive plaited loaf; give a generous sprinkling of ground cinnamon and sugar to a breakfast bread; or encase a whole Camembert cheese topped with chutney in a rich dough to make a decadent starter.

Just as you only need a few staple ingredients, there's also no need to buy a lot of expensive equipment. Paul always prefers to use his hands when baking because you can feel the dough coming together, reaching the right texture. A large bowl, measuring jug, scales and a good heavy baking sheet will get you started. Well-made loaf tins are useful too, and they can also be used for loaf-shaped cakes and terrines. It's easy to make an everyday food like bread into a special treat – just bake it at home, with love.

DON'T FORGET

● Yeast-raised breads need flour that contains more gluten (to give it structure) than mixtures made with chemical raising agents such as baking powder, bicarbonate of soda and cream of tartar, so choose flours labelled 'strong' or 'bread flour' rather than plain, self-raising or cake flour.

● Thorough kneading is a vital step for good bread; it develops the gluten in the flour so it stretches to support the bubbles of carbon dioxide produced by the rapidly growing yeast. It also makes sure the yeast is evenly distributed throughout the dough so it rises evenly and doesn't end up distorted or with huge holes.

● Though a serious investment, a large free-standing electric mixer with a dough hook attachment is a boon if you make a lot of bread and find hand-kneading difficult.

● Freshly baked bread is best cooled on a wire rack.

● Once the bread is cold, if you don't plan to use it immediately, wrap it in a clean tea towel or greaseproof paper, then store it in a bread bin or large paper bag – not a plastic box or container, in a cool airy spot rather than the fridge or under hot kitchen lights.

● Don't throw away leftover bread – it's too good to waste. Use it for croutons or crostini, or for bread and butter pudding. Or turn it into breadcrumbs and freeze.

Brioche Dough

375g strong white bread flour
1 teaspoon sea salt flakes, crushed
1 tablespoon caster sugar
1 x 7g sachet fast-action dried yeast
OR 15g fresh yeast
4 tablespoons milk, chilled
4 large free-range eggs, chilled
175g unsalted butter, at room
temperature, diced

Brioche is the most buttery-rich and golden of breads, with a delicate, sponge-cake-like crumb. Use this dough to create a simple loaf or one of the following Showstopping Challenges: Sweet Brunch Rolls, Camembert Brioche or Herby Brioche Rolls.

1 Put the flour, salt and sugar into a mixing bowl or the bowl of a large free-standing electric mixer and combine with your hand or the dough hook attachment of the mixer. If using dried yeast mix it in. If using fresh yeast, crumble it into a small bowl and mix to a smooth liquid with the milk.

2 Add the milk (or the yeast/milk mixture) and the eggs to the flour and work in by hand, or using the mixer on low speed, to make a very soft and sticky dough. Turn out onto a floured worktop and knead with floured hands for 10 minutes, or knead for 6 minutes in the mixer. Gradually work in the butter, a few pieces at a time, to make a silky-smooth, soft and still sticky dough.

3 Scrape the dough back into the mixing bowl and cover with a snap-on lid, or slip the bowl into a large plastic bag and secure the ends. Put the dough in the fridge to rise for 1–2 hours until doubled in size.

4 Flour your knuckles and punch down the dough to deflate it, then cover again and return to the fridge. Chill for another hour. The dough is now ready for shaping.

TO MAKE A SIMPLE BRIOCHE LOAF

Grease a 450g loaf tin, about 19 × 12.5 × 7.5cm, or line the base with baking paper. Turn out the chilled dough onto a lightly floured worktop and with floured fingers pat out to a rectangle about 18 × 25cm. Roll up from one short side like a swiss roll and pinch the seam to seal. Lift the rolled loaf, seam side down, into the tin, tucking the ends under. Slip the tin into a large plastic bag, slightly inflate to prevent the dough from sticking to the plastic and secure the ends. Leave to rise in a warm place for 1–1 ½ hours until doubled in size.

Towards the end of the rising time preheat the oven to 220°C/425°F/gas 7. Uncover the risen brioche and lightly brush with beaten egg to glaze. Bake for 15 minutes. Reduce the oven temperature to 180°C/350°F/gas 4 and bake for a further 25–30 minutes until a deep golden brown and the turned-out loaf sounds hollow when tapped underneath; if you hear a dull 'thud' instead return the loaf to the tin and bake for a further 5 minutes, then test again. Cool completely on a wire rack before slicing. This loaf freezes well.

Sweet Brunch Rolls

MAKES 10

1 quantity Brioche Dough (see page 121), with ½ teaspoon vanilla extract added with the milk
75g raisins
1 tablespoon orange juice
beaten egg, to glaze
icing sugar, for dusting

FOR THE FRANGIPANE
60g unsalted butter, softened
60g caster sugar
60g ground almonds
finely grated zest of ½ medium orange
1 large free-range egg yolk
1 teaspoon orange juice

10 cardboard mini loaf-cake cases, about 9.5 x 5.5cm; a baking sheet

For a special breakfast or brunch, try these spiralled brioche rolls filled with a rich almond and orange mix. They are perfect enjoyed warm just as they are, or you can serve them with butter and apricot jam, along with plenty of good coffee.

1 Make up the Brioche Dough following the method on page 121. While the brioche dough is chilling in the fridge, soak the raisins in the orange juice for a couple of hours, and make the frangipane mixture by beating all the ingredients together until thoroughly combined. Keep it cool.

2 Turn out the chilled dough onto a lightly floured worktop and punch down to deflate. Divide into 2 equal pieces; cover one piece loosely with clingfilm. Roll out the other piece to a 44 × 12cm rectangle. Spread over half of the frangipane mixture, leaving a 1cm border clear along one long edge. Drain the raisins, if necessary, then scatter half of them over the dough. Roll up like a swiss roll from the long edge without the dough border to make a neat roll 44cm long. Pinch the seam to seal and set the roll seam side down on the worktop. With a floured large, sharp knife, cut the roll across into 5 equal pieces. Set each one, seam side down, in a mini cake case. Repeat with the other portion of dough.

3 Place the cases on the baking sheet and cover loosely with clingfilm. Leave to rise for about 1 hour until doubled in size – the time will depend on the temperature of the dough to start with and the room. Towards the end of the rising time preheat the oven to 200°C/400°F/gas 6.

4 Uncover the rolls and brush the tops very lightly with beaten egg to glaze. Bake for about 30 minutes until well risen and a good golden brown. Transfer the cases to a wire rack and leave to cool. Serve the rolls dusted with icing sugar. They are best eaten warm the same or the next day, or they can be frozen.

TIP
Instead of dusting the rolls with icing sugar, brush them lightly with warmed apricot glaze (sieved apricot jam, gently warmed) and scatter toasted flaked almonds on top.

Camembert Brioche

SERVES

1 quantity Brioche Dough
(see page 121)
1 x 350g Camembert cheese,
about 13cm across
about 5 tablespoons well-spiced
fruity chutney, such as apple and
raisin, or roasted peppers
beaten egg, to glaze

1 baking sheet, lined with baking paper

This is very rich but very good! Serve as a starter to share, with a simple watercress and endive salad with a sharp dressing to contrast the creamy cheese and buttery brioche. You can score the dough in any pattern you like – spirals and sunbursts (as pictured) work best.

1 Make up the Brioche Dough following the method on page 121. Turn out the chilled dough onto a lightly floured worktop. Cut off one-quarter, cover and set aside until needed. Roll out the larger portion of dough to a round about 10cm larger than your cheese (about 23cm across). Gently lift up the dough just to check that it's not sticking to the worktop; dust on more flour if necessary, then lay the dough flat again. Spread the top of the cheese with a thick layer of chutney and set it upside down in the middle of the dough round.

2 With a well-floured sharp knife, trim about 1cm from the edge of the dough round to remove the thick rim. Add the trimmed-off rim to the reserved portion of dough and briefly knead together, then roll out to a round about 14cm across. Trim into a neat round using a small plate as a guide.

3 Brush the exposed surfaces of the cheese and the outer 1cm of the dough border with the beaten egg glaze. Lift up the dough border, in small sections, and wrap over the cheese, leaving the centre exposed. Use more egg glaze as necessary to stick the dough in

place. Brush the dough on top of the cheese with egg glaze, then set the smaller dough round on top and pat gently to seal together thoroughly. With floured hands carefully invert the cheese brioche onto the prepared baking sheet. Gently mould the edges to smooth out any bumps or bulges and to seal any gaps. Cover loosely with clingfilm and leave to rise at room temperature for about 30 minutes until almost doubled in size. Towards the end of the rising time preheat the oven to 190°C/375°F/gas 5.

4 Brush the dough lightly with beaten egg, taking care you don't 'glue' the dough to the baking sheet, then neatly score a pattern in the top with the tip of a sharp knife. Bake for 30 minutes, then brush again with beaten egg and bake for a further 10 minutes.

5 Remove from the oven and leave to cool for 45 minutes before serving – the cheese will still be runny. Alternatively, cool to room temperature (this will take about 4 hours) so the cheese firms up a bit before serving. For a picnic, leave the brioche until cold, then wrap. Take along a sharp knife – the brioche will cut into neat slices.

Herby Brioche Rolls

MAKES
12

1 quantity Brioche Dough
    (see page 121)
100g unsalted butter,
    cool and firm but not hard
1 rounded tablespoon finely
    chopped fresh mixed herbs
    (such as parsley, thyme, rosemary,
    chives, oregano)
beaten egg, to glaze

1 x 12-hole muffin tray, non-stick
    or silicone, well greased

A cross between brioche and croissants, these rolls are an enjoyable challenge for a keen bread-maker. The chilled brioche dough is spread with herb butter, then given several 'turns' of rolling and folding, just like puff pastry. The result is a crisp, flaky, exceedingly buttery roll.

1 Make up the Brioche Dough following the method on page 121. Turn out the chilled dough onto a lightly floured worktop and roll out to a rectangle about 18 × 54cm. Mash the butter with the herbs until spreadable but not oily. Spread the herb butter evenly over two-thirds of the dough rectangle. Fold the butter-free third of the rectangle over the middle section, then fold over the third from the other side to make a 3-layer square 'sandwich'. Seal the open edges with the side of your hand.

2 Give the dough a quarter turn so the rounded folded edge is to the left, a bit like the spine of a book, and the part-open edge is on your right. Roll out the dough to a rectangle as before and fold in 3 again. Seal the edges and give the dough a quarter turn, then repeat the rolling and folding once more. Wrap the dough in clingfilm and chill for 45 minutes to 1 hour until the dough is cool and firm.

3 Roll out the dough on a lightly floured worktop to a 48 × 30cm rectangle. Neaten the edges by trimming with a sharp knife, then roll up the dough like a swiss roll from one long edge. Pinch the seam to seal. Cut the roll across into 12 equal pieces using a floured large, sharp knife. Set one piece cut side down in each hole of the muffin tray. Brush very lightly with beaten egg glaze (take care not to 'glue' the dough to the tray).

4 Slip the muffin tray into a large plastic bag and inflate (by flapping the ends of the bag) so the plastic doesn't stick to the dough, then secure the end. Leave to rise in a warm but not hot place for about 45 minutes until doubled in size. Towards the end of the rising time preheat the oven to 220°C/425°F/gas 7.

5 Uncover the risen rolls and brush once more with beaten egg glaze. Bake for 25–30 minutes until the rolls are a good chestnut brown and smell 'toasty'. Turn out onto a wire rack and leave to cool. Eat warm the same day or the next, or freeze.

Christmas Wreath

SERVES

15

FOR THE BRIOCHE DOUGH
500g strong white bread flour
1 teaspoon salt
50g caster sugar
1 x 7g sachet fast-action dried yeast
¾ teaspoon ground mixed spice
12 cardamom pods, seeds finely ground
6–7 large free-range eggs (350g shelled
    weight), chilled, beaten
250g unsalted butter, at room
    temperature, diced
beaten egg, to glaze

FOR THE ORANGE CURD
85g unsalted butter
170g caster sugar
finely grated zest of 2 oranges
juice of 1 orange and 1 lemon
3 large free-range eggs, at room
    temperature
1 tablespoon orange liqueur

FOR THE FRUIT FILLING
100g sultanas
2 tablespoons orange flower water
100g pistachios, roughly chopped
finely grated zest of 1 orange
200g white marzipan, cut in 1cm cubes

TO FINISH
150g Fondant Icing sugar
about 2 tablespoons orange juice
1 tablespoon each toasted almonds
    and chopped pistachios

1 x 15cm round deep cake tin, greased
    outside and completely covered with
    parchment-lined foil; a 30cm loose-
    based flan tin, greased and lined with
    parchment-lined foil; 4 individual brioche
    moulds or a 6-hole silicon muffin tray,
    greased; a squeezy icing bottle

1 Put the flour, salt, sugar, yeast and spices into a mixing bowl. Add the eggs, then make up the

Here, an egg-rich brioche dough is flavoured with fruit, marzipan, pistachios and oranges and baked as a ring. Afterwards it's filled with orange curd and decorated with an orange fondant icing and more nuts. You can also add sugar paste holly leaves and berries.

brioche dough (follow the method on page 121 up to the end of stage 4). The dough should be thoroughly chilled and firm.

2 While the dough is chilling, make the orange curd (see Lemon Curd on page 306). Add the Cointreau, then cover and chill.

3 For the filling, mix the sultanas with the orange flower water and leave to soak.

4 Roll out the chilled brioche dough on a lightly floured worktop to a square with 32cm sides. Drain the sultanas and scatter over the dough, followed by the pistachios, zest and marzipan. Roll up the dough away from you like a swiss roll, then turn the rolled dough so it is lying vertically. Pat or roll it out to a square once more, then roll it up again as before.

5 Cut the rolled-up dough across into 15 equal portions and shape each into a neat ball with floured hands. Set the covered cake tin in the centre of the lined flan tin to fashion a ring-shaped mould. Arrange 11 of the brioche balls in this ring, setting them slightly apart. Set the remaining balls in the prepared brioche moulds or muffin tray. Cover everything lightly with clingfilm and leave to rise at room temperature for 1–2 hours until doubled in size. Towards the end of the rising time preheat the oven to 220°C/425°F/gas 7.

6 Uncover the risen brioche dough and brush lightly with beaten egg, taking care not to 'glue' the dough to the tin. Bake for 10 minutes, then reduce the oven temperature to 200°C/400°F/gas 6. Bake the individual brioches for a further 10 minutes, and the ring for a further 20–25 minutes, until they are a good rich golden brown (if necessary cover the ring with foil if it is browning too quickly). Leave to firm up for 10 minutes, then carefully turn out the small brioches and unmould the ring. Cool on a wire rack.

7 Fill a squeezy icing bottle with the orange curd. Inject a little into each brioche bun in the ring and into each individual brioche (see page 164 for how to do this).

8 Mix the Fondant Icing sugar with enough orange juice to make a smooth icing that just flows. Drizzle over the wreath and each little brioche (there will be some leftover). Decorate with the nuts, then leave to set before carefully transferring to a serving platter. Pile the little brioches into the ring or serve them separately. Serve with the rest of the orange curd. Best eaten the same day.

Paul's Plaited Loaf

MAKES 1 LOAF

500g strong white bread flour
10g salt
2 x 7g sachets fast-action dried yeast
20ml olive oil
340ml water, at room temperature
1 beaten egg, mixed with a pinch
  of salt, to glaze

1 baking sheet, dusted with flour

1 Put the flour into a mixing bowl. Put the salt on one side of the bowl and the yeast on the other, making sure they don't touch as the salt can kill the yeast. Add the oil, then stir together with your hand or a spoon until everything is evenly mixed.

2 Add three-quarters of the water and bring the mixture together with your hands. Work in the rest of the water. Knead the dough for about 10 minutes until it is silky and very stretchy. The dough should be slightly soft but not sticky, nor dry and tough.

3 Tip the dough into a lightly oiled bowl, cover tightly with clingfilm and leave to rise at room temperature for about 1 hour until doubled in size.

4 Punch down (knock back) the risen dough to deflate, then turn it out onto a lightly floured worktop and shape into a ball. Divide into 8 equal pieces. Using your hands, roll each piece on the worktop until it is a thin, sausage-shaped strand about 40cm long.

5 Lay the strands of dough out on the floured worktop like an octopus and tack all the gathered ends to the table with your thumb.

This is one of Paul's favourite loaves to make. Practise using lengths of string until you get the hang of the plait.

As they are laid out in front of you, number them 1–8 and proceed to plait following the sequence below. Note that every time you move a strand, the order of the numbers will revert to the original 1–8 sequence.

STEP 1: Place strand 8 under strand 7, then over strand 1.

STEP 2: Strand 8 over strand 5.

STEP 3: Strand 2 under strand 3, then over strand 8.

STEP 4: Strand 1 over strand 4.

STEP 5: Strand 7 under strand 6 then over strand 1.

Repeat from step 2 until all the strands are plaited, then tuck the ends under the loaf to neaten.

6 Set the plaited loaf on the floured baking sheet and leave to rise at room temperature for about 1 hour until almost doubled in size. Towards the end of the rising time preheat the oven to 200°C/400°F/gas 6.

7 Brush the risen loaf with seasoned beaten egg to glaze, then bake for 20–25 minutes until golden brown and the loaf sounds hollow when tapped on the underside. Cool on a wire rack.

Pumpernickel Rye

MAKES
2
LOAVES

300g stoneground rye flour
150g stoneground wholemeal
    bread flour
150g strong white bread flour
2 teaspoons sea salt flakes, crushed
1 tablespoon dark brown
    muscovado sugar
1 x 7g sachet fast-action dried yeast
    OR 15g fresh yeast
about 400ml lukewarm water
1 tablespoon black treacle
3 tablespoons low-fat plain yoghurt,
    at room temperature

TO FINISH
rye flakes, for sprinkling

2 x 450g loaf tins, about 19 x 12.5 x
    7.5cm, well greased; a roasting tin

Rye breads come in many styles, from the light, mild New York type, to the darkly bitter, dense sour ryes of Eastern Europe. This one is a pumpernickel style: a flat-topped loaf with a dark, moist and not-too-close crumb that slices well. It has plenty of flavour and is the perfect loaf for breakfast toast, to eat with cheese or for making open sandwiches.

1 Combine the rye, wholemeal and white flours in a large mixing bowl or the bowl of a large free-standing electric mixer. Using your hand or the dough hook attachment of the mixer, stir in the salt and sugar, plus the dried yeast, if using. If using fresh yeast, crumble it into a small bowl and mix to a smooth liquid with 7 tablespoons of the measured water.

2 Make a well in the flour mixture and add the treacle, yoghurt and water (and the fresh yeast liquid, if using). Gradually work the flours into the liquids using your hand, or the dough hook on the lowest possible speed, to make a very heavy, moist and slightly sticky dough. If necessary, work in more water a tablespoon at a time – the dough should not feel dry and stiff.

3 Turn out onto a very lightly floured worktop and knead thoroughly by hand for 10 minutes, or knead for 5 minutes in the mixer using the dough hook. Try not to work in too much additional flour: the dough will firm up as you knead but it should still be very soft and slightly sticky. Return the dough to the bowl and cover with a snap-on lid or clingfilm. Leave to rise in a warm but not too dry place (rye bread needs a steamy kitchen for best results) for 1 ½–2 hours until doubled in size.

4 Punch down the risen dough to deflate, then turn out onto a lightly floured worktop and knead lightly for a few seconds. Divide the dough into 2 equal pieces. Sprinkle the insides of the loaf tins with rye flakes, then flour your fingers and press a portion of dough into each tin, right to the corners, to make a neat, even brick shape. Scatter more rye flakes over the top of each loaf. Slip the tins into a large plastic bag and inflate slightly to prevent the dough from sticking to the plastic, then secure the ends. Leave to rise as before for about 1 ½ hours until doubled in size.

5 Towards the end of the rising time preheat the oven to 200°C/400°F/gas 6. Put the roasting tin half-filled with warm water into the oven to create a moist atmosphere.

6 Uncover the tins and bake for about 35 minutes until the turned-out loaves sound hollow when tapped on the underside. If there is a dull 'thud' instead, return the loaves to the oven (straight onto the shelf) and bake for 5 more minutes, then test again. Leave the turned-out loaves to cool on a wire rack until completely cold, then wrap in greaseproof paper and foil and leave for 24 hours before slicing. Eat the bread within a week or freeze.

RAISIN RYE

The bread can be flavoured to work with your menu: add 85g raisins as you start to knead the dough, or add 1 tablespoon caraway seeds with the sugar.

TIP

Try the following topping ideas for open sandwiches: spread slices with soft, creamy cheese (goats' cheese is very good) mixed with chopped fresh herbs and top with thin slices of smoked salmon, prosciutto, cooked prawns or slices of avocado dipped in lemon juice. Lightly buttered slices can be covered with thinly sliced cold roast beef or flaked smoked trout topped with a dash of horseradish cream; or slices of pear, dipped in lemon juice, and crumbled blue cheese.

Fig, Walnut & Gruyère Bagels

MAKES 12

500g strong white bread flour
1 ½ teaspoons salt
1 x 7g sachet fast-action dried yeast
75g soft-dried figs, roughly chopped
250ml lukewarm water
1 tablespoon runny honey
1 tablespoon olive oil
1 medium free-range egg, at room
   temperature
1 teaspoon yeast extract (e.g. Marmite)

FOR THE TOPPING
beaten egg, for glazing
60g walnut pieces, finely chopped
70g thinly sliced Gruyère, cut into
   1cm squares

2 baking sheets, lined with baking paper

This is the first time that bagels have been made on the Bake Off. These are good filled with cream cheese.

1 Combine the flour, salt, yeast and chopped figs in a large mixing bowl. In a jug, mix together the water, honey, oil, egg and yeast extract. Pour into the bowl and mix with your hand, or the dough hook of a large free-standing electric mixer, to make a fairly firm but not dry dough; add a little more water or flour as needed.

2 Turn out the dough onto a lightly floured worktop and knead by hand for 10 minutes (5 minutes in the mixer) until smooth and elastic. Divide the dough into 12 equal portions and shape each into a neat ball. Set well apart on a well-floured tray or board and cover very lightly with oiled clingfilm. Leave to rise in a warm place for 25 minutes.

3 Push a floured wooden spoon handle through the centre of each ball to make a hole, then gently enlarge it with your fingers to prevent it from closing up as the dough rises again. Take care to make the bagels neat and evenly shaped. Cover and leave to rise as before for 35 minutes.

4 Towards the end of the rising time, preheat the oven to 230°C/450°F/gas 8. Bring a large wide pan, or wok, two-thirds full of water to the boil. Add the bagels, about 3 at a time, and poach for 75 seconds on each side. Remove with a slotted spoon and leave on a wire rack to dry out for about 5 minutes.

5 Lightly brush the top of each bagel with beaten egg. Spread the walnuts on a plate and gently press the top of each bagel onto them to coat. Set well apart on the lined baking sheets and bake for 15 minutes, rotating the sheets after 10 minutes so the bagels brown evenly. Remove the sheets from the oven and quickly top the bagels with the cheese. Bake for a further 3–4 minutes until melted. Transfer the bagels to a wire rack and leave to cool. Best eaten the same day.

BLUEBERRY & CHOCOLATE BAGELS

Make up the dough as before, but omit
the yeast extract and replace the figs with
75g dried blueberries. Poach and glaze the
bagels, but omit the walnuts and cheese.
Bake for about 18 minutes until golden
brown.Allow to cool. Temper 100g white
chocolate (see page 308), then use to pipe
zig-zags across the top of each bagel.
Leave to set.

Cinnamon Breakfast Loaf

MACKES **1 LOAF**

500g strong white bread flour
1 ½ teaspoons sea salt flakes,
    crushed
2 tablespoons caster sugar
1 x 7g sachet fast-action dried yeast
    OR 15g fresh yeast
125ml milk
50g unsalted butter
1 large free-range egg, at room
    temperature

FOR THE FILLING
50g caster sugar
1 teaspoon plain flour or white
    bread flour
1 tablespoon ground cinnamon

TO FINISH
milk, for brushing
small knob of butter

1 x 900g loaf tin, about 26 x 12.5 x
    7.5cm, greased; baking paper

A soft, rich bread with a delightful spicing of cinnamon, this is as good toasted as it is plainly buttered. The key to keeping a neat swirl is to use caster sugar rather than soft brown muscovado, and milk rather than egg for glazing the dough. Use any slightly stale slices for a pretty bread-and-butter pudding.

1 Mix together the flour, salt and sugar in a large mixing bowl or the bowl of a large free-standing electric mixer. If using dried yeast, stir it in. If using fresh yeast, crumble it into a small bowl and mix to a smooth liquid with about 7 tablespoons of the measured milk.

2 Gently warm the (remaining) milk with 125ml water and the butter until lukewarm and the butter has melted. Remove from the heat. Add the egg and beat with a fork until combined, then add to the flour mixture (with the fresh yeast mixture, if using). Work the ingredients together (use the mixer on the lowest speed) to make a very soft but not sticky dough. If there are dry crumbs at the base of the bowl, or the dough seems dry and hard to work, add more milk or water a tablespoon at a time. If the dough sticks to your hands or to the sides of the bowl then work in more flour a tablespoon at a time.

3 Turn out the dough onto a lightly floured worktop and knead thoroughly for about 10 minutes by hand, or knead for 5 minutes with the dough hook on low speed, until the dough is silky-smooth and pliable. Return the dough to the bowl, cover with a snap-on lid or clingfilm and leave to rise in a warm but not hot place for about 1 hour until doubled in size.

4 Meanwhile, prepare the tin. Cut a long strip of baking paper the same width as your tin and long enough to cover both short sides as well as the base. Press the paper into the tin – this makes the loaf easy to remove after baking in case the filling leaks. In a small bowl mix the sugar with the flour and cinnamon for the filling.

5 Punch down the risen dough to deflate, then turn out onto a lightly floured worktop and knead for a few seconds. Pat out to a rough rectangle about 2cm thick. Cover lightly with a sheet of clingfilm and leave to relax for 5 minutes – this will make it easier to roll out.

6 Lightly flour the rolling pin and roll out the dough to a rectangle as wide as the length of the tin and 48cm long. Keep the sides straight and neat. Brush the dough liberally with milk, then sprinkle over the sugar mixture in an even layer, leaving a 1cm border clear at one short end. Roll up the dough, neatly and tightly, from the other short end and pinch the seam together to seal it firmly.

7 Lift the rolled dough into the tin, gently tucking the ends under to make a neat shape. Slip the tin into a large plastic bag and slightly inflate it so the plastic doesn't stick to the dough, then tie the ends. Leave to rise as before until just doubled in size (don't let the loaf become too big or it will lose its shape). Towards the end of the rising time preheat the oven to 180°C/350°F/gas 4.

8 Uncover the dough and brush lightly with milk. Bake for about 35 minutes until a good golden brown and the turned-out loaf sounds hollow when it is tapped on the underside. If it sounds like a dull 'thud' return it to the oven (set straight on the shelf) and bake for a further 5 minutes, then test again.

9 Transfer the turned-out loaf to a wire rack and rub the butter over the top to give a glossy finish. Leave until completely cold before slicing. Eat within 5 days, or freeze.

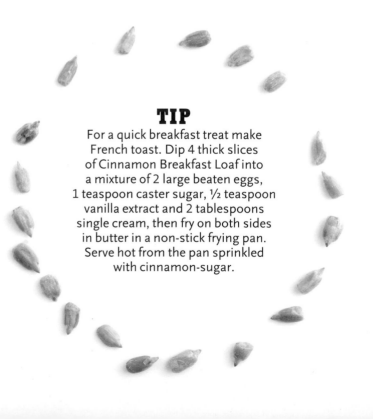

TIP

For a quick breakfast treat make French toast. Dip 4 thick slices of Cinnamon Breakfast Loaf into a mixture of 2 large beaten eggs, 1 teaspoon caster sugar, ½ teaspoon vanilla extract and 2 tablespoons single cream, then fry on both sides in butter in a non-stick frying pan. Serve hot from the pan sprinkled with cinnamon-sugar.

Pick 'n' Mix Rolls

MAKES

350g strong white bread flour
150g plain flour
1 teaspoon sea salt flakes, crushed
1 x 7g sachet fast-action dried yeast
   OR 15g fresh yeast
300ml lukewarm water

TO GLAZE
½ teaspoon sea salt flakes,
   dissolved in 50ml lukewarm water

TO DECORATE (OPTIONAL)
poppy seeds, linseeds and sesame
   seeds

baking paper; 1–2 baking sheets;
   a roasting tin

1 Mix the flours with the salt. Tip half of the mixture into a mixing bowl or the bowl of a large free-standing electric mixer. If using dried yeast, add ½ teaspoon to the flours in the bowl and mix well. If using fresh yeast, mix 5g with the lukewarm water.

2 Work the lukewarm water (or the yeast/water mixture) into the flour with your hand, or the dough hook attachment of the mixer, to make a very smooth, thick batter. Cover the bowl tightly with a snap-on lid or clingfilm and leave at room temperature for 2–3 hours, or overnight in the fridge, until the batter is thick and bubbly.

3 Uncover the bowl and stir the batter well. If using dried yeast, stir 1 tablespoon of water into the batter, and mix the rest of the yeast with the reserved flour mixture. If using fresh yeast, mix the remainder with 1 tablespoon water and stir into the batter.

It's worth the time and effort spent to make these perfect elegant rolls. Vary shapes, sizes and toppings (see page 142).

4 Gradually work the reserved flour mixture into the batter, using your hand or the dough hook attachment of the mixer on low speed, to make a dough that feels slightly soft but not sticky. If the dough sticks to your fingers or the sides of the bowl work in a little more flour. If the dough feels tough and dry or hard to work, or if there are dry crumbs in the base of the bowl, work in a little more water.

5 Turn the dough onto a very lightly floured worktop and knead by hand for 10 minutes, or knead for 5 minutes using the dough hook on the lowest speed, until the dough feels very smooth and elastic. Return the dough to the mixing bowl, cover and leave to rise in a warm place for about 1 hour until doubled in size.

6 Gently turn the risen dough onto the lightly floured worktop, without punching it down or handling it too much. Divide it into 8 equal portions and shape each one into a rough ball. Cover loosely with clingfilm and leave to rest for about 5 minutes, then shape the rolls (see page 142).

7 Set the rolls well apart on baking paper cut to fit your baking sheets and cover loosely with a sheet of clingfilm. Leave to rise until doubled in size – about 30–45 minutes in a warm kitchen.

Recipe continues overleaf

Do Try One!

8 Towards the end of the rising time, preheat the oven to its hottest setting, and put the baking sheets in to heat up. Also put the empty roasting tin in the bottom of the oven. Uncover the risen rolls and brush lightly with the salt glaze. Sprinkle with seeds (about ¼ teaspoon per roll), if using, then slash each roll with a very sharp knife (see page 142 for decorative ideas).

9 Slide the baking sheets out of the oven, on the oven shelves. With great care, lift the rolls – on their baking paper – and place on the hot baking sheets, then slide back into the oven. Pour some cold water into the hot roasting tin to create a burst of steam and quickly close the oven door. Bake for about 10 minutes until golden brown.

10 Push the rolls off the paper-lined baking sheets and straight onto the oven shelves. Bake for a further 2–3 minutes until crisp and a good golden brown. Transfer to a wire rack and leave to cool. Eat warm the same or the next day, or freeze.

TIP
The key to success is a really hot oven with a bit of steam (see step 9). Brushing the risen rolls with a salty glaze before baking on hot baking sheets also helps to achieve the thin and really crisp crust.

Shaping & Finishing Rolls

VARIATION 01

1 To shape a round roll, take one portion of dough and cup it in the palm of your hand. Using the fingers of your other hand, pull the outer edge of the dough outwards, then push it back in towards the centre.

2 Turn the dough over and repeat until the ball is smooth and neat on both sides.

3 Using a sharp knife, make a cross-shaped slash on top of the roll. Leave the rolls plain, or glaze and sprinkle with seeds (see Variations 2 and 3).

VARIATION 02

1 To make a mini baguette, lightly flour your hands and pat out one portion of dough to a rectangle about 10 x 15cm.

2 Tightly roll up from a long side like a swiss roll and pinch the seam to seal. With your hands roll the piece on the worktop to make a neat cigar shape about 20cm long with tapered ends.

3 Using a sharp knife, slash 6 evenly spaced lines diagonally across the baguette. Brush with a salt water glaze (see page 139), then sprinkle with linseeds or a mixture of poppy seeds and linseeds.

VARIATION 03

1 To make a 'squoval' roll, take one portion of dough and shape it into a ball (see Variation 1, steps 1 and 2.

2 Flatten the ball slightly and mould to a square shape with your hands.

3 Using a sharp knife, slash a grid of 2 horizontal and 2 vertical lines across the top (like a noughts and crosses board). Or slash a star shape: start with a cross, then slash across again between the lines so that you have slashed the roll 4 times across the centre.

4 Brush with a salt water glaze (see page 139), then sprinkle with poppy seeds or sesame seeds.

STUART

Blueberry Banana Bread

MAKES 1 LOAF

100g unsalted butter, softened
85g light brown muscovado sugar
85g honey
2 large free-range eggs,
    at room temperature, beaten
300g peeled bananas
    (about 3 medium)
50g walnut pieces
50g soft-dried blueberries
225g stoneground white spelt flour
good pinch of salt
1 ½ teaspoons baking powder

TO FINISH (OPTIONAL)
1 x 170g pot full-fat Greek-style
    yoghurt
1 teaspoon clear honey
75g fresh plump blueberries

1 x 900g loaf tin, about 26 x 12.5
    x 7.5cm, greased and the base
    lined with baking paper

There are plenty of flavours and textures in this tea bread – using stoneground spelt flour gives it a slightly nutty taste and specks of bran. A thick slice (without the blueberry and yoghurt topping) makes a good addition to a lunchbox.

1 Preheat the oven to 180°C/350°F/gas 4. Put the soft butter, sugar and honey into a mixing bowl and beat well with a wooden spoon or electric mixer until soft and light. Gradually add the eggs, beating well after each addition.

2 Coarsely mash the bananas with a fork, leaving some chunks, then add to the bowl together with the walnuts and dried blueberries. Gently stir in using a large metal spoon. Sift the flour, salt and baking powder into the bowl, adding any specks of bran left in the sieve. Gently fold everything together until there are no streaks visible.

3 Spoon the mixture into the prepared loaf tin and spread out evenly. Bake for about 50 minutes until golden brown and a cocktail stick inserted into the centre of the loaf comes out clean.

4 Leave to cool in the tin for 5 minutes, then run a round-bladed knife around the inside of the tin to loosen the loaf. Turn out onto a wire rack and leave to cool completely. Store in an airtight container and eat within 4 days.

5 To decorate the loaf for the tea table, mix together the yoghurt and honey. Dollop on top of the loaf and swirl neatly with the tip of a palette knife. Scatter over the fresh blueberries. Tie a purple ribbon round the loaf, if you like. Cut into thick slices to serve.

TIP
If you don't want to have a yoghurt and blueberry topping, just brush the loaf with 1 tablespoon honey as soon as you take it out of the oven. Slices are very good lightly toasted.

Lardy Cakes

MAKES 10

FOR THE DOUGH

170ml milk, plus extra for brushing
40g unsalted butter, cubed
about 375g strong white bread flour
1 teaspoon salt
2 tablespoons caster sugar
9g fast-action dried yeast
  (from 2 x 7g sachets)
1 small egg, at room temperature

FOR THE FILLING

250g lard, at room temperature
200g caster sugar
¾ teaspoon ground cinnamon
150g dried mixed fruit, soaked in
  2 tablespoons water

TO FINISH

caster sugar and ground cinnamon

1–3 non-stick 4-hole Yorkshire Pudding
  tins (see recipe), buttered and dusted
  with sugar

1 Gently warm the milk with the butter until the butter melts, then set aside to cool to lukewarm. Mix the flour with the salt, sugar and yeast in a large mixing bowl or the bowl of a large free-standing electric mixer. Whisk the egg into the buttery milk until combined, then add to the bowl. Work the mixture with your hand, or the dough hook attachment, to make a very soft but not sticky dough. If necessary, gradually work in extra flour a tablespoon at a time.

2 Turn out the dough onto a lightly floured worktop and knead thoroughly by hand for 10 minutes, or 5 minutes with the dough hook on low speed. Return the dough to the

With their crisp, sweet exteriors, light and flaky crumb and spicy, fruit-filled centres, these are high-class lardy cakes.

clean bowl, cover with clingfilm and leave to rise in a warm place for about 1 hour until doubled in size.

3 Meanwhile, mash the soft lard with the sugar and cinnamon on a large plate to make a soft, very spreadable paste. Divide it into 20 (this makes it easier to use later).

4 Punch down the risen dough to deflate, then divide into 10 equal portions. Shape each into a neat ball. Roll out one of the balls on a lightly floured worktop to a circle about 14cm across. Spread with one portion of the lard mixture (as if you were buttering bread). Fold about one-sixth of the edge of the circle into the centre. Repeat the folding all the way around, rotating the circle, so it becomes a hexagon. Roll out to a 14cm circle again. Repeat with the other 9 balls of dough. Cover the circles with a sheet of clingfilm and leave to rest for 10 minutes.

5 Uncover the circles and spread each with another portion of the lard mixture, then top with the dried fruit mixture (drain off any excess liquid first). Fold the edges of each circle to make hexagons as before.

6 Place each hexagon, with the side with the folded edges uppermost, into a hole in the prepared tin(s). Cover lightly with clingfilm and leave in a warm place to rise for about

45 minutes until doubled in size. (If you have only one 4-hole tin you can bake in batches; spread the rest of the prepared lardy cakes on a baking sheet lined with baking paper and keep them, lightly covered, in a cool spot so they rise slowly, then bake them in batches in the prepared tin.) Towards the end of the rising time preheat the oven to 200°C/400°F/gas 6.

7 Brush the lardy cakes lightly with milk and bake for 15 minutes until golden brown. Turn off the oven, and quickly open and close the oven door (to let out a bit of heat and steam). Leave the cakes in the oven for 5 minutes. Cool in the tin for 10 minutes, then turn out onto a wire rack. Sprinkle with sugar and cinnamon and leave until just warm before eating. Best the same day.

Olive Loaf

MAKES
LOAF

400g strong white bread flour,
    plus extra for optional pattern
100g stoneground wholemeal bread
    flour (or wholemeal spelt flour)
2 teaspoons sea salt flakes, crushed
1 x 7g sachet fast-action dried yeast
    OR 15g fresh yeast
350ml lukewarm water
3 tablespoons olive oil, plus extra
    for kneading
115g pimiento-stuffed green olives,
    drained
50g Manchego cheese, diced

baking paper; a baking sheet; a roasting
    tin; a doily, to decorate (optional)

Stuffed green olives and Manchego cheese
are worked into a simple dough to make this
good-looking loaf that is bursting with colour
and flavour. Serve warm with Spanish tapas,
or with good olive oil for dipping.

1 Mix both flours with the salt in a large
mixing bowl or the bowl of a large free-
standing electric mixer. If using dried yeast,
stir it in. If using fresh yeast, crumble it into
a small bowl and mix to a smooth liquid with
7 tablespoons of the measured water.

2 Add the water (plus the fresh yeast liquid,
if using) and the oil to the flour and work
in with your hand or the dough hook
attachment of the mixer (on low speed),
mixing just enough to make a shaggy-
looking soft, damp dough. Cover the bowl
with a snap-on lid or clingfilm and leave
to rest for 15 minutes.

3 Turn out the dough onto a lightly oiled
worktop. Lightly oil your hands, then knead
the dough for 4 minutes only (set the timer),
or knead for 2 minutes in the mixer. Cover
the dough with a sheet of clingfilm and leave
to rest for 20 minutes, then knead for
another 4 (or 2) minutes.

4 Combine the olives and cheese, then
gently work them into the dough. It should
still be soft but not stick to your hands or the
worktop. Transfer the dough to a sheet of
baking paper cut to fit your baking sheet
and pat out to an oval 1.5cm thick and about
20 × 30cm (it doesn't have to be neat). Cover
the loaf loosely with clingfilm and leave to
rise in a warm place for about 40 minutes
until doubled in size.

5 Towards the end of the rising time,
preheat the oven to 230°C/450°F/gas 8.
Put the baking sheet in to heat up and
place the empty roasting tin in the bottom
of the oven.

6 Uncover the risen loaf. If you're going to
make a pattern, as shown here, lay the doily
gently on top. Sift strong white bread flour
liberally over the doily, then carefully lift it
off the bread, without smudging the shape.
Pull the hot baking sheet out of the oven, on
its shelf, and carefully slide the loaf, on the
baking paper, onto the sheet. Slide it back
into the oven. Pour cold water into the hot
roasting tin to create a burst of steam and
quickly close the oven door. Bake the loaf
for about 20 minutes until a good golden
brown. Cool on a wire rack and eat warm
the same day.

Paul's Chelsea Buns

MAKES 10

FOR THE DOUGH

500g strong white bread flour,
    plus extra for dusting
1 teaspoon salt
1 x 7g sachet fast-action dried yeast
300ml milk
40g unsalted butter, softened
1 free-range egg, at room
    temperature
vegetable oil

FOR THE FILLING

25g unsalted butter, melted
grated zest of 1 orange
75g soft brown sugar
2 teaspoons ground cinnamon
100g dried cranberries
100g sultanas
100g dried apricots, chopped

TO FINISH

1 heaped tablespoon apricot jam
200g icing sugar, sifted
grated zest of 1 orange

1 deep baking tray, lightly greased

1 Put the flour and salt into a large mixing bowl. Make a well in the middle and add the yeast. Heat the milk and butter in a saucepan until the butter melts and the mixture is lukewarm. Add to the flour mixture with the egg and stir until the contents of the bowl come together as a soft dough. (If the dough is too wet, you may need to add a little extra flour.)

2 Tip the dough onto a generously floured worktop. Knead for 5 minutes, adding more flour if necessary, until the dough is smooth and elastic and no longer feels sticky.

Not your usual Chelsea bun! Paul's baked beauties are brimful of dried fruits and finished with an apricot glaze and orange icing.

3 Wash the mixing bowl and lightly grease with a little vegetable oil. Place the dough in the bowl and turn until it is covered all over with oil. Cover the bowl with clingfilm and leave the dough to rise in a warm place for 1 hour until doubled in size.

4 Punch down the dough to its original size, then turn out onto a lightly floured worktop. Roll out the dough to a rectangle about 40cm long and 5mm thick; it should lie horizontally in front of you. Brush all over with the melted butter. Evenly sprinkle the orange zest over the buttered surface, followed by the sugar, cinnamon and fruits.

5 Tack down the long side of the dough rectangle nearest to you (this means pressing it down with your thumb so that it sticks to the table. This will help you roll the dough). Begin to roll the opposite long side towards you, tightening the roll each time you turn it – use the tacked-down edge to help you tighten the roll. Cut across into 10 pieces about 4cm wide. Place them cut side up in the baking tray, leaving a little space around each slice. Cover with a tea towel and set aside in a warm place to rise for 30 minutes.

6 Preheat the oven to 190°C/375°F/gas 5. Bake the buns for 20–25 minutes until risen and golden brown. Check after 15 minutes and cover the buns with foil if they are getting too brown. Transfer the buns to a wire rack and leave to cool.

7 Put the jam in a small saucepan with a splash of water and melt gently until smooth. Brush the jam over the buns to glaze. Allow to cool.

8 Mix together the icing sugar, orange zest and 2 tablespoons water. Drizzle the icing over the cooled buns and allow to set before serving. Best eaten the same day.

Lacy Rye, Honey & Beer Oatcakes

MAKES 9

180g porridge oats
90g rye flour
90g strong white bread flour
10g fast-action dried yeast
1 ½ teaspoons sea salt flakes, crushed
1 tablespoon runny honey
1 ½ teaspoons sunflower oil
300ml warm water
450ml pale ale
butter for frying

These are distinctively flavoured and light pancake-like oatcakes, with crisp edges and spongey centres – perfect with cheese and pickle and a glass of local ale.

1 Grind the oats in a food-processor to make a coarse powder. Tip into a large bowl and mix in the rye and bread flours, the yeast and salt.

2 Combine the honey, oil and water in a jug and pour into the bowl along with the ale. Whisk by hand to make a thick yet runny batter. Cover with a damp tea towel and leave in a warm place for 1 hour until slightly thicker and very bubbly.

3 When ready to cook, heat a large frying pan over medium-high heat. Add a small knob of butter and melt it, then swirl it around the pan. Give the batter a quick stir, then pour a large ladleful into the pan, tilting and swirling the pan so the batter completely and evenly covers the base – as if you are making a pancake. Cook for about 5 minutes until the underside is a rich golden brown and slightly crisp.

4 Loosen the oatcake around the edges and quickly flip it over. Cook the second side for about 5 minutes or until brown and slightly crisp. Flip out the oatcake onto a wire rack to cool. Make 5 more oatcakes from the rest of the batter in the same way. Serve at room temperature the same day.

Gluten-free Sandwich Loaf

400g all-purpose gluten-free
    baking flour
1 ½ teaspoons sea salt flakes,
    crushed
2 teaspoons xanthan gum (unless
    already in your flour mix)
1 tablespoon caster sugar
1 x 7g sachet fast-action dried yeast
1 large free-range egg, at room
    temperature
about 300ml lukewarm water
2 teaspoons low-fat plain yoghurt
1 ½ teaspoons rapeseed oil
2 tablespoons chopped fresh herbs,
    such as chives or rosemary
    (optional)

1 x 450g loaf tin, about 19 x 12.5 x
    7.5cm, well greased

1 Put the flour, salt, xanthan gum, if using, sugar and dried yeast into a mixing bowl and stir until thoroughly combined. Break the egg into a measuring jug and make up to 350ml with lukewarm water. Add the yoghurt, oil and herbs, if using, and mix well. Pour this mixture onto the flour mixture and stir well with a wooden spoon to make a smooth, sticky, batter-like dough.

2 Scrape the dough into the prepared tin and spread evenly. Slip the tin into a plastic bag and inflate so the plastic doesn't stick to the dough, then tie the end securely. Leave to rise in a warm spot for 1–1 ½ hours until doubled in size. Towards the end of the rising time preheat the oven to 200°C/400°F/gas 6.

There are plenty of gluten-free and wheat-free flours on the market, but they do vary in taste and not all are good for making bread. For this loaf we've used a mix that blends flours from potatoes, sorghum, tapioca, chickpeas and broad beans. With the egg and rapeseed oil, the flour mix makes a loaf with a good flavour and colour as well as a moist crumb. Note that some gluten-free flours contain xanthan gum, which takes the place of gluten in giving the dough structure, so check the ingredients list on your pack before adding the 2 teaspoons suggested here.

3 Uncover the loaf. If you like, use a sharp knife to score the top with diagonal criss-cross lines. Bake for about 30 minutes until a good golden brown and the turned-out loaf sounds hollow when tapped on the underside. If not, return the loaf to the oven (straight onto the oven shelf) and bake for a further 5 minutes, then test again. Leave to cool on a wire rack. Once completely cold the loaf can be sliced for serving or wrapped whole in greaseproof and foil and kept for a day. It can also be frozen.

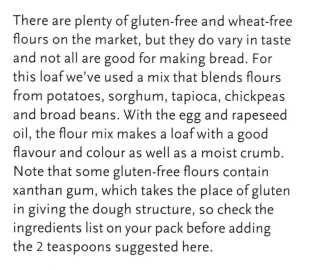

TIP

With the herbs added, this loaf
is delicious served with cheese.
And with or without the herbs
it makes lovely teatime
sandwiches (see page 156).

Teatime Sandwiches

VARIATION 01

MAKES 24 TEA SANDWICHES

1 Make a plain Gluten-free Sandwich Loaf (see page 154). When cold, cut into 12 slices. Spread 6 of the slices with 75g cream cheese or a creamy goats' cheese.

2 Tear 100g smoked salmon into strips and arrange on top of the cream cheese. Drizzle a little fresh lemon juice over the salmon and season with freshly ground black pepper.

3 Set the remaining slices of bread on top and press gently together. Cut off the crusts, if you like, then cut each sandwich into 4 triangles, or into squares or fingers.

VARIATION 02

MAKES 24 TEA SANDWICHES

1 Make a rosemary-flavoured Gluten-free Sandwich Loaf (see page 154). When cold, cut into 12 slices. Mix together 75g cream cheese and 75g grated Wensleydale cheese, and spread over 6 of the slices.

2 Divide 2 tablespoons of tomato chutney among the cheese-topped slices. Set the remaining slices of bread on top and press gently together. Cut off the crusts, if you like, then cut each sandwich into 4 triangles, or into squares or fingers.

VARIATION 03

MAKES 24 TEA SANDWICHES

1 Make a chive-flavoured Gluten-free Sandwich Loaf (see page 154). When cold, cut into 12 slices.

2 Hard-boil 3 large eggs: bring them to room temperature, then put into a pan of boiling water and cook for 10–12 minutes, depending on size. Immediately cool under cold running water for a minute, then peel the eggs. Mash with 2–3 tablespoons mayonnaise using a fork. Season with salt and black pepper.

3 Spread the egg mayonnaise over the slices of bread. Scatter snipped salad cress from a carton over 6 of the slices. Set the remaining slices of bread on top, egg mayonnaise side down, and press them gently together. Cut off the crusts, if you like, then cut each sandwich into 4 triangles, or into squares or fingers.

Once you've made your gluten-free loaf, keep your sandwich fillings simple, to let the flavour of the bread come through. We've paired up some popular filling suggestions with plain, chive and rosemary loaves. These dainty sandwiches are great for afternoon tea, served alongside Fondant Fancies (see page 38) and English Summer Cupcakes (see page 48).

Little Bridge Rolls

MAKES 30

650g strong white bread flour
2 teaspoons sea salt flakes, crushed
1 tablespoon caster sugar
50g unsalted butter, at room
    temperature, diced
1 x 7g sachet fast-action dried yeast OR
    15g fresh yeast
400ml lukewarm milk
1 large free-range egg, at room
    temperature
beaten egg, to glaze

2 baking sheets, lined with baking paper

Small, glossy rolls with a soft white crumb and thin soft crust are perfect split and filled with chipolatas and a spicy ketchup on Bonfire Night as well as with coronation chicken and shredded lettuce for an anniversary party. The rolls freeze well too.

1 Put the flour, salt and sugar into a large mixing bowl, or the bowl of a large free-standing electric mixer, and mix well. Add the butter and rub into the flour using your fingertips until the butter has completely disappeared. If using dried yeast stir it in. If using fresh yeast, crumble it into a small bowl and mix to a smooth liquid with 7 tablespoons of the measured milk.

2 Lightly whisk the milk with the egg until mixed, then add to the flour mixture (and add the fresh yeast mixture, if using). With your hand or the dough hook attachment of the mixer on the lowest speed, mix to a soft and very slightly sticky dough that just leaves the sides of the bowl clean. If the dough feels dry and hard, or there are crumbs at the bottom of the bowl, work in more milk a tablespoon at a time. If the dough feels very wet work in a little more flour.

3 Turn out the dough onto a lightly floured worktop and knead by hand for 10 minutes, or knead for 5 minutes with the dough hook, until very smooth and elastic. Return the dough to the bowl and cover with a snap-on lid or clingfilm. Leave to rise in a warm place for about 1 hour until doubled in size.

4 Punch down the risen dough to deflate, then turn out onto a lightly floured worktop. Divide the dough into 30 equal portions (easy with digital scales). Shape each portion into a ball, then roll with your hands to a neat cigar shape 7cm long with tapered ends. Arrange the rolls, slightly apart, on the prepared baking sheets and cover it loosely with clingfilm. Leave to rise for about 45 minutes until doubled in size. Towards the end of the rising time, preheat the oven to 230°C/450°F/gas 8.

5 Lightly brush the tops of the rolls with beaten egg. Once you've brushed the last one, start again and brush the rolls in the same order as before with a second coat (2 thin coats will give a better finish than one thicker one). Bake for 5 minutes. Reduce the temperature to 200°C/400°F/gas 6 and bake for a further 5–6 minutes until golden.

6 Transfer to a wire rack, cover with a clean, dry tea towel to keep the crusts soft and leave to cool completely. Eat within a day or freeze.

Paul's Camembert & Quince Flatbreads

MAKES

500g strong white bread flour
10g table salt
1 x 7g sachet fast-action dried yeast
320ml lukewarm water
200g Camembert
150g quince jelly
vegetable oil

Incredibly quick to cook in a heavy pan on top of the stove, these light, tasty flatbreads are made from a white yeast dough with rich cheese and fruit jelly carefully worked in. Paul suggests eating these with a fresh green salad.

1 Place the flour, salt and yeast in a large free-standing electric mixer with a dough hook attachment. Start the machine running on low speed while you gradually pour in three-quarters of the water. Leave to mix for a minute, then add the rest of the water. Turn the mixer speed up to medium-high and leave to mix for about 7 minutes to make a shiny, smooth dough.

2 Alternatively, mix together the dry ingredients in a large mixing bowl, then gradually work in three-quarters of the water with your hand. Give the dough a good mix for a couple of minutes, then knead on a lightly floured worktop for about 10 minutes until the dough is shiny and smooth.

3 Tear or cut the cheese into small pieces, and break up the quince jelly. Add to the dough and gently incorporate by hand, mixing the cheese and jelly evenly into the dough. Place the dough in an oiled bowl and turn to coat with oil, then cover with clingfilm and leave to rise at room temperature for 1 hour until doubled in size.

4 Tip out the risen dough onto a lightly floured worktop and punch down (knock back) to deflate. Divide the dough into 16 portions. Roll each portion of dough into a ball, then roll out each ball to a rough disc about 12.5cm wide using a floured rolling pin (Paul decided to make 12 flatbreads from this recipe on the filming day, so feel free to experiment with size and shape, just make sure they are cooked all the way through!).

5 Heat a heavy frying pan over a high heat. Very lightly oil the pan by wiping it with an oiled piece of kitchen paper. Cook the discs of dough, one at a time, for about 2 minutes per side until they look cooked and have a good bit of colour on them. Eat warm.

Autumn Wreath

MAKES 1 LOAF

about 650g strong white bread flour
25g caster sugar
1 x 7g sachet fast-action dried yeast
   OR 15g fresh yeast
300ml lukewarm milk
2 large free-range eggs, at room
   temperature
2 teaspoons sea salt flakes, crushed
finely grated zest of 1 medium
   unwaxed orange
100g raisins or sultanas
100g soft-dried cranberries
100g pecans, roughly chopped
100g unsalted butter, soft but not
   runny, cut in small pieces
beaten egg, to glaze

1 large baking sheet, lined with
   baking paper

A neatly plaited harvest wreath bread looks really impressive on a seasonal buffet table. Rich in fruits and nuts, it goes well with cheese, pâté, salads and soups. The dough is made in stages, with plenty of breaks, to produce a light, fine moist crumb. You can also make a sweet decorated version to serve with coffee (see opposite).

1 Put 400g of the weighed flour into a large mixing bowl and stir in the sugar plus the dried yeast, if using. If using fresh yeast crumble it into a small bowl and mix to a smooth liquid with 7 tablespoons of the measured lukewarm milk.

2 Beat the eggs into the milk (add the fresh yeast liquid, if using) and add to the bowl. Stir into the flour mixture with your hand to make a smooth, thick batter-like dough. Cover the bowl and leave in a warm spot for about 20 minutes until slightly expanded and bubbly.

3 Meanwhile, combine the salt, orange zest, raisins or sultanas, cranberries and chopped pecans with half of the remaining flour in another bowl.

4 Uncover the batter and add the fruit and nut mixture plus the pieces of butter. Using your hands, squeeze everything together between your fingers until thoroughly combined to make a very heavy and sticky dough, which will take about 5 minutes. Cover the bowl and leave in a warm place for 10 minutes.

5 Sprinkle some of the rest of the flour on a worktop and turn out the dough. Flour your hands with more of the remaining flour and gently knead the dough for 2 minutes – set a timer – working in enough of the remaining flour to make a soft dough that doesn't stick to your hands. Cover the dough on the worktop with the upturned bowl and leave to rest for 5 minutes.

6 Knead for another 2 minutes and rest for 5 minutes as before. Knead again for 2 minutes, then return the dough to the bowl and cover as before. Leave to rise in a warm but not hot place for 1 ½–2 hours until doubled in size.

7 Punch down the dough to deflate, then cover and leave to rise once more until doubled in size – about an hour this time. Punch down again, then turn out onto a lightly floured worktop and knead for a few seconds to make a neat ball. Divide the dough into 3 equal portions (digital scales help here).

8 Using your hand, roll each portion to a neat sausage shape 70cm long. Join the 3 pieces at one end and plait together neatly and fairly tightly. Join the ends of the plait neatly to make a wreath about 25cm across. Carefully transfer to the prepared baking sheet and ease back into shape if necessary. Cover loosely with a sheet of clingfilm and leave to rise in a slightly warm place for about 40 minutes until almost doubled in size. (If the room is too hot or the dough rises too much the shape will be lost.) Towards the end of the rising time preheat the oven to 180°C/350°F/gas 4.

9 Uncover the wreath and carefully brush with beaten egg, taking care not to 'glue' the dough to the paper. Bake for about 25 minutes until a good golden brown; if the top starts to become too dark during baking, cover with a sheet of foil.

10 Cool on the baking sheet for 5 minutes before sliding the wreath, on its paper, onto a wire rack. Leave until completely cold before slicing. Best eaten within 5 days, or freeze. Also good toasted.

SWEET HARVEST WREATH

Increase the sugar in the dough from 25g to 50g. Once cooled you can decorate the loaf. Mix 100g sifted icing sugar with about 2 ½ teaspoons orange juice or water to make a smooth, thick icing. Spoon into a disposable piping bag and snip off the tip. Starting from the inside of the wreath, pipe a zigzag pattern backwards and forwards from the inside to the outer edge of the wreath. Leave to set. Where you joined up the plaited dough, tie a big burgundy ribbon in a huge bow so the bread looks like a door wreath.

Paul's Doughnuts

MAKES 10

FOR THE DOUGH
500g strong white bread flour
50g caster sugar
40g unsalted butter, very soft
2 x 7g sachets fast-action dried yeast
10g salt
2 large free-range eggs,
    at room temperature, beaten
150ml lukewarm milk
130ml lukewarm water
oil for deep-frying

FOR FILLED DOUGHNUTS
caster sugar, for rolling
2 jars strawberry jam, sieved to
    remove lumps and seeds

FOR ICED DOUGHNUTS (OPTIONAL)
200g icing sugar
finely grated zest and juice of 1
    medium unwaxed orange

a squeezy bottle, icing syringe or
    disposable piping bag fitted with a
    small plain tube

Paul made his first batch of doughnuts at the age of 11. Following his recipe, you can also make 5 jam-filled and 5 iced ringed doughnuts, if you like – both types are delicious. Paul decided to make jam-filled doughnuts only on the show, which are his favourites! If you want to make iced ringed doughnuts, follow the method below to step 3, but before leaving the doughnut balls to rise, shape them into rings following the method on page 164. To finish, simply halve the jam quantity and make the orange icing instead.

1 Put the flour, sugar, butter, yeast, salt, eggs, milk and three-quarters of the water into a large mixing bowl and mix with your hands to make a firm but not hard or dry dough. Slowly work in the remaining water and massage the dough in the bowl, with your hands, for 4 minutes (you could use an electric mixer fitted with a dough hook to do this instead). The dough should be soft but not sticky.

2 Turn out onto a lightly floured worktop and knead well for 10 minutes to make a very smooth and elastic dough. Shape into a ball, return to the bowl (cleaned and lightly oiled) and cover with a damp tea towel. Leave to rise at room temperature for about 1 hour until doubled in size.

3 Tip out the dough onto a lightly floured worktop and 'knock back' (punching the dough down to remove the excess air). Divide the dough into 10 equal portions and shape into balls. Set them, slightly apart, on a floured tray and leave to rise at room temperature for about 1 hour until doubled in size.

4 Towards the end of the rising time, heat the oil in a deep-fat fryer or large deep pan to 180°C/350°F. Carefully drop the doughnuts, one at a time, in small batches, into the hot oil and fry for 5 minute on each side or until golden brown. Remove with a slotted spoon and immediately roll in caster sugar before leaving to cool.

Recipe continues overleaf

5 When completely cold, make a deep incision into the side of each doughnut using a small, sharp knife. Fill the squeezy bottle, icing syringe or piping bag with the sieved jam, then firmly push in the end of the bottle, syringe or tube and pipe in a generous amount of jam.

6 To make iced ringed doughnuts, use your finger (or the wide end of a piping nozzle) to push a hole through the centre of each shaped ball. Put a finger through the hole and spin the doughnut around to create a big, even hole then leave to rise, as before.

7 Fry the ringed doughnuts, as before, but keep an eye on their colour because they will cook faster than the doughnut balls. Remove the cooked doughnuts from the oil using a slotted spoon and drain on some kitchen paper. Leave to cool completely while you make the icing.

8 To make the icing, mix together the icing sugar, orange zest and juice. Drizzle the icing liberally over the tops of the cold doughnuts before leaving to set.

Cinnamon Apple Doughnuts

MAKES 6

1 large or 2 small sharp eating apples
1 ½ teaspoons ground cinnamon
115g plain flour
good pinch of salt
3–4 gratings of nutmeg
1 teaspoon baking powder
100g caster sugar
2 large free-range eggs, at room temperature
2 tablespoons buttermilk OR low-fat plain yoghurt
3 tablespoons vegetable oil

TO FINISH
3 tablespoons caster sugar
1 teaspoon ground cinnamon

1 x 6-hole doughnut tray (or 6 small savarin moulds), well buttered

This recipe uses a different method from Paul's Doughnuts on page 163 – these little treats are baked in special ring doughnut-shaped trays. They have the look and taste of traditional doughnuts but are quicker and simpler. Buttermilk not only adds flavour but is the secret to the light, moist texture. If you can't find ring trays the mixture can be made into muffins (see opposite).

1 Preheat the oven to 200°C/400°F/gas 6. Peel, quarter and core the apples, then chop roughly into pieces about the size of your little fingernail. Put into a bowl, sprinkle over ½ teaspoon of the ground cinnamon and toss thoroughly. Set aside.

2 Sift the flour into a large mixing bowl with the remaining 1 teaspoon cinnamon, the salt, nutmeg, baking powder and sugar. Whisk the eggs with the buttermilk and oil in another bowl or jug until combined, then add to the flour mixture. Mix together with a wooden spoon, then stir in the apples.

3 Spoon the soft, sticky mixture into the buttered moulds (it's wise to butter even if they are labelled non-stick) to fill evenly. Bake for 12–15 minutes until the doughnuts are well risen and spring back when lightly pressed; if necessary, rotate the tray halfway through baking so the doughnuts cook evenly. The tops of the doughnuts will be pale golden and the undersides a good brown colour (in some fan ovens the tops may not colour much even when the mixture is thoroughly cooked – don't worry).

4 While the doughnuts are baking mix the sugar with the cinnamon in a shallow dish. As soon as the doughnuts are ready, turn them out and quickly coat with the sugar mixture. Leave to cool on a wire rack. These are best eaten the same day.

DOUGHNUT MUFFINS

Divide the mixture evenly among 7 paper muffin cases in a muffin tray. Peel, core and roughly chop a large sharp eating apple and toss with ½ teaspoon ground cinnamon, 1 ½ tablespoons light brown muscovado sugar and 50g pecan pieces or chopped mixed nuts. Carefully spoon on top of the doughnut mixture and bake for about 25 minutes until firm to the touch. Remove the paper cases from the muffin tray and leave to cool on a wire rack. Omit the finishing coating of sugar and cinnamon.

TIP
For an easy dessert, split open the baked doughnuts and fill each with 2 tablespoons full-fat Greek-style yoghurt and 1 tablespoon apple and damson potted fruit.

Tarts

THE BAKERS WERE ASKED TO CREATE an array of tarts this year, from treacle tarts to a tarte tatin as well as classic French recipes. Our first challenge echoes their Designer Fruit Tart Showstopper Challenge which calls for intricate and impressive decoration.

The basic recipe is a Pâte Brisée. French tart pastry is made in a unique way. Rather than rubbing pieces of butter into flour in a bowl and then binding with water into a dough, the ingredients are mixed together directly on the worktop, then worked with the heel of the hand to make a smooth and flexible dough. The beauty of this dough, apart from the taste, is its adaptability – it can be rolled super-thin as the base for a quick and elegant tart, rolled out more thickly to fold around a sweet mixture for a good-looking rustic galette or neatly shaped into a fluted tart case for a glamorous filling.

For the best-tasting pastry you need butter with a fine, distinctive flavour – the French use unsalted lactic butter (made from slightly fermented whole milk) with a low moisture content. A touch of sugar helps ensure a crisp texture, while egg yolk adds richness to the taste, texture and colour of the pastry.

Use this tart pastry to make a Simple Apple Tart. The beauty of the apple slices is adornment enough, but why not complement their golden colour with some edible gold leaf to make it really special? Why not next move onto a seasonal fruit galette, and then a peach frangipane tart that uses a sweeter version of the pastry, Pâte Sucrée? Again, the fruits are the heroes of these recipes – if you take a little extra time cutting and placing them in the pastry, this will make all the difference to your showstopping finish. Not that you should

forget the filling – it has to be as memorable as the tart's appearance.

There is also a second set of Challenge recipes in this chapter – based on the Choux Pastry Gateau Showstopper Challenge from the French episode.

Choux is made only with plain flour, salt, butter and eggs. The magic, which transforms the raw ingredients into lighter-than-air pastry, is in the technique. Choux is twice-cooked, first in a saucepan and then in the oven. The consistency of the dough really matters because it isn't rolled out. So when eggs are beaten into the flour, butter and water paste that's been made on top of the stove, it's vital to get the consistency right – too little beating and too much egg added and the piped dough won't hold a good shape and puff up attractively in the oven; not enough egg and the pastry will be tough and taste more like cardboard. But the real secret to a successful choux dessert is thorough baking – it's so important to bake this pastry until it is really golden and crisp enough to become a firm container.

Because the filling for choux pastries is often soft and delicate – whipped cream, crème pâtissière or ice cream – it's best to serve them as soon as possible after they are assembled. Profiteroles are the classic combination of crisp pastry, simple filling and sauce, but you can make so much more with a choux dough – pipe it into small balls and add a bittersweet caramel-nut topping for a contrast of tastes and textures, or shape into pretty swans or a ring gâteau. To really pull out all the stops, have a look at our spun-sugar technique on page 197.

If you're filling a tart with fruit, pick top-notch fruit. And be sure the fruit is firm enough – upside-down pastries like Mary's Apple Tarte Tatin (see page 202) need apples that will hold together in the heat of the oven so the turned-out tart keeps its shape. If the right fruit isn't available choose another recipe.

The simplest of finishing touches can add glamour to a sweet tart: just a sprinkling of sugar quickly caramelized under the grill, or a brush of warm apricot glaze, will give a professional sheen. Adding pretty pastry leaves or flowers, or an intricately woven lattice of pastry strips, can give a simple homely tart that 'wow' factor. And be sure to have crème fraîche, yoghurt or vanilla ice cream on hand to serve with warm tarts.

DON'T FORGET

Unlike cakes, which are best made with room-temperature ingredients, chill your fat and use ice-cold water to make pastry, unless the recipe specifies otherwise.

Invest in a good-quality rolling pin and a pastry brush, and keep them spotless.

Make sure you have the right size tin for the recipe, to prevent the filling overflowing or the pastry shrinking during baking.

Buy a heavy-duty tin that won't buckle in the hot oven or rust quickly.

Roll the pastry to the correct thickness to prevent the case from collapsing when filled or not cooking properly on the bottom – you don't want a soggy bottom! Follow the recipe instructions and use a ruler, if necessary. For most pastry cases, aim to roll out the dough to the thickness of a pound coin.

Prick the bottom of the pastry case well with a fork so it won't bubble and distort while it bakes.

To prevent the pastry case from shrinking, chill it well before baking.

CATHRYN

Pâte Brisée

200g plain flour
¼ teaspoon salt
100g unsalted butter, chilled
1 large free-range egg yolk
1 tablespoon caster sugar
3 tablespoons cold water

1 Sift the flour and salt onto a clean worktop and make a large well in the centre. Put the butter between sheets of clingfilm and pound with a rolling pin until it is very supple but still cold. Cut the butter into pieces and put into the well with the egg yolk, sugar and water.

2 Put the fingertips of one of your hands together to form a beak shape and use to mash together the ingredients in the well. When they are thoroughly combined gradually work in the flour with your fingers, using a plastic dough scraper (or metal spatula) to help you draw the flour in. When the mixture looks like coarse crumbs, gather the whole lot together to make a ball of dough. If there are dry crumbs and the dough won't come together add more water a teaspoon at a time; if the dough is really sticky work in a little more flour.

Pâte brisée, and its richer, sweeter cousin pâte sucrée (see page 178) – the pastries used for beautiful French pies and tarts – are made from much the same ingredients as shortcrust pastry but in a very different way, giving them an altogether different texture. The dough is mixed by hand straight on the worktop rather than in a mixing bowl or in a food-processor and then it is worked – not kneaded – with the heel of the hand to make it supple and pliable. It can be rolled very thinly without crumbling and bakes to a crisp rather than chewy or crumbly texture.

The recipe here makes enough pastry to line a 23cm deep tart tin. Master this recipe and use to make the following two Showstopping Challenges or why not create your own designer tart filling to rival the bakers of series 3?

3 Lightly dust the worktop with flour and start to gently work the dough: press down on the ball of dough with the heel of your hand and push it away from you, then gather up the dough into a ball once more (using the scraper) and repeat. Continue working for a couple of minutes – no more – until the dough is silky-smooth and very pliable, so pliable it can be pulled off the worktop in one piece. Shape into a ball, then flatten to a thick disc. Wrap tightly in clingfilm and chill for 30 minutes before using.

TIP
A plastic dough or pastry scraper is a big help when mixing in the flour, and when gathering the dough together and working it.

Simple Apple Tart

SERVES 6–8

1 quantity Pâte Brisée
(see page 173)

FOR THE TOPPING
8 medium eating apples
40g unsalted butter, melted
about 2 tablespoons caster sugar
icing sugar, for dusting

2 baking sheets, lined with
baking paper

1 Make the Pâte Brisée following the method on page 173. Lightly dust the worktop with flour, then roll out the well-chilled pastry to a very thin square with sides about 38cm. Using a ruler, trim the sides with a long sharp knife (or a pizza cutter) to make a 36cm square. Cut the square in half and set each rectangle on a lined baking sheet. Prick the pastry all over with a fork, then leave to chill while preparing the apples.

2 Preheat the oven to 200°C/400°F/gas 6. Peel, quarter and core the apples, then slice very thinly. Arrange the apple slices on the pastry rectangles in neat rows, so the slices slightly overlap and completely cover the pastry. Brush or dab lightly with the melted butter, then sprinkle lightly and evenly with caster sugar.

3 Bake for 20–25 minutes until the apples are lightly golden and the underside of the pastry is golden (you can check by carefully lifting an edge with a palette knife).

This is a great tart for a beginner to try – once you've made your pastry, the rest is easy. The great ability of French tart pastry to be rolled paper-thin means you can bake very crisp and light tarts with the minimum of fuss. The tart is pretty enough unadorned, but if you like, decorate with edible gold leaf, as shown here, for that extra 'wow' factor. As there are so few ingredients, it's important to use well-flavoured apples. The recipe makes 2 tarts, and each will serve 3–4.

4 Preheat the grill to maximum. Dust the apples with icing sugar. Slide the tarts off the lining paper but leave them on the baking sheets (to avoid the paper scorching or catching fire), then quickly flash the tarts, one at a time, under the grill to caramelize the sugar and give a shiny glaze. This takes less than a minute, so watch like a hawk to prevent them burning. Leave to cool for a few minutes, then serve warm as soon as possible. Best eaten the same day.

TIP
You can use a kitchen blow-torch to caramelize the sugar, rather than the grill (be sure to slide the tarts off the lining paper first).

Nectarine & Blueberry Galette

SERVES 8

1 quantity Pâte Brisée
(see page 173)

FOR THE FILLING

3 medium nectarines
150g blueberries
1 ½ tablespoons cornflour
50g caster sugar, plus extra for
sprinkling
20g unsalted butter, melted, for
brushing

1 baking sheet, lined with baking paper

1 Make the Pâte Brisée following the method on page 173. Lightly dust a worktop with flour, then roll out the pastry to a neat circle 30cm across. Carefully wrap it around the rolling pin and lift it onto the prepared baking sheet. Cover the pastry with clingfilm and chill while preparing the fruit.

2 Preheat the oven to 200°C/400°F/gas 6. Quarter the nectarines, remove the stones and cut the fruit into thick slices. Put into a bowl with the blueberries. Sprinkle over the cornflour and 50g caster sugar, and toss gently so the fruit is thoroughly coated.

3 Uncover the pastry and pile the fruit into the centre so it is gently mounded, leaving a 5cm border of pastry all around. Carefully fold the pastry up around the fruit, neatly pleating the pastry and leaving plenty of fruit visible in the centre. Brush the pastry edge with melted butter and lightly sprinkle with caster sugar.

You don't need a flan tin or pie dish to make a gorgeous fruit pie – you can simply fold the rolled-out pastry around some luscious fruit. Use the best in season and what you fancy: apricots, peaches or eating apples in place of nectarines, and blackberries or stoned cherries instead of blueberries. Crème fraîche is a perfect partner.

4 Bake for about 40 minutes until the pastry is golden brown. Leave to cool and firm up on the baking sheet for 10 minutes, then slide onto a serving platter. Best eaten warm the same day.

TIP

For tarts with an apple filling, add the finely grated zest of an unwaxed lemon – half to the pastry with the sugar, and the remainder to the fruit when you mix it with the cornflour.

176

TARTS

Peach Frangipane Tart

SERVES

FOR THE PÂTE SUCRÉE

200g plain flour
¼ teaspoon salt
100g unsalted butter, chilled
4 large free-range egg yolks
100g caster sugar
finely grated zest of
   ½ unwaxed lemon

FOR THE FILLING

100g unsalted butter, softened
100g caster sugar
finely grated zest of ½ unwaxed
   lemon
2 large free-range eggs, beaten
100g ground almonds
100g plain flour
4 medium just-ripe peaches
1 tablespoon flaked almonds,
   to decorate
icing sugar, for dusting

1 x 23cm deep loose-based flan tin;
   a baking sheet

This classic combination of fruit and frangipane is baked in a pastry case made from pâte sucrée – a richer and sweeter version of the pâte brisée shown on page 173. There's no water, just egg yolks, and extra sugar, which give the pastry a sandy, biscuit-like taste and texture. Because of the extra sugar the pastry colours more quickly so it is baked at a lower temperature.

1 Make up the Pâte Sucrée following the method for Pâte Brisée on page 173, but omitting the water and adding the lemon zest to the well with the other ingredients. The dough will feel slightly stickier than pâte brisée, but avoid flouring your hands as much as possible. After the dough has been worked and is silky-smooth and pliable, wrap and chill for 30 minutes until firm.

2 Lightly dust the worktop with flour, then roll out the pastry to a circle and use to line the flan tin (see page 312). Save any pastry trimmings to use for decoration. Prick the base of the pastry case, then chill while preparing the filling. Preheat the oven to 190°C/375°F/gas 5 and put the baking sheet into the oven to heat up.

3 Put the butter into a mixing bowl and beat with a wooden spoon or electric mixer until creamy. Add the sugar and lemon zest and beat until the mixture becomes very light in colour and texture. Gradually add the eggs, beating well after each addition. Fold in the ground almonds and flour with a large metal spoon. When thoroughly combined, spoon the mixture into the pastry case and spread evenly. Keep in the fridge while preparing the peaches.

4 Bring a pan of water to the boil. Make a small nick in the skin of each peach at the stalk end, then gently place it in the boiling water. Leave for 12 seconds, then remove. Once the peaches are cool enough to handle, slip off their skins. Halve the fruit and remove the stones.

Recipe continues overleaf

5 Set 7 of the peach halves, rounded side up, on top of the almond filling. Cut the remaining half into thick slices, leaving them attached at the stalk end, and arrange in a fan shape in the centre of the tart. Set the tin on the hot baking sheet and bake for 25 minutes.

6 While the tart is baking, re-roll the pastry trimmings and cut into leaf shapes with a cutter (or cut round a template or free-hand). Remove the tart from the oven – the almond filling will have puffed up around the fruit – and lay the pastry decorations on top. Scatter over the flaked almonds. Dust with icing sugar and return to the oven. Reduce the temperature to 180°C/350°F/gas 4 and bake for a further 25–30 minutes until the pastry and almond filling are golden.

7 Remove from the oven and leave to cool for 10 minutes before carefully unmoulding; the frangipane filling will gradually subside. Serve the tart warm the same day or the next, either at room temperature or reheated in a 160°C/325°F/gas 3 oven for 10–12 minutes.

Raspberry Linzertorte

SERVES 10

FOR THE PASTRY
125g unblanched almonds
225g plain flour
good pinch of salt
½ teaspoon ground cinnamon
grated zest of ½ unwaxed lemon
125g caster sugar
125g unsalted butter, chilled
   and diced
1 large free-range egg plus
   2 egg yolks

FOR THE FILLING
600g fresh raspberries
1 teaspoon lemon juice
6 tablespoons caster sugar
icing sugar, for dusting

1 x 23cm deep loose-based flan tin;
   a baking sheet

1 Grind the almonds in a food-processor to a fine powder. Add the flour, salt, cinnamon, lemon zest and sugar, and 'pulse' a few times until thoroughly combined. Add the butter and process until the mixture looks like fine crumbs. Lightly beat the egg with the yolks, then add to the bowl and process until the mixture comes together to make a ball of fairly soft dough. Form into a thick disc, wrap tightly in clingfilm and chill for about 1 hour until firm enough to roll out.

2 Meanwhile, make the filling. Put the raspberries, lemon juice and caster sugar into a medium-sized pan and heat gently until the juices start to run, then turn up the heat and bring to a fast boil. Cook, stirring frequently, for about 5 minutes until thick and jammy. Pour into a bowl and cool.

The pastry for this pretty Viennese tart is more like shortbread than shortcrust. It's filled with a quick home-made raspberry conserve and finished with an easy lattice, making an elegant jam tart.

3 Preheat the oven to 190°C/375°F/gas 5 and put in the baking sheet to heat up. Set the dough on a lightly floured worktop. Cut off a third, wrap and return to the fridge. Roll out the remaining dough fairly thickly and use to line the flan tin (see page 312). Make sure there are no holes; if there are, just patch them or press together. Trim off the excess dough and add it to the saved portion. Chill the case while making the lattice.

4 Flour the worktop and rolling pin, then roll out the saved dough to a rectangle about 11 × 24cm. Neaten the long sides, then cut lengthways into 10 strips 1cm wide.

5 Spoon the filling into the pastry case. Arrange 5 pastry strips (flat or twisted) over the filling, without pulling or stretching, spacing them equally apart. Press the ends onto the pastry rim and trim off any excess. Arrange the other 5 strips on top at an angle and press to the rim.

6 Set the tart on the heated baking sheet and bake for about 35 minutes until a good golden brown. Remove from the oven and leave to cool and firm up for 10 minutes before carefully unmoulding. Dust with sifted icing sugar and serve warm or at room temperature. Best eaten the same day.

Lychee & Raspberry Tart

SERVES 10

FOR THE SWEET PASTRY
200g plain flour
80g icing sugar
100g salted butter, chilled and diced
2 large free-range egg yolks
about 2 teaspoons rosewater
a little beaten egg, for brushing

FOR THE PRALINE
150g whole blanched almonds
100g caster sugar

FOR THE MACAROONS
75g icing sugar, sifted
75g ground almonds
75g caster sugar
2 large free-range egg whites,
   at room temperature
red edible food colouring gel

FOR THE LYCHEE CRÈME PÂTISSIÈRE
500ml full-fat milk
6 large free-range egg yolks,
   at room temperature
100g caster sugar
3 tablespoons cornflour
25g unsalted butter, at room
   temperature
1 x 425g tin lychees in light syrup,
   drained and finely chopped
icing sugar, to sprinkle

FOR THE CRÈME MASCARPONE
1 large free-range egg, at room
   temperature
30g caster sugar
2 teaspoons raspberry liqueur
1 teaspoon rosewater
½ teaspoon agar flakes
175g mascarpone, well chilled

TO FINISH
150g fresh raspberries
3 tablespoons seedless (or sieved)
   raspberry jam, heated

There's a lot of work in this elaborate designer tart – rich sweet pastry flavoured with rosewater, praline, an unusual lychee crème pâtissière and tiny macaroons, plus a fluffy mascarpone crème – so allow plenty of time.

1 x 23cm deep loose-based flan tin; a sugar thermometer; a piping bag plus a 2cm plain tube; a baking sheet lined with baking paper

1 To make the pastry, put the flour and icing sugar into the bowl of a food-processor and 'pulse' a couple of times to combine. Add the diced butter and process until the mixture looks like fine crumbs. With the motor running, add the yolks and rosewater through the feed tube. Stop the machine when the dough comes together in a ball. If there are dry crumbs work in a little more rosewater. Wrap in clingfilm and chill for 30 minutes.

2 Meanwhile, make the praline (see page 311). When cold and set, crush or coarsely chop into pieces the size of your little fingernail. Set aside until needed.

3 Roll out the pastry on a floured worktop and use to line the flan tin (see page 312). Prick the base and chill for 20 minutes. Meanwhile, preheat the oven to 180°C/350°F/gas 4.

Recipe continues overleaf

4 Bake the pastry case 'blind' (see page 312); after removing the paper and beans, lightly brush the inside of the pastry case with beaten egg, then tip about half of the praline into the case and press onto the sides and base. Return the pastry case to the oven and bake for a further 10–12 minutes until the pastry is golden and crisp. Leave to cool but do not turn out. Leave the oven on.

5 To make the macaroons, combine the icing sugar and ground almonds; set aside until needed. Gently heat the caster sugar with 2 ½ tablespoons water in a small pan until dissolved. Meanwhile, put the egg whites and a little red colouring gel (just dip a cocktail stick into the small pot) into a large mixing bowl and whisk with an electric mixer until soft peaks will form. Bring the sugar syrup to the boil and boil rapidly until it reaches 118°C/245°F on a sugar thermometer, then slowly pour onto the egg whites in a thin, steady stream while whisking on full speed, to make a thick, glossy meringue. Continue whisking until the meringue cools to room temperature, then fold in the icing sugar mixture.

6 Spoon the meringue mixture into the piping bag fitted with the 2cm plain tube and pipe tiny macaroons – about 2.5cm across – on the lined baking sheet (you'll be able to pipe about 48 macaroons). Leave to stand for 15 minutes to form a crust, then bake for about 12 minutes until firm but not turning brown. Leave to cool on the sheet.

7 Next make the crème pâtissière (see page 305 for the instructions). Once the custard has thickened, remove from the heat and leave to cool for 10 minutes before stirring in the butter and lychees. Transfer the

mixture to a bowl. Sprinkle the surface with icing sugar to prevent a skin from forming, then cover and chill for at least 1 hour.

8 Meanwhile, make the crème mascarpone. Put the egg and sugar into a medium-sized heatproof bowl set over a pan of boiling water and whisk with a hand-held electric mixer until frothy and just slightly too hot for your finger to bear comfortably. Add the liqueur, rosewater and agar flakes, then continue whisking until the mixture is thick enough to a leave a ribbon-like trail when the whisk is lifted; take care not to let the mixture get too hot and start to scramble. Remove the bowl, set it in iced water and whisk until cold. Whisk in the mascarpone, then cover and chill until ready to assemble.

9 Lightly brush or paint each raspberry with hot raspberry jam and leave to set on a sheet of baking paper.

10 To assemble the tart, unmould the pastry case and set it on a serving platter. Stir the crème pâtissière until creamy, then spoon into the pastry case and spread out evenly.

11 Carefully spread the crème mascarpone over the top of the crème pâtissière. Arrange the glazed raspberries on top in straight parallel lines, leaving a raspberry's width between each line. Finish with macaroons – you won't need them all – and the rest of the praline. Serve as soon as possible; best eaten the same day.

TIP
Sandwich together any leftover macaroons with crème mascarpone and crème pâtissière and serve alongside the tart as an extra treat.

Mary's Treacle Tart

SERVES

8

FOR THE PASTRY
250g plain flour
130g unsalted butter, chilled and
    diced
about 3 tablespoons cold water
beaten egg, to glaze

FOR THE FILLING
400g golden syrup
about 150g fine, fresh white breadcrumbs
finely grated zest and juice of 2 large
    unwaxed lemons

1 x 18cm deep loose-based flan tin;
    a baking sheet

1 To make the pastry, put the flour into a large mixing bowl, add the pieces of butter and rub in using your fingertips until the pastry resembles fine breadcrumbs. Mix in enough water to bring the ingredients together to make a firm dough. (Or make the pastry in a food-processor.) Wrap in clingfilm and chill for about 20 minutes to making rolling out easier.

2 Cut off about 150g of the chilled pastry; cover and set aside for the lattice. Roll out the rest of the pastry thinly on a lightly floured worktop and use to line the flan tin (see page 312). Prick the base of the pastry case with a fork to prevent it from rising up during baking.

3 Put the reserved pastry onto a sheet of clingfilm, then roll it out to a rectangle about the thickness of a pound coin. Brush the pastry with a little beaten egg, then chill.

Mary made this classic recipe a Technical Challenge because it's a real test of pastry-making skills. Take your time over the lattice, cutting the pastry into strips of even width and spacing them evenly over the filling.

4 To make the filling, gently warm the syrup in a large pan until runny. Take care not to let it boil. Remove from the heat and stir in the breadcrumbs and lemon zest and juice. If the mixture looks runny, add a few more breadcrumbs (it depends on the type of bread you use). Leave to cool, then pour the mixture into the pastry case and spread evenly.

5 Preheat the oven to 200°C/400°F/gas 6, and put the baking sheet into the oven to heat up. Remove the pastry rectangle from the fridge and cut into 10 long strips. Make sure they are all longer than the diameter of the flan tin. Brush the edges of the pastry case with a little beaten egg, then use the strips to make a woven lattice over the filling; let the ends of the strips hang over the sides of the tart.

6 Trim the ends, then press them onto the pastry rim to create a neat finish. Set the tin on the heated baking sheet and bake for 10 minutes. Reduce the oven temperature to 180°C/350°F/gas 4 and bake for a further 25–30 minutes until the pastry is golden and the filling is set. Leave to cool before you remove the tart from the tin. Serve warm or at room temperature.

Banana Tarte Tatin

SERVES

6

FOR THE ROUGH PUFF PASTRY
225g plain flour
good pinch of sea salt flakes,
    crushed
190g slightly salted butter,
    chilled and cut in 2cm cubes
1 teaspoon lemon juice
140ml icy water

FOR THE CARAMEL
100g white granulated sugar
60g salted butter

FOR THE TOPPING
3 large, firm bananas

1 x 22–23cm ovenproof frying pan
    or tatin pan

1 To make the pastry, sift the flour and salt into a mixing bowl. Add the pieces of butter and toss until coated in flour. Mix the lemon juice with the icy water and add to the bowl. Using a round-bladed knife, work in the liquid, cutting the butter slightly as you mix and rotating thc bowl with your other hand. As soon as the dough comes together into a shaggy lump, turn it out onto a lightly floured worktop and shape it into a block about 10 × 14cm.

2 Roll out the dough away from you to a rectangle about 20 × 35cm. Fold in 3 like a business letter (bottom third up to cover the centre third, then top third down to cover the other 2 layers and make a neat square). Give the dough a quarter turn, then roll out again and fold as before. Wrap and chill for about 20 minutes. Repeat the rolling, folding and chilling twice so the pastry has been folded

Lovely light, crisp pastry contrasts with bittersweet caramel and sticky, fragrant bananas in this scrumptious tart.

a total of 6 times. Wrap and chill for an hour at least, preferably overnight, before using.

3 When ready to assemble, preheat the oven to 200°C/400°F/gas 6. To make the caramel, put the sugar in the frying pan or tatin pan with 1 tablespoon water and heat gently, without boiling or stirring, until the sugar has completely melted. Turn up the heat and bring to the boil. Cook until the syrup turns a light golden brown (see page 197 for tips when making caramel). Remove the pan from the heat. Add the butter and tip and swirl the pan until the butter has completely melted, then leave to cool for 5 minutes.

4 Meanwhile, cut the bananas into 1.5cm thick slices. Arrange the slices in a neat pattern in the caramel.

5 Roll out the pastry on a lightly floured worktop about 3mm thick. Cut out a circle slightly larger than your pan – use a plate or cake tin as a guide. Lift the pastry, using the rolling pin to help you, and gently drape it over the bananas in the pan. Tuck the edge of the pastry lid down inside the pan. Prick the pastry in several places with a fork.

6 Bake for 35–40 minutes until the pastry is a good golden brown, puffed up and crisp. Carefully invert onto a deep serving plate – the caramel will be hot and runny so take care. Serve warm.

Choux Dough

100g plain flour
¼ teaspoon salt
75g unsalted butter, diced
3 large free-range eggs, at room
  temperature, beaten

1 Sift the flour onto a sheet of greaseproof paper and set aside until needed. Put the salt, butter and 175ml water in a medium-sized pan and heat gently until the butter has completely melted – don't let the water boil and begin to evaporate. Quickly bring the mixture to the boil, then tip in the flour all in one go.

2 Take the pan off the heat and beat furiously with a wooden spoon – the mixture will look a hopeless, gluey, lumpy mess at first, but as you beat it will turn into a smooth, heavy dough. Put the pan back on low heat and beat at a more gentle speed for a couple of minutes to slightly cook the dough until it will come away from the sides of the pan to make a smooth, glossy ball.

Choux is unlike any other pastry in that it is cooked twice: first water, butter and flour are cooked to a heavy lump of paste in a pan before eggs are beaten in; then the now silky-smooth paste is shaped and baked. The heat of the oven transforms the dough – it puffs up and turns golden and crisp – into a container that can be filled with whipped cream, fruit, crème pâtissière or ice cream.

Choux is, of course, the basis for éclairs, but in the following Showstopping Challenges, it is transformed into Salambos, which are pingpong-sized balls dipped in caramel and pistachios and filled with orange cream; pretty strawberry and Chantilly cream swans; and, for the really adventurous cook, an exquisite Gâteau Paris-Brest decorated with spun sugar. The dough here can also be used to make 48 profiteroles or 8 cream puffs.

3 Tip the dough into a large mixing bowl and cool until barely warm. Using an electric mixer (a wooden spoon won't give the same result), gradually add the eggs, beating well after each addition. Add enough of the beaten eggs to make a very shiny, paste-like dough that just falls from the spoon when lightly shaken; you may not need the last tablespoon or so of egg (save it for glazing). The dough must be stiff enough to pipe or spoon into shapes. If it is too wet it will spread out rather than puff up in the oven.

4 Use the choux dough immediately or cover tightly, keep at cool room temperature and use within 4 hours.

TIP

Choux must be thoroughly baked so it is really crisp and dry. It is better to slightly over – rather than under – bake, so don't rush the cooking time and be prepared to return the pastry to the oven if the interior looks damp when split open.

Pistachio Salambos

SERVES 6–8

1 quantity Choux Dough
(see page 191)

FOR THE CARAMEL TOPPING

25g unsalted shelled pistachios,
blanched (see page 312) and
finely chopped
175g caster sugar
green edible glitter
(optional, see page 310)

FOR THE FILLING

250ml whipping cream, well chilled
2 tablespoons icing sugar
finely grated zest of 1 medium
unwaxed orange
1 teaspoon orange liqueur
(optional)

1 piping bag plus a 2cm and a 1cm
plain tube (optional); 2 baking trays,
lined with baking paper

1 Make the Choux Dough following the method on page 191. Preheat the oven to 200°C/400°F/gas 6. Spoon the dough into the piping bag fitted with the 2cm plain tube and pipe mounds about 4cm across and 3cm high on the lined baking sheets, spacing them well apart to allow for rising and spreading. Bake for 25 minutes.

2 Reduce the oven temperature to 180°C/350°F/gas 4. Open and quickly close the oven door to get rid of the steam, then bake for a further 5 minutes until the pastry is crisp and golden, and the cracks are coloured rather than pale white.

These tiny balls of crisp choux pastry are filled with orange-flavoured whipped cream and finished with a crunchy caramel and pistachio topping. Add sliced oranges in caramel sauce for a really lovely dessert (see Mini Ricotta Cheesecakes on page 261).

3 Remove the baking sheets from the oven and make a small hole at one side of each choux ball to let out the steam. Return to the oven and bake for a further 5 minutes until firm. Cool on a wire rack.

4 For the topping, spread the pistachios on a plate and have a skewer or cocktail stick for holding the choux balls ready at hand. Make the caramel with the sugar and 3 tablespoons water (see page 197). Working quickly, dip the top of each choux ball first in the hot caramel and then into the chopped nuts. Leave to set on a sheet of baking paper. (Once set, the choux balls can be kept in a dry, airy spot for up to 4 hours before filling.)

5 To make the filling, put the cream, sugar, orange zest and liqueur, if using, into a well-chilled bowl and whip until the cream is stiff enough to hold a peak. Spoon into the piping bag fitted with the smaller tube and pipe into each ball through the steam hole (or split each ball horizontally and spoon in the cream with a teaspoon).

6 Arrange in a serving dish or on individual plates and eat as soon as possible. Sprinkle the Salambos with green edible glitter for extra sparkle, if you like.

Swan Lake

MAKES 10

1 quantity Choux Dough
    (see page 191)
beaten egg, to glaze
10 large ripe strawberries, at room
    temperature, thinly sliced
1 quantity Chantilly Cream
    (see page 305)

FOR THE RASPBERRY SAUCE
250g fresh raspberries
1 teaspoon lemon juice
4 tablespoons icing sugar,
    or to taste

1 piping bag plus a 6–7mm plain tube
    and a large star tube (optional);
    2 baking sheets, lined with
    baking paper

These elegant pastry swans, dusted with icing sugar and floating on a lake of raspberry sauce, are as pretty as a picture. Each swan is shaped from 2 pieces of choux pastry: an oval-shaped mound for the body and wings, and a piped S-shape for the head and neck. With their filling of vanilla-flavoured whipped cream and sweet strawberries, the swans are quite special.

1 Make the Choux Dough following the method on page 191. Preheat the oven to 200°C/400°F/gas 6. Spoon some of the dough into the piping bag fitted with the small plain tube (you could also use a disposable piping bag with the tip snipped off). To form the necks for the swans, pipe 12 S shapes (extra to allow for breakages), each about 9cm long, on one of the prepared baking sheets, setting them well apart to allow for expansion. Brush very lightly with beaten egg to glaze, taking care not to 'glue' the dough to the paper. Bake for about 15 minutes until a good golden brown and very crisp. Leave to cool on a wire rack.

2 Return any leftover dough from piping the necks to the rest of the choux dough. To make the bodies, spoon the dough (using 2 kitchen spoons) onto the other baking sheet to make 10 ovals about 8cm long, 4cm wide and 2.5cm high. Set the shapes well apart to allow for expansion. Brush lightly with egg glaze as before and bake for about 30 minutes until a good golden brown.

3 Reduce the oven temperature to 180°C/350°F/gas 4. Open and quickly close the oven door to let out the steam, then bake for a further 5 minutes until the cracks are also coloured. Remove the baking sheets from the oven and make a small hole at one end of each oval to let the steam escape. Return to the oven and bake for another 5 minutes or so until really crisp and dry. Cool on a wire rack. (The cooled baked choux shapes can be kept in a dry airy spot, lightly covered, for up to 4 hours before assembling the swans.)

4 To make the sauce, put the raspberries, lemon juice and icing sugar into a food-processor and purée. Press through a fine sieve to remove the seeds. Taste and add more sugar if needed. Cover and chill for up to 12 hours.

5 When ready to assemble, spoon a little pool of raspberry sauce onto each individual serving plate. Cut the choux ovals in half horizontally, then slice the top section in half lengthways to make the wings. Arrange the sliced strawberries in the base of each oval. Spoon the Chantilly cream into the piping bag fitted with the star tube and pipe cream over the berries to cover (or simply spoon the cream neatly on top of the strawberries). Gently stick a neck into one end of each oval, then set pairs of wings into the cream, on either side of the neck, at an angle so they tilt upwards. Dust with icing sugar and set a swan on the sauce on each plate. Serve as soon as possible.

Caramel & Spun Sugar

EQUIPMENT NEEDED
small, heavy-based saucepan
pastry brush
sugar thermometer
1 rolling pin
1 metal spoon (or 2 forks)

1 Fill the sink with cold water. Put your measured sugar and water into a heavy pan and heat gently, without boiling, until the sugar has completely melted. Tip and swirl the pan to move the sugar around but don't stir; use a wet pastry brush to brush down any sugar that gets stuck to the sides of the pan. Bring the syrup to the boil and boil until it turns a good chestnut brown (photo 1).

2 Immediately plunge the base of the pan into cold water to stop the cooking. As soon as the caramel has stopped bubbling, remove the pan from the water. The caramel is now ready to use.

3 Turning caramel into spun sugar can be messy (cover the floor with newspapers) and will take some practice to get right, but spun sugar is a stunning and cheap way to decorate a dessert. It's best if your kitchen is cool and steam-free.

4 Make the caramel as above, but put a sugar thermometer into the pan when the syrup starts to boil. When it turns golden and reaches 160°C/320°F on the thermometer, dip the base of the pan in cold water to halt the cooking and stop any further colouring. Set the pan on a heatproof surface and leave to firm up briefly.

5 Dip a metal spoon (or 2 forks) into the hot, liquid caramel, then lift out and quickly flick trails of caramel back and forth over the rolling pin (photo 2). As the caramel is flicked it instantly cools. If you keep it moving it will form long strands; if you stop it will set into a clump. You will get the best result if you hold the spoon high and allow plenty of room underneath the rolling pin for the sugar strands to hang down. Continue until the caramel in the pan firms up too much to flick into fine strands. (You can very gently warm the caramel so it just melts, then make more spun sugar, but the strands will tend to be a bit thicker.)

6 Gently lift the spun sugar off the rolling pin, handling it as lightly as possible, and drape it over the dessert. It will only last about an hour before it starts to melt, so serve soon.

Gâteau Paris-Brest

SERVES 10

1 quantity Choux Dough
   (see page 191)
beaten egg, to glaze
3 tablespoon flaked almonds
icing sugar, for dusting
spun sugar, made with 175g sugar
   and 3 tablespoons water (see
   page 197 for the method), and
   gold almond dragees, to decorate

FOR THE PRALINE
75g unblanched almonds
75g caster sugar

FOR THE CRÈME PÂTISSIÈRE
250ml creamy milk
1 vanilla pod, split open
3 large free-range egg yolks,
   at room temperature
50g caster sugar
1½ tablespoons cornflour
250ml whipping cream, well chilled

1 piping bag plus a 2cm plain tube and
   a large star tube; a baking sheet;
   baking paper

1 Make the Choux Dough following the method on page 191. Preheat the oven to 200°C/400°F/gas 6. Draw a circle 20cm in diameter on a piece of baking paper; turn it over and use to line the baking sheet. Spoon the choux dough into the piping bag fitted with the plain tube and pipe a ring over the drawn circle on the lined sheet. Pipe another ring inside the first ring. Pipe a third ring on top of both rings to cover the 'seam'.

2 Brush with beaten egg to glaze, taking care not to 'glue' the dough to the sheet, then sprinkle with the flaked almonds. Bake for

The ring shape of this splendid confection represents a bicycle wheel, to commemorate a cycle race between Brest and Paris in 1891. After baking, the choux ring is split and filled with a rich praline cream. It's a lot of work but the last-minute assembly is fairly quick.

about 30 minutes until puffed and golden. Reduce the temperature to 180°C/350°F/gas 4. Open and quickly close the oven door to let out the steam, then bake for a further 10 minutes until the pastry feels crisp.

3 Remove from the oven and make a few steam holes around the middle of the choux ring to let out the steam. Return to the oven and bake for a further 5 minutes until the ring is really crisp and dry. Transfer to a wire rack and cool until warm. Split in half horizontally using a sharp knife, then cool.

4 Meanwhile, make the praline (see page 311). When it is cold, break up and grind to a fine powder in a food-processor.

5 Make the crème pâtissière (see page 305), adding the praline powder before folding in the whipped cream. Cover and chill for up to 2 hours.

6 Set the bottom half of the choux ring on a serving platter. Spoon the praline cream into the piping bag fitted with the star tube and pipe into the choux, saving a little for the decoration. Top with the upper half of the choux ring. Dust with icing sugar, then decorate with piped praline cream, spun sugar and dragees. Serve within an hour.

Delux Dobos Torte

SERVES
12

FOR THE SPONGE
225g unsalted butter, softened
225g caster sugar
finely grated zest of 1 medium
    unwaxed orange
4 large free-range eggs, at room
    temperature, beaten
200g self-raising flour
25g cornflour

FOR THE CHOCOLATE BUTTERCREAM
175g caster sugar
120ml water
4 large free-range egg yolks, at room
    temperature
300g unsalted butter, softened, cut
    into pieces
150g dark chocolate (70% cocoa
    solids), melted (see page 308)
2 teaspoons orange liqueur, or to
    taste (optional)

FOR THE CARAMEL GLAZE
175g caster sugar

2 x 20.5cm sandwich tins, greased and
    the bases lined with baking paper;
    a baking sheet, oiled

In this extravagant creation, 6 very thin orange sponge layers sandwiched with a silky-smooth chocolate buttercream have a glass-like topping of bittersweet caramel. Both the sponge and chocolate filling were invented in Hungary in 1887 and made the chef, Jozsef Dobos, an overnight sensation.

1 Preheat the oven to 180°C/350°F/gas 4. To make the sponge mixture, put the soft butter into a large mixing bowl and beat until very creamy using a wooden spoon or an electric mixer. Gradually beat in the caster sugar and orange zest, and continue beating until the mixture is very light in colour and texture.

2 Gradually add the eggs, beating well after each addition, and adding 1 tablespoon of the weighed flour with each of the last few additions of egg. Sift the rest of the flour and the cornflour into the bowl and gently but thoroughly fold in with a large metal spoon until there are no streaks of flour.

3 Divide the mixture into 6 equal portions, either by eye or using a digital scale. Spoon a portion into each of the 2 prepared tins and spread evenly – the cake mixture will only be about 5mm deep. Bake for about 15 minutes until firm and just starting to turn golden. Run a round-bladed knife around the inside of each tin to loosen the sponge, then leave to cool for 2 minutes before turning out onto a wire rack covered with a sheet of baking paper. While the sponges cool, wipe out the tins, grease and re-line, then repeat to bake the remaining 4 sponges. (Baked this way, the sponges are moist but a bit crisper and firmer than a sponge that has been split into layers after baking.)

4 Make the chocolate buttercream (see page 305), adding the optional orange liqueur after the melted chocolate has been worked in. Set aside the best-looking sponge layer for the top, then use the buttercream to sandwich the other layers and coat the top and sides of the assembled cake.

5 Before you make the caramel topping, get everything ready: set the top sponge layer on a wire rack placed over the oiled baking sheet (to catch the drips); brush off any loose crumbs that might spoil the glass-like finish; and lightly oil a large sharp knife.

6 Make the caramel with the caster sugar and 6 tablespoons water (see page 197 for help with making caramel). As soon as the caramel is chestnut-brown, remove from the heat and carefully pour it over the top sponge layer to coat completely (the caramel will burn you if you accidentally touch it).

7 Working quickly, mark the caramel topping into 12 segments with the oiled knife – this will make it easy to slice the cake neatly once the caramel has set hard. Leave the caramel sponge layer to cool for at least 30 minutes (don't touch it). When it is completely cold and hard, set it on top of the assembled cake.

8 Break up the pieces of caramel that dripped onto the baking sheet and use to decorate the top of the cake. Keep in a cool, dry spot until ready to serve. This cake is best the same day or the next, before the caramel starts to soften, although it will still taste just fine.

TIP
The sides of this elaborate cake are usually left unadorned, but you could add a chocolate ribbon (see page 46) or cover with a chocolate transfer strip (see page 309).

Mary's Apple Tarte Tatin

SERVES 6

FOR THE PASTRY
50g unsalted butter
25g lard
200g plain flour
4 tablespoons cold water

FOR THE TOPPING
175g granulated sugar
6 tablespoons water
900g red eating apples
finely grated zest and juice
   of 1 lemon
75g caster sugar

1 x 23cm sandwich tin (not
   loose-based), lined on the
   base with baking paper

A classic 'upside-down' French tart, usually served warm as a pudding. Mary uses red-skinned eating apples, which look really lovely when the Tarte Tatin is cooked.

1 To make the pastry, chill the butter and lard in the freezer until it is very cold and firm. Sift the flour into a mixing bowl and grate in the butter and lard. Toss with the flour so that all the pieces of butter and lard are coated. Add the cold water and toss together until the mixture comes together.

2 Roll out the pastry on a lightly floured worktop to make a rectangle, rolling it out away from you so the rectangle is vertically in front of you. Fold the top third down, then fold the bottom third up over the top to make 3 layers. Wrap in clingfilm and chill for about 20 minutes. Repeat the rolling out, folding and chilling process 2 more times.

3 Put the granulated sugar into a small pan with the water and heat until melted, then cook to make a caramel (see page 197). Pour the caramel into the cake tin, and tilt and rotate it so the caramel covers the base evenly.

4 Preheat the oven to 220°C/425°F/gas 7. Core and slice the apples (without peeling); sprinkle with the lemon zest and juice.

5 Arrange a single layer of the best apple slices in a circular pattern over the caramel. Cover with the remainder of the apple slices and press down firmly.

6 Roll out the chilled pastry on a lightly floured worktop to a disc about 28cm in diameter. Drape over the apples, then tuck the edges of the pastry disc down inside the tin. Cut a small cross in the centre of the pastry lid. Bake for 40 minutes until the pastry is crisp and golden brown (it will have shrunk a little when cooked).

7 Tip the cake tin carefully and pour off the juices into a small pan. Turn out the tart onto a deep plate or plate with a rim, with the pastry on the bottom. Add the caster sugar to the juices and boil to reduce to a syrup, then pour over the apples. Serve warm with cream or crème fraîche.

Wild Mushroom & Gorgonzola Tart

SERVES
6–8

FOR THE PASTRY
200g plain flour
good pinch of salt
50g walnut pieces
120g unsalted butter, chilled
 and diced
1 large free-range egg yolk
3 tablespoons icy water

FOR THE FILLING
25g dried porcini mushrooms
3 tablespoons white wine
1 tablespoon olive oil
2 red onions, thinly sliced
3 garlic cloves, crushed
10 sprigs of fresh thyme
200g chestnut or portobello
 mushrooms, thickly sliced
2 large free-range eggs
150ml single cream
60g Gorgonzola piccante,
 thinly sliced
50g walnut pieces or halves
black pepper

1 x 23cm deep loose-based flan tin;
 a baking sheet

Just a few dried porcini mushrooms have the power to add an intensely deep flavour to this savoury tart filling. Walnut pastry and sharp Gorgonzola add contrast and texture. Enjoy this as a main dish with a colourful salad and new potatoes. This tart is made in a food processor for ease.

1 Make the rich pastry in a food-processor: put the flour, salt and walnuts into the processor bowl and run until the nuts are finely chopped and the mixture looks sandy. Add the butter and process until the mixture looks like fine crumbs.

2 Mix the egg yolk with the icy water, then with the machine running add to the mixture through the feed tube and process just until the mixture comes together to make a ball of dough. If there are dry crumbs and the mixture won't form a dough add more icy water a teaspoon at a time. Flatten the dough to a thick disc, then wrap and chill for about 20 minutes.

3 Roll out the pastry on a lightly floured worktop and use to line the flan tin (see page 312). While it is chilling, preheat the oven to 190°C/375°F/gas 5.

4 Bake the pastry case 'blind' (see page 312). Remove it from the oven and set aside on a wire rack. Reduce the oven temperature to 180°C/350°F/gas 4 and put in the baking sheet to heat up.

5 While the pastry case is baking, make the filling. Put the dried mushrooms into a heatproof bowl. Bring the wine and 2 tablespoons water to the boil in a small pan, then pour over the mushrooms and leave to soak for 25 minutes.

6 Meanwhile, heat the oil in a non-stick frying pan, add the sliced onions, garlic and thyme and stir well. Cover with a dampened disc of greaseproof paper, pressed directly onto the surface of the onions, and cook over low heat for about 25 minutes until very soft but not coloured.

7 Remove the paper and stir the onions well, then add the fresh mushrooms together with the dried mushrooms and their soaking liquid. Fry over medium heat, stirring constantly, for about 5 minutes until the mushrooms are softened and all the liquid has evaporated. Remove from the heat and season with plenty of pepper. Leave to cool.

8 Beat the eggs into the cream to mix, then stir into the cooled mushroom mixture. Spoon into the pastry case. Scatter the cheese over the top followed by the walnuts.

9 Set the pastry case on the heated baking sheet and bake for about 35 minutes until the filling is set in the middle. Leave the tart to settle for about 5 minutes before carefully unmoulding. Serve warm.

Goats' Cheese Filo Cups

MAKES 8

4 x 100g firm mini goats' cheeses
about 180g filo pastry
    (4 sheets, each 25.5 x 48cm),
    thawed if frozen
50g crustless white bread
15g parsley sprigs without stalks
1 tablespoon olive oil
50g shelled unsalted pistachios
about 75g unsalted butter,
    melted, for brushing
salt and pepper

1 x 12-cup loose-based mini sandwich
    pan or non-stick muffin tray;
    a baking sheet

For these good-looking, great-tasting and easy little pastries, individual goats' cheeses are baked in filo with a crunchy herb and pistachio topping. You'll need a food processor to mince the filling really fine. Go for a cheese that's firm and well-flavoured rather than soft and mild – as it bakes it melts like a fondue, making a good contrast to the crisp pastry and nuts.

1 Preheat the oven to 180°C/350°F/gas 4. Freeze the cheeses for about 15 minutes until very firm (this makes slicing easier). Unwrap the filo, but keep it covered with clingfilm to prevent it from drying out.

2 While the cheese is chilling, spread out the bread on a baking sheet and bake for 5 minutes until firm and fairly dry but not coloured. Break up and put into the bowl of a food-processor with the parsley. Process to make fine green crumbs. Add the oil, a pinch of salt and several grinds of pepper, and process briefly just to combine. Add the nuts and process until roughly chopped. Transfer the mixture to a bowl. Turn the oven up to 190°C/375°F/gas 5.

3 Brush one filo sheet lightly with melted butter. Using kitchen scissors, cut the sheet into 8 squares with 12cm sides. Layer up 4 of the squares so the tips point in different directions (like tulip cupcake cases), making

sure that there are 4 layers of pastry in the centre. Repeat with the remaining 4 squares and then the rest of the filo sheets to make 8 filo stacks in all.

4 Unwrap the partially frozen cheeses and check that they will fit, when wrapped in pastry, into the cups in your tray – if the cheeses are a bit wide, carefully pare away the rind. Cut each cheese in half horizontally and set one half, cut side up, in the middle of each pastry stack.

5 Gather up the pastry around the cheese and gently set each into a cup in the tray. Carefully open up the pastry 'leaves' to expose the surface of the cheese. Spoon the green crumb mixture onto the cheese to cover completely. (At this point the little pastries can be left at cool room temperature for 1–2 hours before baking.)

6 Set the tray on the baking sheet and bake for 12–15 minutes until the pastry is golden brown and crisp. Leave to cool for 5 minutes before carefully unmoulding – the cheese will be molten. Serve warm.

Roast Beef Tartlets

MAKES **12**

1 x 500g fillet of beef
2–3 tablespoons olive oil
½ quantity Puff Pastry (see page 312) OR 375g all-butter puff pastry, thawed if frozen
beaten egg, to glaze
1 x 125g wedge blue cheese, such as Stichelton, Blue Monday, Cashel Blue or Stilton (without rind)
salt and pepper

1 x 12-hole bun/mince pie tray; 2 baking sheets; greaseproof paper

The most tender, luxurious cut of beef, simply roasted, and just-melting piquant blue cheese fill these puff pastry tartlets. This is a classy dish that can be prepared well ahead, then assembled and quickly baked to serve, with watercress or salad leaves.

1 Rub the fillet of beef all over with salt and pepper and the oil, then leave to come to room temperature – about 1 hour. Towards the end of this time, preheat the oven to 230°C/450°F/gas 8.

2 Heat a heavy-based roasting tin or an ovenproof frying pan until hot, then add the meat and briefly sear and brown on all sides. Transfer to the oven to roast – 12 minutes for a thin piece of fillet and 15 minutes for the thicker end. The meat will be very rare. Remove from the pan and cool, then wrap tightly and chill for 2 hours. Reduce the oven temperature to 200°C/400°F/gas 6.

3 Roll out the pastry to about 28 × 37cm, then trim off the edges to make a neat 27 × 36cm rectangle. Cut into 12 squares with 9cm sides. Gently press 6 of the squares into the bun tray, using alternate holes so the pastry doesn't overlap. Prick the bases, then chill for 15 minutes. Lay the remaining 6 squares on a baking sheet lined with greaseproof paper, cover lightly and keep in the fridge.

4 Lightly brush the edges of the pastry cases in the bun tray with beaten egg. Set a paper bun or fairy-cake case (or a small square of greaseproof paper) filled with baking beans into each tartlet. Bake 'blind' for 10 minutes until lightly coloured and firm. Carefully remove the paper and beans, then bake for a further 5 minutes until the base is completely cooked and dry. Leave to cool for 5 minutes before removing the tartlet cases to a baking sheet.

5 When the tray is cold, line 6 alternate holes with the remaining pastry squares and bake in the same way. (The tartlet cases can be baked up to 4 hours ahead; keep lightly covered until needed.)

6 When ready to assemble, preheat the oven to 230°C/450°F/gas 8. Set all 12 tartlet cases back into the bun tray. With a large sharp knife, cut the beef fillet into slices about 1cm thick, then cut across into 1cm wide strips. Arrange in the tartlet cases and season with pepper only. Slice the wedge of cheese across into 12 thin triangles and set one on top of the meat in each tartlet case. Bake for 5–8 minutes until piping hot. Serve immediately.

Pies

THERE'S AN OLD SAYING: tarts for tea and pies for pudding (and of course for supper too). Perhaps substance makes a pie seem less fancy, more down-to-earth than a tart. Whether it has one crust or two – underneath, on top or both – a pie makes a fine dish to set before friends and family.

A wide variety of pastries are used for pie crusts, from familiar crumbly shortcrust and crisp, firm American pie pastry to sturdy hot-water crust, rich puff, and flaky strudel or filo as well as suet-crust and scone doughs, which are more spongy.

Pie pastry is also a great opportunity to show off your pastry finishes. For the Pie Showstopper Challenge, the bakers were asked to make American Pies, which are traditionally baked for festive occasions such as Thanksgiving. As well as perfectly baked pastry and a generous filling, the bakers embellished the pie crust for a showstopping finish. Our chapter begins with a basic recipe for this pastry, which you can use to make a great Pecan Pie, a double-crust Pear Pie and finally a Cranberry Pie.

Paul asked the bakers to make a Hand-raised Pie for his Technical Challenge. The secrets to success with Paul's pies include shaping the pastry cases so that they are the right thickness and height to encase the filling but don't buckle or collapse in the oven; dicing the filling and layering it to achieve a good apricot to meat ratio – it is important that the layers are attractively even when the pie is cut open. The pies also had to be cooked to perfection and sufficient jelly added at the right time to combine the filling ingredients – not easy but the bakers really rose to the challenge, albeit with varying results!

The pastry ingredient list is usually short and simple – flour, fat, liquid and salt, plus sometimes sugar, eggs and nuts. The proportions used and the method of combination define the type of pastry you make for your pie.

From an eating point of view, it's clear what makes a good pie crust – pastry with excellent texture and taste. For many pastries, it's best to use butter because it gives a unique flavour. Recipes usually call for chilled butter for good reason – if it is soft it will make the pastry difficult to handle, and you'll be tempted to add more flour to your worktop and hands, throwing out the proportions and in the end baking a tough crust.

Other fats, such as lard for hot-water crust and beef or vegetable suet for suet-crust dough, give their own special qualities and flavours. Lard, made from pork fat, makes a distinctively flavoured pastry that's crisp and short when served cold; for hot-water crust it's melted to form an easily mouldable paste that then sets rigid enough to be filled without collapsing. Suet comes ready-shredded so it just needs to be mixed with flour and water to make a soft, moist dough to top a pie.

Plain white flour is the most common pastry flour, although strong or bread flour is used in hot-water pastry for raised pies, and for strudel dough, as the extra gluten helps them stretch. Self-raising flour is used for scone or cobbler toppings, as well as some suet crusts, to produce the desired soft, spongy quality. If you want to experiment with spelt or wholemeal flours in your pie crusts, you will need a bit more liquid to bind the dough; the pastry will be slightly chewier and not as light, but the flavour will be nuttier and more interesting.

A little salt is added to enhance the flavour of pastry, and sometimes sugar for sweetness as well as crispness and colour. Moisture is usually provided by water, or sometimes egg and milk. Too much or too little moisture can spell disaster: a sticky wet dough is as difficult to roll out neatly as a crumbly dry one. Do take a little time to measure carefully.

Rolling out most types of pastry to line a pie plate or tin, or lay over a filling, is much easier if the pastry has been chilled well first. It is less likely to stick to your hands, the rolling pin or the worktop. In addition, the time spent resting in the fridge allows the pastry to relax so it is less likely to shrink in the oven. The exceptions to this rule are hot-water crust pastry, which is shaped as soon as it is cool enough to be handled and before it has time to set, then chilled before baking, and suet-crust and cobbler doughs made with self-raising flour, which should be quickly made, shaped and baked for maximum lightness.

Once you've tackled the pastry, you need a filling with excellent flavour.

Finally, a pie must look as fine as it tastes, but that can be achieved very easily. Do aim for a golden-coloured pastry and finish with a bit of panache – we show you four ways to edge a pie on pages 216–217. And for a sweet pie, one of the simplest finishes is to dust it with caster or icing sugar. Or you could add a quick chocolate lattice as on the Cranberry Pie or use a doily as a stencil to create a pretty pattern.

DON'T FORGET

🧁 A general rule for shortcrust and American pie pastry as well as scone and suet doughs is to handle them as little as possible. Overworked pastry will be hard and prone to shrinking in the oven.

🧁 Lightly dust the worktop with flour when rolling out pastry and keep a dry pastry brush at hand to brush excess flour off the underside of the rolled-out sheet.

🧁 Gently lift rolled-out pastry with the help of the rolling pin, then drape it over the pie dish or tin to avoid stretching it.

🧁 Neatly trim the edges of the pastry case with a small, sharp knife.

🧁 For top-crust and double-crust pies, seal the edges firmly to prevent the filling from bubbling out.

🧁 Keep ready-made filo pastry tightly wrapped while thawing and bringing to room temperature and keep it covered while assembling the pie, to prevent it from drying out.

🧁 When shaping a hot-water crust case, make sure there are no holes for the filling to leak through. Seal any cracks with your fingers before adding the filling.

🧁 Bake a pie with a bottom crust on a heated baking sheet to avoid a soggy base.

SARAH JANE

Pie Pastry

200g plain flour
good pinch of salt
1 tablespoon caster sugar
120g unsalted butter, chilled
 and diced
1 large free-range egg yolk
1 ½ tablespoons icy water

1 To make the pastry in a food-processor, put the flour, salt and sugar into the bowl and 'pulse' a few times just to combine. Add the pieces of butter and process just until the mixture looks like fine crumbs. Add the egg yolk and icy water through the feed tube while the machine is running, to bring the mixture together into a ball of dough. If the dough is dry and hard, and won't form a ball, add more water a teaspoon at a time. If the pastry feels soft, wrap it in clingfilm and chill for about 15 minutes to firm up before rolling out.

2 To make the pastry by hand, sift the flour, salt and sugar into a mixing bowl and rub in the butter with your fingertips until the mixture looks like fine crumbs. Using a round-bladed knife, work in the egg yolk and enough icy water to bring the mixture together to make a ball of dough that's firm but not dry or hard. Wrap and chill if necessary before rolling out.

When the bakers of series 3 tackled Showstopper pies, they looked across the Atlantic for inspiration. Three elements make home-made American pies outstanding: superlative pastry that really does melt in the mouth, a fine-tasting filling, and the 'I can't wait for a slice' appearance and aroma of the warm pie.

The filling should be generous – American pies are more lavish than their European cousins – and offer contrasts in texture. Layered fillings look and taste very appealing.

To make pie pastry with the best flavour and short, almost crumbly texture you need to use unsalted butter – anything else just won't taste as good. Eggs, or just yolks, and sugar boost the flavour but also give the pastry structure, helping it to be a firmer, crisper container for the filling. American pies are made in a deep loose-based flan tin – with a pastry case or with a pastry lid too for a double-crust pie – but you could also use a traditional deep pie plate or round pie dish.

The recipe here makes enough pie pastry to line a 23cm deep loose-based flan tin. Make this pastry and then try one of the following three Showstopping Challenges, which take inspiration from the bakers' American pies.

Pecan Pie

SERVES
10

1 quantity Pie Pastry (see page 213)

FOR THE FILLING
100g unsalted butter, diced
125g dark brown muscovado sugar
85g maple syrup
85g golden syrup
3 large free-range eggs, beaten
½ teaspoon vanilla extract
300g pecan halves
icing sugar, for dusting

1 x 23cm deep loose-based flan tin;
   a baking sheet

For the moist, sticky filling in this all-time favourite, you must use very fresh nuts and real maple syrup or the flavour will be disappointing. The taste gets better and better, so plan to bake the pie a day ahead of serving and have plenty of vanilla ice cream to enjoy with it.

1 Make the Pie Pastry following the method on page 213. Roll out the pastry on a lightly floured worktop and use to line the flan tin (see page 312). While the case is chilling, preheat the oven to 190°C/375°F/gas 5. Bake the pastry case 'blind' (see page 312). When you remove it from the oven, reduce the oven temperature to 180°C/350°F/gas 4 and put the baking sheet into the oven to heat up. Do not unmould the pastry case.

2 While the pastry case is baking, make the filling. Put the butter, sugar, maple syrup and golden syrup into a pan large enough to hold all the ingredients. Melt gently over low heat, stirring occasionally, then bring to the boil, stirring constantly, and boil (still stirring) for 1 minute. Remove from the heat and leave to cool until just warm. Beat the eggs with the vanilla and stir into the melted mixture. Save 50g of the best-looking pecans for the decoration and roughly chop the rest. Add to the pan and stir well, then pour the filling into the pastry case.

3 Decorate the filling with the saved pecan halves. Set the tin on the heated baking sheet and bake for 30–35 minutes until the filling is just firm and set (the pie will continue cooking for a few minutes after it comes out of the oven). Leave to cool on a wire rack until just warm, then carefully unmould.

4 For a simple decoration, place a 21cm doily upside-down and flat on the pie and dust liberally with icing sugar, then carefully remove the doily stencil. Alternatively, just dust with sifted icing sugar. Eat warm or at room temperature.

Double-crust Pear Pie

SERVES 10

FOR THE PIE PASTRY
300g plain flour
good pinch of salt
3 tablespoons caster sugar
175g unsalted butter,
    chilled and diced
1 large free-range egg, beaten
1 tablespoon icy water

FOR THE FILLING
225g marzipan, diced
100g unsalted butter, softened
    and diced
2 tablespoons plain flour
2 large free-range eggs, at room
    temperature, beaten
4 large pears
caster sugar, for sprinkling

1 x 23cm deep loose-based flan tin,
    lightly greased; small shaped cutters
    or card shapes; a baking sheet

Sweet pears baked on a creamy almond mixture make a simple yet elegant filling for this double-crust American pie. The pastry top can easily be decorated with cut-outs – leaves are traditional – and the edge can be fluted, ridged or given a starburst design (for details, see page 218). Serve with cream or lemon ice cream.

1 Make the Pie Pastry following the method on page 213. Cut off two-fifths and save for the top. Roll out the rest of the dough on a lightly floured worktop and use to line the flan tin (see page 312); do not trim off the excess pastry. While the pastry case is chilling, preheat the oven to 190°C/375°F/gas 5 and put in the baking sheet to heat.

2 To make the filling, put the pieces of marzipan and butter into a food-processor and blend until smooth. Add the flour and eggs and process until the mixture is really creamy. Spoon into the pastry case. Peel, quarter and core the pears, then cut each quarter into 2 or 3 thick slices. Set on top of the almond mixture.

3 Roll out the reserved pastry to a round slightly larger than the top of the flan tin. Lightly brush the rim of the pastry case with cold water. Roll up the pastry lid around the rolling pin and lift it over the pastry case, then gently unroll the lid so it drapes over the case to cover the filling. Gently but firmly press the edges together to seal and cut off the excess pastry with a sharp knife. Finish the edges as you like (see page 218).

4 Cut 3 small slits in the centre of the lid. Gather up the pastry trimmings and re-roll. Cut out small shapes using a cutter, or cut around card shapes. Dampen the underside of each shape and attach to the pie.

5 Set the pie on the heated baking sheet and bake for 40–45 minutes until a light golden brown. Remove from the oven and sprinkle with caster sugar. Leave to cool and firm up for about 15 minutes, then carefully unmould the pie. Eat warm, or at room temperature the same or the next day.

Crimping & Decorating

EQUIPMENT NEEDED
small knife
small leaf cutters
pastry brush
fork

1 For a simple but attractive fluted or crimped edge, be it a single crust on the top or bottom of a pie or a double-crust pie, you only need your fingers. If you've made a double-crust pie, first 'knock up' the edge: use a small knife to make tiny, shallow, horizontal cuts ('knocks') all around the edge of the sealed pastry rim, so looked at side on the edge resembles the pages of a book. To flute the edge, flour a fingertip of one hand and a knuckle on the other and gently press the pastry rim between the 2 at regular intervals all around the pie, to make a neat wavy finish.

2 For a pretty leaf edging, roll out chilled pastry scraps, or reserved pastry, on a lightly floured worktop to about the thickness of a pound coin. Cut out oval-shaped leaves 1.5–2.5cm long, using a small leaf or oval cutter or cutting the shapes free-hand with a small knife. Mark lightly with the back of the knife to make 'veins'. Brush the pastry rim with cold water, then gently press on the leaves so they slightly curl and overlap.

3 For an easy ridged effect, dust a fork with flour, then lightly press the back of the fork tines down on the pastry rim, either in straight lines or a criss-cross pattern, all the way around. Re-flour the fork if it starts to stick.

4 For a decorative folded or starburst edging, start off by making small cuts in the rim, 1–2cm long and at 1cm intervals, all around the pie. Brush lightly with cold water, then diagonally fold over one corner of each cut section to make a tiny triangle and press to seal firmly.

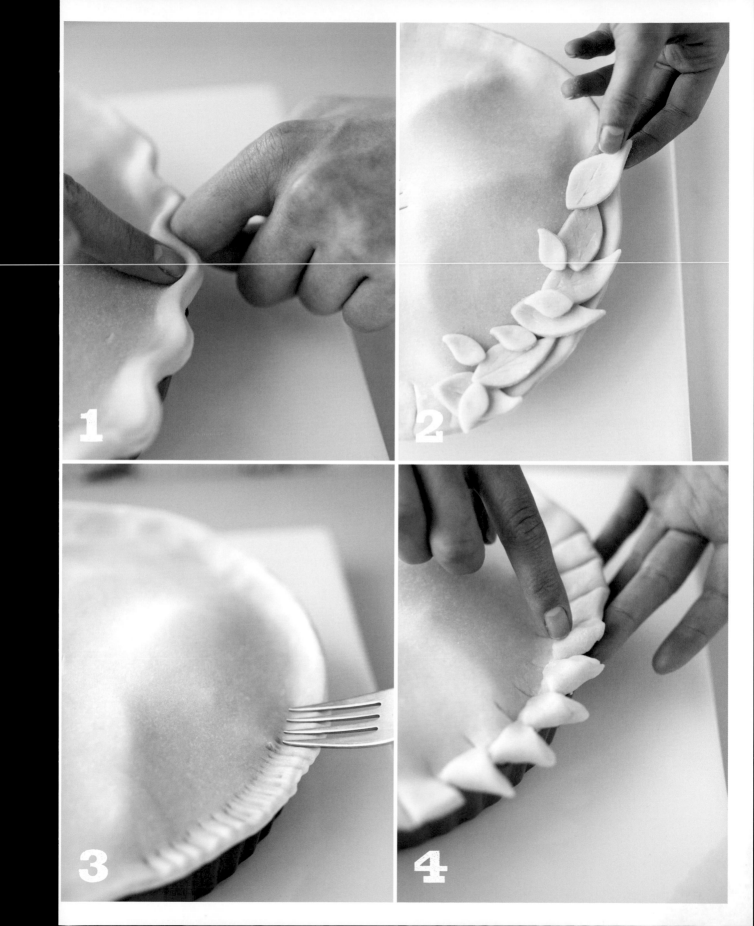

Cranberry Pie

10

FOR THE PIE PASTRY

175g plain flour
25g ground almonds
good pinch of salt
3 tablespoons icing sugar
125g unsalted butter,
    chilled and diced
1 large free-range egg yolk
1 tablespoon icy water

FOR THE FILLING

350g fresh or frozen and
    thawed cranberries
1 cinnamon stick
finely grated zest and juice
    of 1 large unwaxed orange
100g demerara sugar

FOR THE TOPPING

75g marzipan, diced
100g demerara sugar
85g unsalted butter, cut into pieces
100g plain flour
1 teaspoon ground cinnamon
1 tablespoon lemon juice

TO DECORATE

50g dark chocolate (70% cocoa
    solids), melted (see page 308),
    OR icing sugar

1 x 23cm deep loose-based flan tin,
    lightly greased; a baking sheet;
    a disposable piping bag (optional)

We all love a colourful sauce of cranberries to go with the Christmas turkey, but they make an excellent pie filling too. Their juicy tartness contrasts perfectly with the rich and buttery almond pastry case and crunchy, cinnamon-sweet topping here. All of the elements can be made in advance, ready to assemble just before baking. Serve with whipped cream or cinnamon ice cream for a festive treat.

1 Make the Pie Pastry following the method on page 213, adding the ground almonds with the flour. Wrap tightly and chill until firm, if necessary. Roll out on a lightly floured worktop and use to line the flan tin (see page 312).

2 While the pastry case is chilling, preheat the oven to 190°C/375°F/gas 5. Bake the pastry case 'blind' (see page 312). Because it contains icing sugar instead of caster, this pastry colours quickly, so watch it carefully. Remove and leave to cool. Do not unmould the pastry case.

3 Put all the filling ingredients in a heavy-based medium pan and simmer gently, stirring frequently, for about 15 minutes until the mixture is very thick. Pour into a heatproof bowl and leave to cool, then cover and chill until needed (up to a day).

4 To make the topping, put the marzipan and the sugar in a food-processor and run the machine until the mixture looks like coarse crumbs. Melt half of the butter and

Recipe continues overleaf

leave to cool. Add the rest of the butter to the processor and process until the mixture looks sandy. Add the flour and cinnamon and 'pulse' just to combine, then add the lemon juice and melted butter and process until the mixture comes together in a ball. Form into a brick shape, wrap tightly in clingfilm and freeze for at least 2 hours until hard. (The topping can be kept in the freezer for up to a week until needed.)

5 When ready to assemble the pie, preheat the oven to 180°C/350°F/gas 4 and put the baking sheet in to heat.

6 Spoon the cranberry filling into the pastry case, discarding the cinnamon stick, and spread evenly. Unwrap the topping, leaving just enough of the wrapping for holding the brick, and grate it straight onto the cranberry mixture using the coarse side of a cheese grater. Make sure the filling is completely covered by the topping, right up to the edges, and that the topping forms an even layer – use the tip of a knife to move the strands of topping rather than your fingers. Set the pie on the heated baking sheet and bake for about 35 minutes until the topping is soft and lightly coloured.

7 Remove the pie from the oven and set it on a wire rack. Leave to cool and firm up for about 30 minutes before carefully unmoulding. Once the pie has cooled to room temperature, you can decorate with a lattice of chocolate, if you like: spoon the melted chocolate into the disposable piping bag and snip off the tip. Pipe 7–8 lines, about 2cm apart, across the top of the pie, then turn the pie and pipe again in the opposite direction; leave to set. Or simply dust with sifted icing sugar and eat warm or at room temperature.

American Lime Pie

SERVES 12–16

FOR THE SWEET PASTRY
300g plain flour
60g icing sugar
1 tablespoon ground ginger
pinch of salt
180g unsalted butter,
    chilled and diced
3 large free-range egg yolks
about 2 tablespoons icy water

FOR THE FILLING
4 pieces stem ginger in syrup,
    drained and finely chopped
finely grated zest and juice
    of 6 limes
1 x 397g tin condensed milk
4 large free-range egg yolks
300ml double cream, well chilled

FOR THE ITALIAN MERINGUE
250g granulated sugar
5 tablespoons water
4 large free-range egg whites,
    at room temperature

TO DECORATE
2 limes, thinly sliced
few small sprigs of mint

1 x 30cm loose-based flan tin;
    a piping bag fitted with a 2cm
    plain tube; a blowtorch

A beautifully light and refreshing pie, this has a crisp, biscuit-like pastry, cool and creamy filling, and fluffy meringue, all set off with a touch of hot stem ginger. You'll need a small blowtorch to brown the meringue topping.

1 To make the pastry, sift the flour, icing sugar, ginger and salt into a mixing bowl. Add the diced butter and rub in until the mixture looks like fine crumbs. Mix the yolks with the icy water and stir in with a round-bladed knife to make a soft but not sticky dough; add more water if necessary. Wrap the dough in clingfilm and chill for about 20 minutes until firm.

2 Roll out the dough on a lightly floured worktop to a circle about 37cm across and the thickness of a pound coin. Use to line the flan tin (see page 312). Prick the base of the pastry case with a fork and chill for about 20 minutes. Meanwhile, preheat the oven to 200°C/400°F/gas 6.

3 Bake the pastry case 'blind' (see page 312 for instructions); after removing the paper and beans, reduce the oven temperature to 180°C/350°F/gas 4 before baking for a further 8–10 minutes until the pastry is a light golden brown. Leave to cool but do not unmould.

4 For the filling, scatter the chopped ginger over the base of the pastry case. Set aside half of the lime zest for the decoration and put the rest into a mixing bowl with the juice, condensed milk and yolks. Whisk with a wire whisk for a couple of minutes until the mixture thickens slightly.

5 Whip the cream just until it falls in a thick ribbon-like trail from the whisk (the stage before soft peak), then fold into the lime mixture using a large metal spoon – the mixture will thicken considerably. Pour into the pastry case and chill for about 1 hour until firm.

6 Next, make the Italian meringue (see page 250 for the method), whisking until the mixture has cooled to room temperature. Spoon the meringue into the piping bag.

7 Unmould the pie and set it on a serving platter. Pipe the meringue in a thick rope of continuous loops around the edge of the pie.

8 Use a kitchen blowtorch to lightly brown and highlight the meringue curves. Decorate with lime slices, the remaining lime zest and sprigs of mint. Serve immediately or keep chilled until serving. Best eaten the same day, but can be kept, well wrapped, overnight in the fridge.

Guinea Fowl Croustade

SERVES 8–9

1 quantity Strudel Dough (see page 281), made but not stretched, OR about 360g filo pastry (8 sheets, each 25.5 x 48cm), thawed if frozen
about 100g unsalted butter, melted, for brushing

FOR THE FILLING

1 guinea fowl, about 1.25kg
2 tablespoons olive oil
2 onions, finely chopped
1 ¼ teaspoons ground cinnamon
½ teaspoon ground ginger
good pinch of saffron threads
1 tablespoon lemon juice
small bunch of fresh coriander, leaves finely chopped
1 small preserved lemon, rinsed, pulp discarded and peel finely chopped
75g blanched almonds, toasted and roughly chopped
salt and pepper

FOR POACHING

1 onion, roughly chopped
1 carrot, roughly chopped
1 celery stick, roughly chopped
1 cinnamon stick
6 black peppercorns

1 x 23cm springclip tin, greased; a baking sheet

The exotic cuisine of Morocco, where rich and spicy mixtures of pigeon, eggs, nuts and preserved lemons are baked in many layers of thin, crisp pastry, is the inspiration for this unusual guinea fowl pie. You could also use 450–500g cooked chicken or turkey instead.

1 Put the guinea fowl into a large saucepan with the poaching ingredients and add cold water to cover. Bring to the boil, then reduce the heat to a simmer, cover and poach gently for 1 ¼–1 ½ hours until tender. Remove from the heat and leave the bird to cool in the liquid.

2 As soon as the guinea fowl is cool enough to handle, remove from the pan, draining it well. (The poaching liquid can be boiled down until reduced by two-thirds, then strained and used for a soup or gravy.) Remove all the meat from the guinea fowl, discarding the skin and bones. Tear or shred the meat into bite-sized pieces. Cover and keep in the fridge until ready to assemble the pie – up to 24 hours.

3 Heat the oil in a heavy-based frying pan and add the onions, 1 teaspoon of the cinnamon, the ginger and saffron. Stir well, then cover and cook over very low heat, stirring occasionally, for about 20 minutes until very soft. Uncover and stir in the lemon juice and coriander. Season with a little salt and plenty of pepper. Leave to cool.

4 Stretch the strudel dough now, if using. Or if using filo, unwrap it, but keep it covered with clingfilm to prevent it from drying out.

5 Preheat the oven to 190°C/375°F/gas 5. Using kitchen scissors, cut the stretched strudel dough into 8 sheets about 20 × 40cm; save all the torn sections and scraps for the topping and use the large sections to assemble the pie. You will need 6 sheets of strudel or filo for the base.

6 Brush one sheet with a little melted butter, then arrange in the tin so it covers the base and drapes over one side. Brush another sheet with butter and arrange at a right angle to the first sheet. Continue in this way with 4 more sheets so the base has 6 layers and the sides of the tin are completely covered with pastry.

7 Arrange the shredded guinea fowl on the pastry base and cover with the onion mixture. Scatter the preserved lemon peel on top. Fold over one of the overhanging flaps of pastry and brush with butter, then fold over a couple more and brush with butter. Scatter the almonds and the remaining ¼ teaspoon cinnamon over the pastry. Fold over the remaining flaps of pastry, buttering as you go.

8 Trim off any thick, unsightly or dry edges with kitchen scissors. Brush the remaining 2 sheets of pastry (and the saved scraps) with melted butter, then tear into strips and drop them, like a crumpled handkerchief, on top of the pie.

9 Set the tin on the baking sheet and bake for about 50 minutes until the pastry is crisp and a good golden brown. Serve the pie hot or warm, with salad.

Paul's Hand-raised Pies

MAKES 2

FOR THE HOT WATER CRUST PASTRY
200g plain flour
40g strong white bread flour
50g unsalted butter,
    chilled and diced
60g lard
100ml boiling water
1 teaspoon salt
beaten egg, to glaze

FOR THE FILLING
300g uncooked chicken meat, free
    of skin and bones, roughly diced
300g smoked back bacon rashers,
    cut into narrow strips
1 teaspoon chopped thyme
240g dried apricots, chopped
salt and pepper

TO FINISH
1 chicken stock cube
2 leaves gelatine (about 4g total)

2 medium pie dollies, about 13cm wide
    and 7.25cm high, greased with olive
    oil; a baking sheet, lined with
    baking paper

1 To make the pastry, put both the flours in a mixing bowl and rub in the butter until the mixture looks like fine crumbs. Put the lard, boiling water and salt into a small pan and heat until the lard has melted, then pour onto the flour mixture. Stir with a wooden spoon until the mixture comes together into a dough.

The bakers got themselves into a sticky situation with the hand-raised pies. The key is to shape the pastry as quickly as you can. The 'dollies' in this recipe are wooden moulds used by pie-makers to shape hand-raised pies. Alternatively, Mary suggests that you could use 2 jam jars of similar dimensions. Fill the jam jars with hot water before you remove the pastry from around them – the hot water will help the pastry come off. The recipe makes 2 pies and each will serve 3–4.

2 Tip the warm dough onto a lightly floured worktop and gently work until it forms a smooth ball. Divide it in half. Set aside one-quarter of each portion for the lids and keep covered with clingfilm until needed. Form the rest of one portion of dough into a ball, then flatten slightly. Set a dolly on top of the flattened disc. Using your hands, mould the still warm dough around the dolly. Try to make sure the dough is the same thickness on the sides, that the dough on the base is not too thick and that there are no holes. Repeat with the other portion of dough. Set the moulded pie cases on the lined baking sheet and chill for about 20 minutes or until really firm.

Recipe continues overleaf

3 Roll out the 2 saved portions of dough to make discs 13cm across, or to fit the size of the pies you've moulded. Make a hole in the centre of each lid, then chill them for about 20 minutes.

4 Meanwhile, keeping the chicken and bacon strips separate, season them with salt, plenty of pepper and the thyme.

5 Preheat the oven to 200°C/400°F/gas 6. Take the pie cases out of the fridge and very carefully coax the hard pastry off each dolly in one piece. If the pie cases soften in handling, return them to the fridge for about 10 minutes until really firm again. Trim the top of the pie cases so the sides are of even height all around and not too tall (Paul trimmed his pies so that they were 10cm tall). Now layer up the filling: start with bacon, then add chicken and then a layer of apricots, and repeat – the filling should be well packed in.

6 Set a top on each pie and crimp (see page 218) the lid and the rim of the pastry case together with your thumb and forefinger

to seal thoroughly. Set the pies on the unlined baking sheet and brush the tops with beaten egg to glaze. Bake for 50–60 minutes until the pastry is crisp and a good golden brown all over.

7 Dissolve the chicken stock cube in 150ml of hot water. Soak the leaves of gelatine in a small bowl of cold water for about 5 minutes until soft, then squeeze out the excess water. Whisk the gelatine into the hot but not boiling stock until melted.

8 Remove the cooked pies from the oven, set them on a wire rack and leave to cool. While the pies are still hot, carefully pour the stock into each pie through the hole in the pie lid to fill up any cavities (this must be done while the pies are hot, otherwise the jelly will sit on the top of the filling only). Leave to cool completely, then cover and chill in the fridge overnight so the stock has time to set to a firm jelly.

Chickpea, Spinach & Mushroom Wellington

SERVES 8–9

1 quantity Rough Puff Pastry
   (see page 188)

FOR THE DUXELLES

1 large onion, quartered
1 large garlic clove, peeled
225g chestnut mushrooms
25g unsalted butter
salt, black pepper and grated nutmeg

FOR THE PANCAKES

50g plain flour
1 large free-range egg
150ml semi-skimmed milk
1 tablespoon each finely chopped
   thyme and parsley
1 tablespoon sunflower oil

FOR THE FILLING

2 tablespoons olive oil
1 onion, finely chopped
1 garlic clove, finely chopped
1 small red pepper, cored and
   finely chopped
½ teaspoon each red chilli paste,
   cumin seeds and crushed
   coriander seeds
1 x 200g bag washed baby spinach
   leaves
120g drained chickpeas
   (from a 410g tin)
1 tablespoon tahini
40g fresh breadcrumbs
2 teaspoons each lemon juice and
   natural yoghurt
about 10 sprigs each thyme,
   coriander and parsley,
   leaves finely chopped
beaten egg, to glaze

baking paper; a baking sheet

A colourful and well-spiced combination of vegetables and chickpeas and flaky, buttery pastry. Serve with plenty of watercress and a herb sauce, as the baker did in series 3 (see TIP) OR Beurre Blanc (see page 307). When Mary tried this Wellington, she thought it tasted lovely without any additional sauce, so see what you think!

1 Make the Rough Puff Pastry following the recipe on page 188. While it is chilling, make the duxelles. Finely chop the onion, garlic and mushrooms in a food-processor. Heat the butter in a 20–23cm non-stick frying pan and cook the mushroom mixture over medium-low heat, stirring frequently, until cooked down and the liquid has evaporated. Season to taste with salt, pepper and nutmeg, then tip into a bowl and cool.

2 To make the herb pancakes, sift the flour into a bowl, make a well in the centre and add the egg and half the milk. Whisk until smooth, gradually working in the rest of the milk to make a smooth batter. Add the herbs and a good pinch of salt. Pour the batter into a measuring jug and note the volume.

3 Wipe out the non-stick frying pan with a sheet of oiled kitchen paper, then set over medium-high heat. Pour exactly one-third of the batter into the hot pan, tipping and swirling it so the batter evenly covers the base. Cook for 1–2 minutes until the

Recipe continues overleaf

underside of the pancake is golden brown, then flip the pancake over and cook the other side for 1–2 minutes. Tip out onto a plate and leave to cool while you make 2 more pancakes in the same way. Cover the herb pancakes with a sheet of baking paper and set aside until needed.

4 Next make the chickpea filling. Heat the olive oil in a wok (or a very large, deep frying pan) set over medium-low heat and cook the chopped onion, garlic and red pepper, stirring frequently, for about 4 minutes until softened. Stir in the chilli paste and cumin and coriander seeds, and cook for a further 5 minutes, stirring frequently. Add the spinach and cook, stirring, for 5 minutes until the spinach has wilted. Turn up the heat and stir for a minute until excess liquid has evaporated. Tip the mixture into a large heatproof bowl and stir in the chickpeas, tahini, breadcrumbs, lemon juice, yoghurt and herbs. Taste and add salt, black pepper and more chilli paste as needed. Cover and chill for about 30 minutes until firmed up.

5 To assemble the Wellington, remove the pastry from the fridge and leave to 'come to' for 10 minutes. Meanwhile, arrange 2 of the pancakes, side by side and slightly overlapping, on a large sheet of baking paper. Cut the third pancake in half and place one piece over the gap in the middle of each side of the 2 overlapped pancakes to make a near rectangular shape about 42 × 25cm. Carefully spread the duxelles over the pancakes, leaving a 2cm border clear all the way around.

6 Spoon the chickpea filling down the centre of the duxelles and shape with your hands to a neat log, leaving a 2cm border of duxelles

showing. Fold the short ends of the pancakes over the filling, then both long sides. Use your hands to mould and press the pancakes around the filling to make a firm, neat log shape about 32 × 10cm. Bring the baking paper up around the log to hold it firmly in place and fold the ends so it stays in place. Chill while rolling out the pastry.

7 Roll out the pastry on a floured worktop to a rectangle about 42 × 30cm. Trim the edges straight. Unwrap the pancake log and gently roll it onto the middle of the pastry so the seam side of the pancake log is underneath. If necessary, tuck in any loose ends so the filling is completely enclosed. Brush the pastry edges with beaten egg, then fold the short ends of the pastry over the pancake log, followed by the long sides. Neatly trim off the thick excess pastry at each corner, then press all the pastry seams well to seal.

8 Roll the Wellington, seam side down, onto the baking sheet lined with baking paper. Cut leaves from the pastry scraps (see page 218) and stick on with beaten egg. With the tip of a small knife, make 3 steam holes in the pastry lengthways down the middle of the Wellington. Chill for 1 hour.

9 Towards the end of this time, preheat the oven to 220°C/425°F/gas 7. Lightly brush the Wellington with beaten egg to glaze, then bake for about 50 minutes until golden brown. Serve hot or warm, the same day.

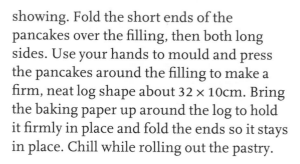

TIP
For a quick herb sauce, press the yolks of 2 hard-boiled eggs through a fine sieve and mix with 1 tablespoon herby French mustard and 300g natural yoghurt. Season to taste with salt, paprika and lemon juice.

Mini Turkey Pies

MAKES

10

FOR THE PASTRY
450g plain flour
¼ teaspoon salt
1 ½ teaspoons icing sugar
250g unsalted butter,
    chilled and diced
2 large free-range egg yolks
5 tablespoons icy water
beaten egg, to glaze

FOR THE FILLING
350g skinless uncooked turkey
    breast meat or escalopes
275g herby pork sausages (3–4)
50g cranberries, fresh or frozen
    and thawed
1 tablespoon Madeira
pepper

2 round cutters, 11cm and 7cm; a
    12-cup loose-based mini sandwich
    pan or 12-hole non-stick muffin tray,
    greased; a baking sheet

Christmas in a pie – turkey, sausagemeat and cranberries, baked in a rich shortcrust case. Serve with cranberry sauce or chutney.

1 To make the pastry, sift the flour, salt, sugar and a pinch of pepper into a mixing bowl. Rub in the butter with your fingertips until the mixtures resembles fine crumbs. Mix the yolks with the water and stir in with a round-bladed knife to bind to a just-firm dough, adding more water as necessary a teaspoon at a time. Wrap and chill for 15 minutes.

2 Roll out the pastry on a lightly floured worktop to the thickness of a pound coin. Cut out 10 discs with the 11cm cutter (or a size suitable to line the cups in your tray) and 10 discs with the 7cm cutter (or a size suitable for a lid). Gather up the trimmings, re-roll and cut more discs as needed. Gently ease a larger disc into each cup in the tray, pressing out any gathers or pleats. Make sure the pastry is pressed neatly onto the base and sides, without any pockets of air, easing the pastry up over the rim of each cup to make a rim for the lid to stick to.

3 Cut the turkey into 1cm chunks, discarding any sinews, and put into a mixing bowl. Skin the sausages and add the meat to the bowl with the cranberries, Madeira and a little pepper. Mix well with your hand. Pack the filling into the pastry cases, slightly doming the filling (it will shrink a little during baking). Brush the rim of each case with a little beaten egg, then press on a pastry lid. Seal by pressing round the edge with the back of a fork (or see page 218 for crimping ideas). Chill for 15 minutes. Meanwhile, preheat the oven to 180°C/350°F/gas 4.

4 Lightly brush the tops of the pies with beaten egg to glaze, and make a small steam hole in the centre with the tip of a knife. Set the tray on the baking sheet. Bake for about 35 minutes until a good golden brown. Remove from the oven and leave for 5–10 minutes to allow the pastry to firm up, then carefully unmould. Serve warm or at room temperature the same day; or cool, then cover and chill overnight (reheat in a 180°C/350°F/gas 4 oven for 8–10 minutes before serving).

Paul's Beef Wellington

SERVES 8

FOR THE PUFF PASTRY
150g strong bread flour
150g plain flour
2 large free-range eggs. beaten
100ml icy water
160g unsalted butter, well chilled

FOR THE FILLING
1 x 750g beef fillet
olive oil
100g chicken liver pâté
1 free-range egg
salt and freshly ground black pepper

1 baking sheet

Start this recipe at least one day before you want to serve it because the pastry needs plenty of chilling time. Paul advises on long chilling times, but if you don't have as much time, just chill at each stage for as long as you can. The most important thing is that your pastry is well chilled at all times.

1 To make the pastry, put the flours, eggs and water in a large bowl and gently mix everything together to make a stiff dough. Transfer the dough to a lightly floured worktop and knead it well for 10 minutes. The dough will feel tight but elastic, so the kneading will take a bit of effort. When the dough is smooth, shape it into a ball, put it in a plastic bag and chill for 7 hours, or overnight.

2 Roll out the chilled dough on a lightly floured worktop to a rectangle about 60 × 20cm and about 1cm thick, rolling away from you so the rectangle is lying vertically. Put the rolled out dough back into the fridge.

3 Flatten the butter by pounding with a rolling pin into a 40 × 20cm rectangular slab about 5mm thick. Wrap in clingfilm and chill to harden the butter again.

4 Take the chilled butter and dough out of the fridge and arrange the slab of butter so that it covers 2/3 of the dough. Make sure that the butter is positioned neatly and comes almost to the edges of the dough. Fold in the edges slightly so the butter does not escape during the rolling and folding process (a little fold will do).

5 Fold the 1/3 of dough without butter down over one half of the butter slab. Gently cut off the exposed bit of butter and set it on top of the dough you have just folded down. Fold the remaining third of the dough over the butter. You now have a sandwich of 2 layers of butter and 3 of dough. Put it in a plastic bag and chill for 1 hour (or as along as you can).

6 Take the dough out of the bag and place it on the lightly floured worktop with a short side towards you. Roll out the dough into a rectangle as before, then fold the top one-quarter down and the bottom one-quarter up so they meet neatly in the middle. Then fold the dough in half along the middle line. This is called a 'book turn'. Chill in the bag for a further hour.

7 Take the dough out of the bag and put it on the lightly floured worktop with a short end towards you. Roll out into a rectangle as

Recipe continues overleaf

before. This time fold the top third of the dough down and then the bottom third up on top to make a neat square. This is called a 'single turn'. Chill in the bag for another hour.

8 Roll out the dough again and repeat a single turn, then chill in the bag overnight.

9 Trim the fillet, carefully removing any sinew and squaring off the ends. Put a large frying pan on a high heat. Drizzle a little oil over the fillet, sprinkle on some salt and massage into the meat. When the frying pan is very hot, sear the fillet to brown well all over. Set aside to cool.

10 Roll out the pastry into a rectangle with appropriate dimensions for your fillet – about 10cm longer than the fillet and wide enough to wrap around it with an overlap. Paul 'tacked down' the short side of the rolled pastry rectangle nearest to him,

which means pressing it down with his thumb so that it sticks to the table. (This helps when you seal the Wellington.)

11 Spread the pâté evenly over the area of the pastry rectangle that will be in contact with the fillet (the majority of the pastry, leaving a border). Place the fillet on top of pâté, then wrap the pastry around the beef. Press the joins along the length and at the ends to seal well. Place on the baking sheet.

12 Beat the egg with a little salt and brush all over the pastry. Chill for 1 hour, then repeat the egg wash and chilling.

13 Preheat the oven to 220°C/425°F/gas 7. Score the top of the pastry decoratively (Paul scored diagonal stripes over his Wellington), then bake for 20–25 minutes until a deep golden brown. Allow to rest for 20 minutes before carving.

Rich Beef Cobbler

SERVES 6

FOR THE FILLING

2 tablespoons olive oil
600g very lean minced beef
1 large or 2 medium onions,
    very finely chopped
2 celery sticks, very finely chopped
1 carrot, very finely chopped
75g mushrooms, very finely chopped
2 teaspoons plain flour
250ml good beef stock
125ml red wine
1 tablespoon Worcestershire sauce,
    or to taste
1 tablespoon tomato purée
salt and pepper

FOR THE SCONE TOPPING

175g self-raising flour
25g fresh white breadcrumbs
90g shredded suet
2 tablespoons each chopped fresh
    parsley and chives
1 large free-range egg
about 100ml milk, plus extra
    for brushing

1 large baking dish, 1–1.25 litre capacity;
    a 6cm round or shaped cutter(s)

A posh cottage pie – lean minced beef slowly cooked in a red wine gravy, topped with light, herby scones before baking. The scones are made quickly from a suet pastry, so they have a good flavour with a delightfully crunchy top.

1 Preheat the oven to 160°C/325°F/gas 3. Heat the oil in a flameproof casserole (one with a lid), add the minced beef and stir over high heat until it is broken up and lightly browned. Reduce the heat, push the meat to one side and add the chopped onions, celery, carrot and mushrooms. Cook gently, stirring frequently, for about 5 minutes until they soften, then mix in the browned mince. Sprinkle over the flour and stir in, followed by the stock, wine, Worcestershire sauce, tomato purée and a little seasoning. Bring to the boil, stirring, then cover and transfer to the oven. Cook, stirring occasionally, for 1–1 ½ hours until the meat is very tender.

2 Taste and add more Worcestershire sauce or salt and pepper as needed. Transfer the mixture to the baking dish (at this point the filling can be left to cool, then covered and kept chilled for up to 2 days or frozen).

3 When ready to finish, preheat the oven to 220°C/425°F/gas 7. To make the topping, combine the flour, breadcrumbs, suet and half of the chopped herbs in a mixing bowl. Add a good pinch each of salt and pepper. Beat the egg with the milk until combined, then stir in using a round-bladed knife to make a very soft scone-like dough, adding more milk as necessary.

4 Turn out the dough onto a lightly floured worktop and knead a couple of times, then pat out about 1.5cm thick. Cut out 8 rounds or other shapes with a floured cutter. Arrange the scones over the meat filling in the baking dish and brush the tops lightly with milk. Bake for 20–30 minutes until the filling is bubbling and the scone topping is golden brown. Scatter the remaining herbs over the top and serve immediately.

Desserts

WHO DOESN'T HAVE an all-time best-ever dessert? Everyone remembers just where and when they first enjoyed eating their favourite sweet treat and who made it. Desserts are cherished like no other part of a meal, particularly those made for a special, or a seasonal, celebration. The dessert recipes here are worth taking time over – both creating them in the kitchen and then enjoying them at the table. This doesn't mean that they are all difficult, but that a little extra time spent making them will be richly rewarded.

The bakers invented some incredible meringue desserts for the Showstopper Challenge as well as some stunning flourless desserts, and we have 3 of the best in this chapter. Mary's Technical Challenge of Crème Caramel (see page 258) is also featured here – her tip is to not let the caramel around the custard bubble during baking, which leaves marks on the pale gold desserts when they are turned out. Setting the correct oven temperature is essential too.

The show desserts might be wonderful for a special occasion, but not all desserts that look beautiful and taste sublime are expensive or difficult to make. Many of the recipes in this chapter are straightforward but have a few extra stages of preparation – if you set aside enough time, you'll be fine.

Meringue desserts are a great showpiece, but can be as simple or extravagant as you like. Eggs whipped to a stiff foam with sugar make a mixture that is infinitely adaptable: it can be baked in simple shapes to serve sandwiched with cream or melted chocolate, or with fresh berries. With a piping bag and star tube the same meringue mixture can be fashioned into pretty swirls and small nests to hold fruit or ice cream, or transformed into a stunning 3-tier gâteau. Another advantage of meringues is that they can be baked well ahead, then stored carefully in airtight containers, ready to be assembled quickly at the last minute.

Other desserts are better made a day or so before they're eaten. Flavours mellow and deepen, and slicing often becomes easier with a bit of distance between oven and plate. Cheesecakes are easy to make, but should ideally spend at least a night in the fridge and nearly every chocolate recipe invented tastes richer if it's allowed to age gracefully.

And speaking of chocolate, here you'll find it in a striped black- and white- cheesecake and an impressive layer cake that is bound to thrill any chocoholic but is really just three different layers – just take your time.

There are lots of ways to dress up a favourite, well-loved dessert – some very easy. Edible gold dust (see page 310) will instantly add a 'wow' factor to a very dark chocolate dish – try dusting a chocolate log with a mixture of gold dust and cocoa powder (for the best flavour use really good cocoa powder, never drinking chocolate powder). Or why not have a go at making your own chocolate decorations (see pages 308–309 for ideas and directions)?

Having created your beautiful dessert, be sure to take as much care with its presentation. Make sure you have a serving plate that is the right size and shape, and decorate with edible leaves or pretty berries. If your dessert needs to be chilled or kept cool before serving, do check in advance that you have enough fridge space.

DON'T FORGET

🎂 Leftover egg whites can be stored in the freezer, then thawed when you want to make meringues.

🎂 Use the correct sugar for the best results – meringues are best made with caster sugar, or muscovado sugar for golden brown 'toffee' meringues.

🎂 For the best meringues, have the egg whites at room temperature and use a perfectly clean, dry and grease-free bowl and whisk. If you get a tiny speck of egg yolk in the whites by mistake, you'll still be able to make meringues, but they won't be as fluffy.

🎂 Don't overbeat: stiffly whisked whites should just hold a peak when the whisk is lifted out of the bowl. The mixture should still look smooth and satiny – it will look grainy or 'bobbly' when overbeaten and will start to lose bulk.

🎂 Meringues are notorious for sticking, so always line baking sheets with baking paper or re-usable non-stick liners.

🎂 For perfectly whipped cream, chill not only the cream, but the bowl and the whisk too. If using an electric mixer, start whipping on low speed, then gradually increase the speed as the cream thickens. Stop when it forms a peak that just starts to flop over when the whisk is lifted (this is slightly less stiff than for whisked egg whites) and the mixture is smooth and silky. If the cream starts to look grainy or as if it is breaking up, it has gone too far to pipe neatly, but it's fine to use it for filling or spreading on cakes.

🎂 Take care when grinding nuts in a food-processor – they can easily become oily if they're overworked. If possible, add a tablespoon or so of the measured flour or sugar before you start.

🎂 White chocolate varies in flavour and quality (you get what you pay for). The type sold in bars or buttons for children isn't suitable for baking.

Simple Meringue

4 large free-range egg whites,
   at room temperature
2 good pinches of cream
   of tartar
225g caster sugar

1 Put the egg whites into a large, spotlessly clean and grease-free bowl (any trace of fat – either specks of yolk or stuck to the bowl or whisk – will prevent the whites from being beaten to their full volume). Whisk with an electric mixer for 20–30 seconds until the whites become foamy. Add the cream of tartar and keep whisking until the mixture forms a soft peak when the whisk is lifted out of the bowl.

2 Whisk in 4 tablespoons of the measured sugar (1 tablespoon for each egg white), one at a time, and continue whisking for a minute or so until the meringue is glossy and forms a stiff peak when the whisk is lifted out of the bowl.

3 Sprinkle the rest of the sugar over the meringue and very lightly fold it in with a large metal spoon. The sugar needs to be combined with the whites, but it's important not to over-mix or the sugar will start to dissolve and the meringue will lose volume and 'weep' during baking. The meringue is now ready to use.

With just egg whites and sugar, you can make 3 types of heavenly light, snowy meringue – a simple meringue, Italian meringue and cooked meringue. Simple meringue is the most familiar in home baking, and it is used in the first and second Showstopping Challenges that follow. It can be piled on top of pies or piped into different shapes and then baked until crisp and dry, or folded into mousses and soufflés to make them fluffy. It should be used as soon as it is made.

Italian meringue, which is used for the Celebration Vacherin (see page 250), is made by whisking the egg whites to soft peak stage, then whisking in a hot sugar syrup. The heat stabilizes the meringue, producing more volume, and enables it to be kept for several hours. It can be piped into more elaborate designs than simple meringue.

Cooked meringue, which is even firmer than Italian meringue and keeps longer, is made by whisking the egg whites and sugar together over heat.

The bakers of series 3 made decadent meringue desserts, sandwiching meringue layers with cream, fruit, mousses and chocolate. If you've not made meringues before, start with the Pretty Meringue Sandwiches on page 246, which are simple but still impressive.

This basic recipe can be used to make 14 meringue sandwiches, 6 meringue nests or a Celebration Vacherin.

Pretty Meringue Sandwiches

MAKES 14 PAIRS

1 quantity Simple Meringue
(see page 245)
2 edible food colourings
(we used pink and lilac)

TO SANDWICH
150ml double cream, well chilled

2 or more baking sheets, lined
with baking paper; 2 disposable
piping bags plus a large
star tube

Pretty, dainty meringues simply sandwiched with whipped cream make an elegant treat for a special tea party. If you don't want to tint and pipe them, you can spoon the white meringue onto the baking sheet to make about 20 ovals, using a rounded kitchen spoon of meringue for each, then swirl through a little food colouring (also see TIP).

1 Make the Simple Meringue following the method on page 245. Preheat the oven to 120°C/250°F/gas ½. Divide the meringue equally between 2 bowls. Add a little edible (pink or other) food colouring to one portion of meringue to tint it. Spoon the meringue into one of the piping bags fitted with the star tube. Pipe 14 small swirls about 5.5cm diameter on a prepared baking sheet (see page 253 for help with piping meringue).

2 Wash the star tube and fit it into the other (clean) piping bag. Tint the other portion of meringue with a little edible (lilac or other) food colouring. Spoon into the bag, then pipe 14 small swirls on a baking sheet as above. If you really want to show off, dip a cocktail stick into the food colouring and mark a couple of lines along the swirls of the piped shapes.

3 Bake all the meringue swirls for 1–2 hours until they are crisp and dry. Remove from the oven and leave to cool.

4 Once the meringues are completely cold, they can be peeled off the lining paper. (They can be kept in an airtight container for up to 3 days.)

5 When ready to serve, whip the cream until thick and use to sandwich the meringue swirls together in pairs. Set in paper muffin cases and serve as soon as possible – within 4 hours of assembling.

TIPS
Instead of tinting with food colouring, sift a little cocoa powder into the meringue mix and swirl through gently. Sandwich pairs together with scoops of coffee or chocolate ice cream. These are great with Bitter Chocolate Sauce (see page 307).

Black Forest Meringues

MAKES

1 quantity Simple Meringue
(see page 245)
100g dark chocolate (70% cocoa
solids), chopped

FOR THE FILLING
200ml double cream, well chilled
1–2 tablespoons icing sugar,
or to taste
1 tablespoon kirsch or Cointreau
(optional)
250g fresh large cherries, stalks
removed, pitted and quartered

TO DECORATE
icing sugar
cocoa powder
6 whole fresh cherries (optional)

1 baking sheet; baking paper; a piping
bag fitted with a large star tube

A modern twist on the favourite gâteau of the early 1970s, here meringue nests are lined with melted chocolate and filled with cream and fresh cherries, then decorated with flakes of chocolate. The combination of chocolate, cherries and cream is still irresistible. Once they are cold, the meringue nests can be stored in an airtight container for 2–3 days.

1 Preheat the oven to 110°C/225°F/gas ¼. Draw six 7.5cm circles on a piece of baking paper, spacing them well apart; turn the paper over and lay it on the baking sheet.

2 Make the Simple Meringue following the method on page 245. Spoon the meringue into the piping bag. Starting in the middle of each drawn circle, pipe a neat spiralled disc of meringue, finishing just inside the drawn line. Then pipe a 'wall' on top of the edge of each disc to make a nest shape. Bake for about 2 hours until completely dry and crisp, without allowing the meringues to colour. Leave to cool.

3 Melt the chocolate (see page 308). Using a pastry brush, coat the inside of each meringue nest with melted chocolate, then leave to set. Pour the remaining chocolate onto a sheet of baking paper (or a reusable non-stick liner) and spread fairly thinly. Leave to set.

4 When ready to assemble, arrange the meringue nests on a serving platter or individual plates. Whip the cream with the icing sugar and kirsch until thick. Gently fold in the pitted cherries. The juice will run a bit but don't worry: it gives the cream a pretty marbled effect. Pile the whipped cream and cherry mix into the nests.

5 Break up the chocolate on the baking paper into shards and scatter over the top. Dust with a little sifted icing sugar and cocoa powder and finish with a whole fresh cherry, if you wish. Serve within an hour of assembling.

Celebration Vacherin

SERVES 12–16

1 quantity Simple Meringue
(see page 245)
edible coloured sprinkles,
to decorate

FOR THE ITALIAN MERINGUE
225g caster sugar
4 large free-range egg whites,
at room temperature
½ teaspoon vanilla extract

FOR THE FILLING
750ml raspberry sorbet
200ml double cream, well chilled
1 tablespoon caster sugar
½ teaspoon vanilla extract
500g fresh berries – strawberries,
raspberries, blueberries, dessert
blackberries

3 baking sheets; baking paper;
a piping bag plus a large star tube

This spectacular dessert is a modern twist on a classic. The basket is made from 2 types of meringue: simple meringue for the base and sides, and Italian meringue to 'glue' it all together. In this version, the sides are made from pretty piped swirls. Rather than rosettes of cream to finish, whipped cream is swirled loosely on top of the filling and decorated with colourful sprinkles. Inside the meringue basket, underneath all the berries, is a tangy raspberry sorbet. You can make the basket the day before, but serve the dessert as soon as you've assembled it, before the sorbet starts to melt!

1 Preheat the oven to 120°C/250°F/gas ½. Draw a 20.5cm circle on a piece of baking paper, turn it over and lay it on one baking sheet. On 2 more pieces of baking paper, draw 24 circles about 5cm across, spacing them well apart; turn the paper over and lay it on the other baking sheets.

2 Make the Simple Meringue following the method on page 245. Spoon into the piping bag fitted with the star tube. Pipe into a large spiralled disc inside the drawn 20.5cm circle, starting in the centre and keeping the piping bag upright as you pipe. This will form the base of the basket. Now make the shapes for the 'walls': pipe a loose swirl inside each circle on the other baking sheets.

3 Bake the base disc and small swirls for 50–70 minutes until dry and very crisp, but not coloured. Leave to cool. (Once cold, the meringues can be stored in an airtight container for 2–3 days.)

4 When ready to assemble the basket (on the day of serving), make up the Italian meringue. Put the sugar and 150ml water into a medium pan and heat gently, stirring frequently, until the sugar has completely dissolved. Turn up the heat and boil steadily, without stirring, until the syrup reaches 120°C/248°F on a sugar thermometer (make sure the thermometer isn't touching the bottom of the pan, otherwise it will give an incorrect reading and your meringue will separate later.)

5 While the syrup is cooking, put the egg whites into a spotlessly clean and grease-free

Recipe continues overleaf

250

DESSERTS

large mixing bowl. Beat with an electric mixer until stiff peaks form when the beaters are lifted. As soon as the syrup reaches the correct temperature, pour it in a steady stream onto the egg whites (not down the sides of the bowl), beating on the highest possible speed. When the meringue is very stiff and glossy, add the vanilla. Keep beating for 5–7 minutes until the mixture cools down to room temperature. Spoon into the clean piping bag fitted with the star tube.

6 Preheat the oven to 120°C/250°F/gas ½. If necessary, remove some of the oven shelves to make space for the basket.

7 Set the meringue base on a baking sheet lined with fresh baking paper. Pipe a thick rope of Italian meringue on the outside edge of the base, about 5mm from the edge. Stick half of the meringue swirls, on edge with the swirled side out, onto the base to make a ring, pressing them gently into the Italian meringue. Pipe Italian meringue over the joins at the back of the swirls as 'mortar' to glue them together, then build up a second ring of swirls on top in the same way to form a basket. Smooth a thin layer of Italian meringue over all the joins on the inside. Finish by piping stars in the gaps between the swirls on the outside of the basket.

8 Carefully set the baking sheet in the oven and bake for 1–1 ½ hours until the Italian meringue is very firm but not coloured. Remove and leave to cool, then set on a serving platter.

9 While the meringue basket is baking, make scoops of sorbet and open-freeze on a tray lined with baking paper. Loosely whip the cream with the sugar and vanilla. Halve or quarter any large strawberries.

10 Just before serving, fill the basket with the scoops of sorbet, then top with the berries. Decorate with swirls of loosely whipped cream and coloured sprinkles.

TIP
A large free-standing electric mixer is a great help when making Italian meringue.

Piping Meringue Swirls

EQUIPMENT NEEDED
baking paper
baking sheet
piping bag fitted with a large star tube

1 Cut a piece of baking paper to fit the baking sheet. Use a pencil to draw circles of the diameter required on the paper, spacing them well apart. Turn the paper over and secure to the baking sheet using 4 blobs of your meringue mixture.

2 Spoon the meringue into the piping bag (see page 312 for tips on how to fill the bag), twisting the top to gently compact the meringue. Test the flow speed of the meringue.

3 Holding the piping bag upright, about 1cm above the centre of one of the drawn circles on the baking paper, gently squeeze the bag with your other hand, keeping the tube steady. Continue squeezing out the meringue, keeping the pressure consistent, as you work your way from the centre around inside the circle, spiralling the meringue until you reach the edge.

4 To finish, move the tube back to the centre while still squeezing out a little more meringue. Then release the pressure on the piping bag as you lift it off, to make a peak.

Hazelnut and Pear Dacquoise

SERVES 20

FOR THE FRUIT LAYERS
4 large Comice pears
3 tablespoons runny honey, warmed

FOR THE DACQUOISE LAYERS
125g blanched hazelnuts
20g cornflour
300g caster sugar
125g ground almonds
8 large free-range egg whites,
   at room temperature
pinch of salt
1 teaspoon vanilla extract

FOR THE GANACHE
450g dark chocolate (54% cocoa
   solids), finely chopped
600ml double cream, very hot
4 tablespoons hazelnut paste
2 tablespoons hazelnut oil
3 tablespoons Frangelico
   (hazelnut liqueur)

FOR THE MOUSSE FILLING
2 teaspoons powdered gelatine
180g hazelnut paste
200g mascarpone
1 ½ tablespoons cocoa powder
700ml double cream, well chilled
80g caster sugar

TO FINISH
3 tablespoons finely chopped
   toasted hazelnuts
20 whole toasted hazelnuts
edible gold leaf (see page 310)

2–3 baking sheets, lined with baking
   paper; 3 disposable piping bags
   plus a medium star tube

An intricate layering of hazelnut and almond meringue layers, hazelnut and mascarpone mousse, honey-baked pears and a hazelnut and chocolate ganache.

1 Preheat the oven to 180°C/350°F/gas 4. Peel, quarter and core the pears, then cut into slices about 4mm thick. Arrange in a single layer in a baking dish and brush lightly with the honey. Bake for about 15 minutes until tender. Leave to cool, then drain thoroughly.

2 Using a ruler draw 5 rectangles each 10 × 28cm on the baking paper cut to fit your baking sheets (you should be able to fit 2 rectangles onto a sheet). Turn the paper over on the sheets.

3 To make the dacquoise, toast the hazelnuts in a small tin in the oven for 6–7 minutes until golden. Cool, then grind in a food-processor with the cornflour and 30g of the caster sugar to make a coarse powder. Add the ground almonds and 'pulse' a couple of times to combine. Set aside.

4 Put the egg whites, salt and vanilla into a bowl and whisk with an electric mixer to the soft peak stage. Whisk in the remaining caster sugar a tablespoon at a time to make a stiff, glossy meringue. Fold in the ground nut mixture using a large metal spoon. Spoon the mixture into a piping bag and snip off the tip to make a 1.5cm wide aperture.

Recipe continues overleaf

5 Pipe the meringue onto the baking paper to fill the drawn rectangles – it's easiest to pipe zig-zags from side to side. Bake the 5 meringue strips for 15 minutes, then reduce the oven to 150°C/300°F/gas 2 and bake for a further 30 minutes. Turn off the oven and leave the meringues inside to dry for about 45 minutes. Then remove and leave to cool. Peel carefully off the lining paper – the meringues will be golden brown, crisp and fragile.

6 To make the ganache, put the chocolate in a heatproof bowl, pour over the very hot cream and leave to soften for a minute. Stir gently until smooth, then stir in the paste, oil and liqueur. Set aside until the ganache is starting to thicken, but is still spreadable, then beat with a wooden spoon or mixer until thick enough to pipe.

7 While you're waiting for the ganache to thicken, make the mousse. Pour 6 tablespoons water into a small pan, sprinkle the gelatine on top and leave to soak for a couple of minutes, then heat gently to dissolve. Beat together the paste, mascarpone and cocoa powder in a large mixing bowl with a wooden spoon until smooth. Beat in the gelatine mixture. Whip the cream with the sugar until it stands in soft peaks, then fold into the mascarpone mixture in 3 batches using a large metal spoon. Spoon into a large piping bag and snip off the end to make 1.5cm aperture.

8 To assemble the dacquoise, put a small blob of mousse on a serving board or platter. Set a meringue layer in the centre and cover with a layer of piped mousse. Top with a quarter of the drained pears. Repeat until you have 4 layers of meringue covered with mousse and pears. Set the last meringue layer on top. (In warm weather chill thoroughly until firm.)

9 Cover the top and sides of the dacquoise with a thick layer of ganache. Using a palette knife dipped in warm water (and dried), quickly smooth and neaten the ganache. Spoon the remaining ganache into a piping bag fitted with the star tube. Decorate the top of the dacquoise with neat lines of chopped hazelnuts, then pipe 10 small rosettes of ganache along each long edge, and finish with the whole hazelnuts and gold leaf. Chill thoroughly before slicing very thinly.

Raspberry Dacquoise

SERVES 8–10

FOR THE MERINGUE
10 large free-range egg whites,
   at room temperature
good pinch of cream of tartar
400g caster sugar
1 teaspoon vanilla extract
50g light brown muscovado sugar
2 tablespoons cornflour
200g unblanched almonds

FOR THE FILLING
600ml double cream, well chilled
2 tablespoons icing sugar,
   plus extra for dusting
1 teaspoon vanilla extract or kirsch
450g raspberries

3 baking sheets; baking paper

1 Preheat the oven to 150°C/300°F/gas 2.
Cut 3 pieces of baking paper to fit the baking
sheets and draw a 25cm circle on each; turn
the paper over and lay on the baking sheets.

2 Put the egg whites into a large, spotlessly
clean and grease-free bowl and whisk with
an electric mixer until frothy. Add the cream
of tartar and continue whisking until stiff
peaks start to form. Gradually whisk in
10 tablespoons of the caster sugar and the
vanilla to make a stiff, glossy meringue.

3 Mix the rest of the caster sugar with the
muscovado sugar. Put the cornflour and
unblanched almonds into a food-processor
and process until finely ground. Stir the nut
mixture into the sugar mixture, then fold
into the meringue in 3 batches using a
large metal spoon.

Three layers of crunchy, nutty meringue
sandwiched with fresh raspberries and
whipped cream make a dessert that everyone
will love. It looks very special, but it's actually
quite easy to make because the meringue is
spread into discs, rather than piped. If you
like, serve with raspberry sauce (see page
194) and decorate with fresh rose petals.

4 Divide the meringue into 3 equal portions.
Spoon one portion onto each lined baking
sheet and gently spread out to a disc just
inside the drawn line. Bake the meringue
discs for 45–50 minutes until very crisp, dry
and golden; rotate the baking sheets during
baking so the meringue discs cook evenly.
Remove from the oven and leave to cool.
Once cold, peel the discs carefully off the
baking paper. (The meringue discs can be
stored in an airtight container for a day
before assembling.)

5 Whip the cream until thick, then add the
icing sugar and vanilla and whip until stiff.
Set one meringue disc on a serving platter
and cover with half of the whipped cream.
Arrange half the raspberries on top. Set
another disc of meringue on top and spoon
the remaining cream over it. Top with the
remaining raspberries and then the final
meringue disc. Chill for at least 30 minutes
before serving, dusted with icing sugar.
The dacquoise can be kept in an airtight
box in the fridge for 2–3 hours.

Mary's Crème Caramel

MAKES 6

FOR THE CARAMEL
160g granulated sugar

FOR THE CUSTARD
4 large free-range eggs,
   at room temperature
1 teaspoon vanilla extract
25g caster sugar
600ml full-fat milk
a little unsalted butter, for greasing

6 x 150ml (size 1) ramekins;
   a roasting tin

This baked custard dessert can be very tricky to make, but actually very easy if you know how! Make these the day before and turn out just before serving – if you turn out the crème caramels too soon after cooking, the caramel will lose its colour and stay in the base of the ramekins. If you'd prefer one large crème caramel use a 1.2 litre capacity deep dish and bake for 40–50 minutes.

1 Preheat the oven to 150°C/300°F/gas 2. Put the ramekins into the oven to warm them gently while you make the caramel.

2 Combine the granulated sugar and 6 tablespoons water in a clean stainless-steel pan (not a non-stick pan, which would cause the syrup to crystallize). Dissolve the sugar slowly over low heat, stirring with a wooden spoon. When there are no sugar granules left, stop stirring and bring to the boil. Boil rapidly for a few minutes until the sugar turns a dark caramel colour (be careful not to let the caramel burn). Remove from the heat and pour into the base of the warmed ramekins. Set aside to cool.

3 Once the caramel is hard, carefully butter the sides of the ramekins above the caramel level. Leave in a cool place.

4 To make the custard, whisk the eggs, vanilla and caster sugar together in a large heatproof bowl until well mixed. Gently warm the milk in a saucepan over low heat. Don't let it get too hot – you should still be

able to dip your finger in for a moment. Strain onto the egg mixture in the bowl and whisk together until just smooth but not frothy. Pour into a jug and then into the prepared ramekins.

5 Set the ramekins in the roasting tin and pour enough boiling water into the tin to come halfway up the sides of the ramekins. Bake for 20–30 minutes until the custard is set – check with the tip of a knife inserted into the middle. Do not overcook the custards and make sure no bubbles appear around the edges of the dishes as they cook.

6 Remove from the oven and lift the dishes from the roasting tin. Leave to cool on a wire rack. When cold, chill in the fridge overnight to allow time for the caramel to be absorbed into the custard.

7 To serve, loosen the custards by tipping each ramekin and running a small palette knife around the sides, then place a small plate on top of the ramekin; turn upside down and lift off the ramekin. Serve with pouring cream.

Strawberry Roulade

SERVES

8

FOR THE SPONGE

4 large free-range eggs,
    at room temperature, separated
good pinch of cream of tartar
75g caster sugar
pinch of salt
1 teaspoon vanilla extract
25g unsalted butter, melted
50g plain flour
2 tablespoons flaked almonds

FOR THE FILLING

150ml whipping cream, well chilled
½ teaspoon vanilla extract
100g mascarpone cheese
3 tablespoons icing sugar, or to
    taste, plus extra for dusting
300g ripe strawberries

1 Swiss roll tin, 20 x 30cm, well greased
    and the base lined with baking paper

1 Preheat the oven to 160°C/325°F/gas 3.
Using an electric mixer, whisk the egg
whites in a large mixing bowl until frothy.
Add the cream of tartar and continue
whisking until the whites form soft peaks.
Gradually whisk in 2 tablespoons of the
measured sugar and whisk until stiff
peaks form. Set aside until needed.

2 Add the remaining sugar, the salt and
vanilla to the egg yolks and start whisking
with the electric mixer (there's no need to
wash the beaters), slowly adding the barely
warm butter. Keep whisking until the yolk
mixture is very thick and mousse-like and
the mixture makes a ribbon-like trail.

3 Sift the flour onto the yolk mixture and
gently fold in using a large metal spoon.

When strawberries are at their seasonal peak,
use them with rich mascarpone cream to fill
this feather-light rolled cake. It's made with
a sponge that just melts in the mouth.

Fold in the whisked egg whites in 3 batches.
Transfer the mixture to the prepared tin and
spread out evenly. Scatter the almonds over
the top. Bake for 10–12 minutes until the
sponge is light gold and springs back when
lightly pressed in the centre. Set the tin on
a wire rack and leave to cool.

4 Lay a sheet of baking paper on the worktop
and turn out the cold sponge onto it. Gently
peel off the lining paper – the sponge will be
slightly mousse-like. Make a deep cut across
the sponge about 1cm from one short side.

5 Whip the cream with the vanilla until stiff.
In another bowl stir the mascarpone with the
icing sugar until very smooth, then stir into
the whipped cream. Taste and stir in more
sugar if necessary. Spread evenly over the
sponge to within 2cm of the uncut short side.

6 Halve small strawberries and thickly slice
large ones, then arrange evenly over the
cream. Roll up the sponge from the cut end,
using the paper to help guide the roll into a
neat and fairly tight shape. Keep the paper
around the roll to hold it in shape and
transfer it to a serving platter. Chill for about
4 hours until firm (the roll can be kept for
a day in the fridge if it is well wrapped).
To serve, carefully remove the paper and
dust with icing sugar.

Mini Ricotta Cheesecakes

MAKES 12

FOR THE BASES
150g digestive biscuits, crushed
75g unsalted butter, melted

FOR THE FILLING
500g ricotta
200ml soured cream
2 large free-range eggs, beaten
100g icing sugar
2 tablespoons ground almonds
finely grated zest of 1 large unwaxed
    lemon and 1 medium unwaxed
    orange

FOR THE TOPPING
2 medium oranges
100g caster sugar

1 x 12-cup loose-based mini sandwich
    tin, greased; a baking sheet

Very light and fluffy, these individual cheesecakes are made with low-fat ricotta rather than cream cheese, and are finished with a caramelized orange topping and sauce.

1 Preheat the oven to 150°C/300°F/gas 2. To make the base, mix the biscuits with the melted butter. Divide evenly among the cups of the tin (about 1 ½ tablespoons crumbs for each). Press onto the base and halfway up the sides of each cup using a teaspoon; be sure there are no holes or gaps in the crust. Set the tin on the baking sheet and bake for 10 minutes. Remove and leave to cool while making the filling. Leave the oven on.

2 Put the filling ingredients into a food-processor and process until very smooth, then pour into a jug. Carefully pour the mixture into the cups in the sandwich tin (still on the baking sheet) to fill completely.

3 Bake for about 25 minutes until just firm, then remove from the oven – the mixture will continue cooking so don't overbake.

When the cheesecakes are cold, cover the tin and chill for at least 2 hours, but preferably overnight.

4 To make the topping, peel the oranges (work over a bowl to catch the juices). Cut each orange into 6 thin slices and add to the juice in the bowl. Make a caramel with the sugar and 3 tablespoons water (see page 197). Remove from the heat, then carefully pour in 3 tablespoons water. Return to the heat and stir gently until the caramel melts to make a thick sauce. Remove the pan from the heat and add the orange slices and juice. Tip the pan back and forth so the slices are coated in caramel, then leave to cool.

5 When ready to assemble, remove the sandwich tin from the fridge and leave at room temperature for 5 minutes to 'come to', then gently unmould the cheesecakes by pushing up the base of each cup. Remove the cup bases with a small, round-bladed knife. Arrange the cheesecakes, biscuit side down, on a serving platter or individual plates.

6 Set an orange slice on top of each cheesecake and spoon over a little of the caramel. Serve the remaining caramel in a small jug. Best eaten within a couple of hours of decorating.

Chocolate, Macadamia & Coffee Torte

SERVES 12

FOR THE SPONGE LAYERS

200g macadamia nuts
75g ground almonds
200g white chocolate, finely chopped
6 large free-range eggs, separated,
    plus 2 yolks, at room temperature
180g caster sugar
1 teaspoon vanilla paste
2 tablespoons milk,
    at room temperature

FOR THE FILLING

1 tablespoon brandy
1 tablespoon instant espresso powder
250g mascarpone
about 1 tablespoon icing sugar

TO DECORATE

200g white chocolate
50g macadamia nuts
1 tablespoon chocolate-covered
    coffee beans

FOR THE GANACHE

170g white chocolate, finely chopped
100ml double cream
2 teaspoons brandy
1 ½ teaspoons instant espresso
    powder

2 x 20.5cm loose-based sandwich tins,
    buttered, base lined with baking
    paper and dusted with caster sugar;
    chocolate transfer sheets; a small
    disposable piping bag

Two light but richly flavoured sponge-like nut and chocolate layers are sandwiched with a smooth layer of mascarpone, brandy and coffee. The torte is exquisitely finished with a feathered white chocolate ganache and patterned chocolate triangles.

1 Preheat the oven to 160°C/325°F/gas 3. Coarsely grind the macadamia nuts in a food-processor for a few seconds – watch carefully and stop the machine as soon as they start to clump together. Tip onto a plate lined with kitchen paper, spread out and leave to dry out for 5 minutes, then mix with the ground almonds.

2 Melt the chocolate (see page 308) and leave to cool. Put the 8 egg yolks into a large mixing bowl with the sugar and vanilla and whisk with an electric mixer until very thick and the mixture forms a ribbon-like trail when the whisk is lifted. Fold in the nuts with a large metal spoon, then fold in the melted chocolate and milk. Whisk the egg whites in another large mixing bowl until stiff, then gently fold into the yolk mixture in 3 batches.

3 Divide the mixture evenly between the prepared tins. Bake for 35–40 minutes until the sponges are golden brown and firm when gently pressed in the centre. Cool in the tins for 10 minutes, then turn out onto a wire rack and leave until cold.

Recipe continues overleaf

4 Meanwhile, make the filling. In a mixing bowl, stir the brandy with the espresso powder until dissolved. Add the mascarpone and a little icing sugar to taste (the sponges are sweet). Cover and chill until needed.

5 Next, make the decorations. Cut the chocolate transfer sheets into strips about 9cm wide and set shiny side down on a clean worktop. Temper the white chocolate (see page 308), then spread over the strips to the thickness of a pound coin. Just before the chocolate is completely set, score with a sharp knife into triangles. Leave to set before peeling away the acetate layer to reveal the design (see page 309 for information about chocolate transfers).

6 To make the ganache, put the chocolate into a heatproof bowl. Heat the cream until almost boiling, then pour onto the chocolate in a thin stream, whisking constantly with a balloon whisk. As soon as the mixture is smooth, whisk in the brandy. Spoon a quarter of the mixture into a small bowl and stir in the instant espresso powder. Cover both bowls and leave the ganache to thicken until firm enough to hold its shape.

7 To assemble the torte, put a small blob of the filling in the centre of a serving plate to secure the torte, then set one layer of sponge on top. Spread over the mascarpone filling, then cover with the second sponge. Spread the white ganache over the top of the cake (gently warm the ganache if it has become too firm to spread).

8 Spoon the coffee ganache into a small piping bag and snip off the tip, then pipe parallel lines across the top of the torte. Feather with a cocktail stick (see page 69 for details of how to do this). Leave in the fridge until set. Decorate with the macadamia nuts, chocolate coffee beans and white chocolate triangles just before serving.

Stripey Chocolate Cheesecake

FOR THE BASE
75g unsalted butter, melted
2 tablespoons cocoa powder
175g digestive biscuits, crushed
2 tablespoons caster sugar

FOR THE WHITE MIXTURE
500g full-fat cream cheese
140g caster sugar
2 large free-range eggs, beaten
1 ½ teaspoons vanilla extract

FOR THE DARK MIXTURE
150g dark chocolate (70% cocoa
    solids), broken up
500g full-fat cream cheese
140g caster sugar
2 large free-range eggs, beaten
1 ½ teaspoons vanilla extract

1 x 23cm springclip tin, greased;
    a baking sheet

1 Preheat the oven to 150°C/300°F/gas 2. To make the base, mix the butter with the cocoa, then stir in the crumbs and sugar. Tip into the prepared tin and press firmly and evenly over the base and about 2cm up the sides. Set on the baking sheet and bake for 10 minutes. Cool. Leave the oven on.

2 To make the white mixture, put the cream cheese in a food-processor and process until smooth. Add the sugar, eggs and vanilla and process until thoroughly combined. Scrape the mixture into a measuring jug.

3 For the dark mixture, melt the chocolate with 3 tablespoons water (see page 308); cool

With a food-processor and 2 measuring jugs, you can easily make this rich, glamorous cheesecake. Decorate simply with chocolate buttons or more elaborately, as you wish.

to room temperature. Put the cream cheese into the food-processor (there's no need to wash it) and process until smooth. Add the sugar, eggs and vanilla and process until combined. Add the chocolate and process to mix. Pour into another measuring jug.

4 With the tin still on the baking sheet, slowly pour one-third of the dark mixture onto the very centre of the biscuit base. Next, pour one-third of the white mixture into the very centre of the dark mixture. Repeat with half of the remaining dark mixture, then half the white mixture. Finish with the rest of the dark and white mixtures in the same way. As the mixtures are poured in they will spread out and the filling will end up with alternate rings of dark and light.

5 Carefully transfer to the oven and bake for 1–1 ¼ hours until just set, still with a slight wobble. Turn off the oven and leave the cheesecake inside for 1 hour. Then remove from the oven and run a round-bladed knife around the inside of the tin to loosen the cheesecake. When completely cold, cover and chill overnight. To serve, unclip the tin and remove the cheesecake. Store, tightly covered, in the fridge and eat within 5 days.

Hazelnut Torte

SERVES
12-16

FOR THE SPONGE
250g unsalted butter, at room
    temperature, diced
255g dark chocolate (about 70%
    cocoa solids), chopped
3 passion fruit
160g hazelnuts
6 large free-range eggs,
    at room temperature, separated
200g caster sugar

FOR THE GANACHE
300ml double cream
4 passion fruit
300g dark chocolate (about 70%
    cocoa solids), chopped
cocoa powder, for dusting

1 x 23cm springclip tin, greased and
    the base lined with baking paper

A rich but not heavy concoction with an intriguing flavour – plenty of chocolate and nuts with a dash of passion fruit.

1 Preheat the oven to 160°C/325°F/gas 3. Put the butter and chocolate into a heatproof bowl. Halve the passion fruit and scoop the pulp and seeds into a sieve set over the bowl. Press to extract the juice; discard the seeds. Set the bowl over a pan of steaming hot but not boiling water and melt gently. Remove the bowl from the pan and cool.

2 Grind 120g of the hazelnuts in a food-processor to a fine powder. Add the remaining 40g nuts and 'pulse' 3 or 4 times to roughly chop. Set aside until needed.

3 Whisk the egg whites with an electric mixer until they stand in soft peaks. Whisk in a tablespoon of the weighed sugar until stiff and glossy. Whisk the yolks with the remaining sugar until the mixture is very pale and thick, and will make a ribbon trail.

4 Using a large metal spoon, fold the chocolate mixture into the yolk mixture. When thoroughly combined fold in the nuts. Finally, fold in the egg whites in 3 batches.

5 Spoon the mixture into the prepared tin and spread evenly. Bake for 45–55 minutes until a skewer inserted in the centre comes out clean. Cool in the tin for 5 minutes – the torte will shrink slightly – then turn out onto a wire rack and leave to cool completely.

6 To make the ganache, put the cream into a pan. Halve the passion fruit and scoop out the pulp and seeds into the cream. Heat until the cream just comes to the boil, then remove from the heat and leave to infuse while melting the chocolate (see page 308).

7 The cream and chocolate should be the same temperature, so gently warm the cream if it has cooled too much. Strain the cream into the chocolate to remove the passion fruit seeds and stir until the ganache is smooth and glossy. It should thicken slightly but still be pourable.

8 Set the torte upside down on a serving platter (the flat underside makes a better surface for covering). Pour four-fifths of the ganache onto the cake and let it flow evenly over the top and down the sides, helping it as little as possible. Leave to set, then clean up the excess ganache.

9 Leave the remaining ganache to thicken until almost setting, then drop teaspoons onto a sheet of baking paper. Once firm, dust your hands with cocoa powder and roll into neat small balls. Arrange around the edge of the cake and dust the whole torte with cocoa powder. Can be kept, well covered, in a cool spot – not the fridge – for up to 48 hours.

Divine Chocolate Layer Cake

FOR THE SPONGE LAYER

200g dark chocolate (70% cocoa
    solids) OR espresso-flavoured
    dark chocolate, broken up
85g unsalted butter, diced
4 large free-range eggs, at room
    temperature
80g light brown muscovado sugar

FOR THE DARK CHOCOLATE LAYER

75ml boiling water
2 tablespoons cocoa powder
200g dark chocolate (70% cocoa
    solids), broken up
300ml whipping cream, at room
    temperature
2 tablespoons icing sugar

FOR THE WHITE CHOCOLATE LAYER

3g leaf gelatine
300ml whipping cream, at room
    temperature
175g good-quality white chocolate,
    finely chopped
1 teaspoon vanilla extract
dark chocolate decorations,
    such as discs, curls or cigarellos
    (see page 308)

1 x 23cm springclip tin, greased and
    the base lined with baking paper

Here is a truly impressive dessert – a 3-layer
confection for ardent chocolate-lovers. It
may look like hard work, but in fact it's made
in straightforward stages: first a flourless
dark chocolate sponge base, then a bitter
chocolate cream layer and finally a cream
and white chocolate top. Leave the
decorations fairly simple, using dark
chocolate for contrast.

1 Preheat the oven to 180°C/350°F/gas 4.
Start with the chocolate sponge layer. Melt
the chocolate with the butter (see page 308).
Leave to cool until needed.

2 Separate the eggs, putting the whites into
a large mixing bowl and the yolks into
another. Using an electric mixer, whisk
the whites until they form soft peaks, then
whisk in half of the sugar. Using the same
beaters – no need to wash – whisk the yolks
with the remaining sugar until thick and
mousse-like. Gently fold in the chocolate
mixture using a large metal spoon, then
fold in the whites in 3 batches. Spoon the
mixture into the prepared tin and spread
level. Bake for 20–25 minutes until just
firm to the touch. Remove from the oven
and leave to cool (do not unclip the tin
or remove the cake from the tin).

3 Once the sponge is cold, gently press it with your hand so the surface is flat and level, and the cake – which will have shrunk – touches the sides of the tin. Wipe any crumbs off the sides of the tin.

4 To make the dark chocolate layer, whisk the boiling water into the cocoa in a heatproof bowl; leave to cool while melting the chocolate (see page 308). Whisk the warm cocoa liquid into the chocolate, then cool to room temperature. Meanwhile, whip the cream until quite thick; add the icing sugar and whip until the cream stands in soft peaks. Using a large metal spoon, fold the whipped cream into the chocolate mixture in 3 batches. Spoon into the tin and spread evenly over the sponge base. Wipe any splashes off the sides of tin. Chill for about 30 minutes until set.

5 Once set, make up the white chocolate layer. Soak the gelatine in a bowl of cold water for about 5 minutes until soft. Meanwhile, gently heat 100ml of the measured cream, and put the chocolate into a large heatproof bowl. Squeeze out the soaked gelatine, then whisk into the hot cream off the heat until melted. Pour the hot cream over the chopped chocolate and leave to stand for 3 minutes, then whisk gently until melted and smooth. Leave to cool to room temperature. Meanwhile, whip the remaining cream with the vanilla until it stands in soft peaks. Fold into the white chocolate mixture in 3 batches, using a large metal spoon.

6 Spread the white chocolate cream evenly over the dark layer. Cover the tin with clingfilm (don't let it touch the surface of the top layer) and chill for at least 4 hours, or preferably overnight. Remove from the fridge about 30 minutes before serving.

7 To serve, run a round-bladed knife carefully around the inside of the tin to loosen the cake, then unclip the side and remove the cake. Neaten up the sides if necessary with a palette knife, then arrange chocolate decorations on top. Store in an airtight container in the fridge and eat within 4 days.

TIP
For neat slices, use a large, sharp knife, dipping it into a jug of hot water and drying before cutting each slice.

Rich Coffee & Walnut Torte

SERVES 12

FOR THE SPONGE

175g walnut pieces
1 x 20g slice crustless bread
6 large free-range eggs,
   at room temperature
110g caster sugar
2 tablespoons dark rum
2 teaspoons instant coffee powder
   or granules

FOR THE FILLING

200ml double cream, well chilled
1 tablespoon dark rum
1 tablespoon instant coffee powder
   or granules
100g mascarpone
75g icing sugar
25g walnut pieces and/or chocolate
   coffee beans, to decorate

3 x 20.5cm sandwich tins, greased and
   the base lined with baking paper

1 Preheat the oven to 180°C/350°F/gas 4.
Tip the walnut pieces into a baking dish
or small tin and toast in the oven for 6–8
minutes until lightly coloured; leave to cool.
At the same time, put the slice of bread into
the oven to dry for 2–3 minutes, without
colouring. Remove, but leave the oven on.

Although light in texture, this coffee and
walnut cake with a mascarpone cream filling
is rich and very moist, yet not overly sweet –
perfect for a special dessert. The flavours
intensify as the cake matures, so plan to
bake it a day or so ahead.

2 Roughly break up the bread, put into the
bowl of a food-processor and process to fine
crumbs. Tip into a medium bowl. Finely
chop the walnuts in the processor – they
should be about the same size as instant
coffee granules, not as finely ground as
ground almonds. Set aside 3 tablespoons
of the walnuts for the decoration and put
the remainder into the bowl with the
breadcrumbs.

3 Separate the eggs, putting the whites into
a large mixing bowl, or the bowl of a large
free-standing electric mixer, and the yolks
into another bowl. Whisk the egg whites
until stiff peaks form; set aside. Add the
caster sugar to the yolks and whisk with
the same beaters (no need to wash) until
thick and pale and the mixture leaves a
thick, ribbon-like trail when the whisk is
lifted from the bowl.

4 Gently warm the rum in a small pan, add the coffee and stir until dissolved. Gently fold into the whisked egg yolks together with the nut and crumb mixture, using a large metal spoon. Very carefully fold in the egg whites in 3 batches. When thoroughly combined divide the mixture evenly among the 3 prepared sandwich tins and gently spread to level the surface. Bake the sponges for 12–15 minutes until just firm to the touch. Set the sandwich tins on a wire rack and leave to cool completely.

5 To make the filling mixture, whip the cream until thick. Gently warm the rum in a small pan, add the coffee and stir until dissolved, then cool. In another bowl, stir the mascarpone until creamy, then stir in the icing sugar followed by the rum mixture. Fold this mixture into the whipped cream. (At this point the filling can be covered tightly and kept chilled for up to 8 hours.)

6 To assemble the torte, turn out one of the sponges onto a serving plate; turn out the other 2 sponges onto a large sheet of baking paper lightly sprinkled with caster sugar (the sponge discs will be fragile and a little sticky). Divide the filling mixture into 4 portions. Spread one portion over the sponge on the plate. Top with a second sponge and spread with the second portion of filling, then put the third sponge in place. Spread another portion of filling evenly over the sides of the torte and press on the reserved chopped walnuts. Spread the remaining mascarpone cream filling neatly on top of the torte and decorate with walnut pieces or chocolate coffee beans. Put the torte into a large airtight container and chill for at least 12 hours before serving.

Triple Chocolate Log

SERVES

10–12

FOR THE SPONGE

6 large free-range eggs,
   at room temperature
good pinch of cream of tartar
140g caster sugar
50g cocoa powder
1–2 tablespoons dark rum
   (optional)

FOR THE DARK MOUSSE

200g dark chocolate (about 70%
   cocoa solids), chopped
4 large eggs, at room
   temperature, separated
1–2 tablespoons dark rum
   (optional)
1 tablespoon caster sugar

FOR THE WHITE MOUSSE

200ml whipping cream, well chilled
½ teaspoon vanilla extract
75g best-quality white chocolate,
   well chilled, finely grated

TO FINISH

75g dark chocolate (about 70%
   cocoa solids), broken up
edible gold lustre (see page 310)
cocoa powder, for sprinkling

1 swiss roll tin, baking tray or roasting
   tin, 25 x 30.5cm (see recipe);
   parchment-lined foil or baking paper

1 Preheat the oven to 190°C/375°F/gas 5.
Line the tin or tray with the parchment-lined
foil or baking paper, folding it so it makes a
25 × 30.5cm rectangular container with 2cm
sides (it doesn't matter if your tin or tray is
larger than this; just make sure the 'liner'
is the right size).

This is a very rich, spectacular chocolate
dessert to make during the holiday season –
a light sponge rolled around dark and white
chocolate mousse layers. It's topped with
chocolate and gold leaves. You could also
simply dust with sifted icing sugar and add
grated white chocolate or chocolate curls.

2 Make the sponge first. Separate the eggs,
putting the whites into a large mixing bowl
or the bowl of a large free-standing electric
mixer, and the yolks in another. Using an
electric mixer, whisk the egg whites until
frothy. Add the cream of tartar and continue
whisking until the whites stand in stiff
peaks. Whisk in 3 tablespoons of the
measured caster sugar, a tablespoon at
a time, to make a stiff, glossy meringue.
Set aside until needed.

3 Add the remaining caster sugar to the egg
yolks and whisk with the same beaters (no
need to wash) until the mixture is very thick
and mousse-like and forms a thick ribbon-
like trail when the beaters are lifted from
the bowl. Sift the cocoa powder into the
bowl and gently fold in with a large metal
spoon. Fold the whisked egg whites into
the yolk mixture in 3 batches.

4 Transfer the mixture to the prepared 'liner'
and spread evenly. Bake for 15–18 minutes
until the sponge is springy when gently
pressed. Meanwhile, cover a wire rack with
a clean, dry tea towel topped with a sheet
of baking paper.

Recipe continues overleaf

5 Tip the baked sponge out onto the lined rack and peel off the paper 'liner'. Sprinkle the rum over the sponge, if using, then leave to cool completely.

6 Meanwhile, make the dark mousse. Melt the chocolate with 100ml water in a large bowl (see page 308). Off the heat, gently stir in the egg yolks, one at a time, followed by the rum, if using. Whisk the egg whites until stiff as before, then whisk in the sugar. Very gently fold the whites into the chocolate mixture in 3 batches. Cover and chill for 30 minutes until starting to set.

7 To make the white mousse, whip the cream with the vanilla until it thickens and stands in stiff peaks. Fold in the chocolate. Cover and keep in the fridge until needed.

8 To assemble the log, make a deep cut across the sponge about 1.5cm away from one short end. Spread the dark chocolate mousse over the sponge, leaving a 2cm border clear all around. Cover the dark mousse with the white mousse.

9 Roll up from the short end with the cut, using the baking paper to help you pull and mould the roll into a neat shape. Wrap the roll in the paper to give it a neat shape, then chill for at least 2 hours until firm (or up to a day if the roll is well covered).

10 When ready to finish, remove the paper and transfer the log to a serving platter. Trim off the ends, if you like. Temper the chocolate (see page 308), then use to make leaves (see opposite page). Brush half of them with edible gold lustre. Leave to set.

11 Arrange the chocolate leaves down the length of the cake, then sprinkle with sifted cocoa powder. Any leftover cake can be kept in an airtight container in the fridge for up to 3 days.

TIP
Spoon the tempered dark chocolate into a disposable piping bag, snip off the tip and pipe 'Buche de Noel' on a strip of acetate or Perspex (see page 309); leave to set before peeling from the acetate and placing gently on the cake.

Making Chocolate Leaves

EQUIPMENT NEEDED

rose, bay, lemon or camellia leaves,
    free from pesticides
dark chocolate or good-quality white
    or milk chocolate
baking paper
small paintbrush
edible gold lustre (see page 310)

1 Leaves with a visible veining are the best to use. When you cut your leaves, take a bit of the stem, which you can use as a 'handle'. Thoroughly clean the leaves by wiping with damp kitchen paper, then dry well with kitchen paper.

2 Temper the chocolate (see page 308). To make 12 chocolate rose leaves for the Triple Chocolate Log (see page 272) we used about 75g tempered dark chocolate.

3 Put a sheet of baking paper or a tray on the worktop. Hold a leaf by its stem. Using a small paintbrush, brush a thin layer of tempered chocolate on the underside of the leaf. Make sure the chocolate covers evenly and completely to the edge of the leaf all round.

4 Place the leaf carefully on the baking paper. Cover the rest of your leaves with tempered chocolate. (Make extra to allow for breakages.) Leave to set, then paint on another thin layer of tempered chocolate.

5 When the chocolate is firm, peel away and discard the leaves. Do this gently and carefully, handling the chocolate leaves as little as possible.

6 To add extra sparkle, finish your chocolate leaves with gold. Dip a small paintbrush in gold lustre and brush gently onto the leaves. Another finish is to paint delicate patterns or leaf veining on the chocolate leaves using a contrasting tempered chocolate.

Puddings

A HOME-COOKED PUDDING EVOKES a feeling of old-fashioned warmth and comfort, and it's as satisfying to make as to eat. So, how do you give a favourite homely pud the special treatment? The simple answer is to make it taste and look fabulous.

If fruit is the basis for your pudding, then only buy fresh fruit with real taste, in season, and allow for ripening time, if necessary. Don't settle for anything dud, over-ripe and bruised or musty-smelling just because it's fresh – top-quality frozen and bottled berries and cherries would make a better choice.

Then there's the trick of subtle enhancement – adding a little something to bring out the flavour of the fruit without overwhelming it. Finely grated lemon or orange zest can lift an apple or pear mixture, just as lime zest and juice work so well with perfectly ripe mangoes. Warm, fragrant spices like cardamom, cinnamon, ginger and mixed spice develop enticing, sweet aromas as they cook, scenting stone fruit – plums, cherries, peaches, apricots and greengages. A split vanilla pod added while poaching dried fruits (apricots, prunes, figs and apples) or fresh (peaches, apricots and pears) will give a delicious flavour to fruit and syrup. A dash or two – or three – of rum, brandy, kirsch or other fruit-based liqueur adds a festive boost.

There are a whole host of comforting puddings from the series here. For the first time, the bakers were challenged to make Strudel and we have a basic recipe for Strudel Pastry at the beginning of the chapter. It's a tricky technique to perfect as you have to stretch the pastry as thinly as you can, but you can easily patch tears or, if you prefer, you can use ready-made filo pastry instead. We also give you two classic strudel recipes – one with a slightly more complicated filling, and then an apple pudding that is delicately encased in the pastry.

There are also some simple fruity puddings as well as the Technical Challenge recipes including Mary's Queen of Puddings and Paul's Rum Babas and the best Sticky Toffee Pudding from the bakers. Mary's Toffee Apple and Pecan Pudding is a classic sponge recipe which looks stunning but is actually very simple to make.

There are some easy things you can do to make even the simplest pudding look particularly tempting. Use good-looking baking dishes (make sure they're the right size so the mixture doesn't overflow). For sponge puddings that don't need to be turned out, bake in a nicely shaped dish – look out for pretty fluted ovenproof glass pudding basins. Rather than just dusting the pudding with icing sugar to serve, set a paper doily over the top as a stencil (we've used this technique on bread and pies with great success).

Also think about what will best accompany your pudding. Home-made egg custard is always a treat with sponges, crumbles and fruit puddings. A quickly made hot cherry sauce, spiked with a touch of kirsch, is perfect with a light sweet-cheese strudel. A jug of warm maple syrup makes a cosy winter pudding of fruit and nuts even more delicious. Frothy whipped cream or Chantilly cream is the classic final touch for apple strudel.

Whether made in advance and gently reheated, or popped into the oven to bake as the main course is set on the table, there's always time and room for pudding.

DON'T FORGET

Thaw frozen filo pastry according to the packet instructions – never use the microwave. Use at room temperature and keep tightly covered until needed, because the delicate pastry leaves quickly dry and become fragile and easily shattered.

To stop the filling bursting out, make sure the ends of the strudel rolls are securely folded and pressed together.

Lining baking sheets with baking paper ensures easy removal of strudels so they keep a good shape.

Serve strudels gently warm rather than piping hot from the oven.

Prepare pudding basins and moulds carefully so a sponge mixture doesn't stick – use very soft or melted butter and a pastry brush to coat all over.

Make a sponge pudding mixture as you would make a cake: take time creaming the soft butter with the sugar. Use room-temperature eggs and beat them in a little at a time. Carefully fold in the flour with a large metal spoon so you don't knock out all the air you've beaten in.

Don't overfill the basin or mould – make sure there is room for the mixture to rise during baking.

Strudel Dough

300g strong white bread flour,
plus extra for dusting
pinch of salt
1 large free-range egg, at room
temperature
30g unsalted butter, melted,
plus extra for brushing
150ml water, at room temperature

1 Sift the flour and salt into a large mixing bowl. Make a well in the centre. Beat the egg and melted butter into the water, then pour into the well. Using your hand, work the ingredients together to make a very soft paste, adding more water if necessary a tablespoon at a time. Slap the paste up and down in the bowl with your hand until it leaves the sides of the bowl clean.

2 Turn out onto a lightly floured worktop and knead thoroughly for 10 minutes until very smooth and elastic. The easiest way to start is to pick the dough up and throw it down onto the worktop, then gather it up again. Repeat until the dough leaves your hand easily, then knead as if making bread. Upturn the bowl over the ball of dough to cover and leave to rest for 15–30 minutes.

3 When you are ready to start stretching the dough, spread a cloth flat on a tabletop so there are no wrinkles. Lightly dust with flour. Set the ball of dough in the middle and lightly brush the surface of the dough with melted butter. Roll out the dough to a square with sides about 45cm (or about 3mm thick if using half quantity). Remove all your rings, watches and bangles and flour your hands. Slip them, palm down, under the dough and

Making ultra-thin, crisp sheets of strudel pastry is a challenge but it's a lot of fun. Use this strudel dough to make the following Showstopping Challenges: Classic Apple Strudel, Sweet Cheese Strudel and Spiced Apple Croustade.

Unlike other pastries, strudel is made with strong white flour – the kind you use for bread – and is kneaded to develop the gluten, which is what enables it to become very elastic when it is pulled and stretched out by hand to the thinness of a paper tissue.

The stretched sheet of pastry will be very large, so you'll need to work on a tabletop covered with a cloth. If you don't have that much space, either divide the rested ball of dough in half and stretch each piece in turn to make 2 smaller strudels, or make up half quantity of dough for a smaller strudel. It won't matter if your first attempt has a few holes or tears, because strudel pastry is used in layers, so is easily patched up.

Fresh or frozen filo pastry is very similar to strudel and can be used instead.

gently move them apart to stretch the dough over your hands. Move around the table as you work so the dough is evenly stretched. Gradually the dough will become very thin – you will have a sheet about 82 × 82cm.

4 Trim off thick edges with kitchen scissors. The strudel dough is now ready to use. It will rapidly dry out, so cover with clingfilm if not using immediately. Cut the sheet of dough to size with kitchen scissors.

Classic Apple Strudel

SERVES 12–14

1 quantity Strudel Dough (see page 281), made but not stretched, OR about 360g filo pastry (8 sheets, 25.5 x 48cm), thawed if frozen
about 100g unsalted butter, melted
icing sugar, for dusting

FOR THE FILLING
100g large raisins
1 tablespoon dark rum or lemon juice
75g unsalted butter
100g fresh white breadcrumbs
5 tablespoons caster sugar
1kg eating apples, peeled, cored and sliced
1 teaspoon ground cinnamon
finely grated zest of 1 large unwaxed lemon
100g ground almonds

1 baking sheet, lined with baking paper

Sweet-tart apples and raisins soaked in rum or lemon juice fill this layered pastry roll. Arranging the filling on ground almonds helps keep the pastry crisp. Serve warm, in thick slices, with cream or crème fraîche.

1 Soak the raisins in the rum or lemon juice for at least 1 hour, or overnight. Make the Strudel Dough following the method on page 281, but don't stretch it yet; if using filo, unwrap it but keep it covered with clingfilm to prevent it from drying out. Preheat the oven to 190°C/375°F/gas 5.

2 To make the filling, heat the butter in a frying pan, add the breadcrumbs and fry, stirring, over medium heat until golden brown. Add 1 tablespoon of the sugar and stir over the heat for 1 minute, then tip into a heatproof bowl and cool.

3 Put the apples in a large mixing bowl and mix in the remaining sugar, the cinnamon, lemon zest and raisin mixture.

4 Stretch the strudel dough, if using, then trim the sheet of dough, on the cloth, to a square with 80cm sides; if using filo, overlap the sheets on a cloth to make a square about that size. Brush lightly with some of the melted butter, then scatter the browned breadcrumbs evenly over the pastry. About 8cm in from one side of the pastry square, spoon the ground almonds in a 78cm band that is about 8cm wide (leave a small gap at each end of the band). Pile the apple mixture on top of the almonds, then fold over the flap of pastry to cover the filling.

5 Lifting the cloth to help, roll up the pastry, tucking in the ends as you go and pulling the cloth towards you each time the roll flops over. After each roll use a dry pastry brush to remove as much excess flour as possible.

6 Use the cloth to tip the rolled strudel, seam side down, onto the lined baking sheet and gently shape into a crescent or horseshoe to fit. Make sure the ends of the pastry are tucked in. Brush the roll with melted butter, then bake for 30–35 minutes until a good golden brown and crisp.

7 Finish with a good dusting of icing sugar. The strudel is best eaten warm the same day or the next (reheat on a baking sheet in a 180°C/350°F/gas 4 oven for 10 minutes).

Sweet Cheese Strudel

SERVES 12

1 quantity Strudel Dough (see page 281), made but not stretched, OR about 360g filo pastry (8 sheets, 25.5 x 48cm), thawed if frozen
about 100g unsalted butter, melted
icing sugar, for dusting
2 quantities Black Cherry Sauce (see page 308), to serve

FOR THE FILLING
100g whole blanched almonds
150g caster sugar
75g sultanas or crimson raisins
1 tablespoon rum
3 large free-range eggs, at room temperature, separated
50g unsalted butter, softened
finely grated zest of 1 large lemon
1 tablespoon plain flour
450g curd cheese
good pinch of salt

2 baking sheets, lined with baking paper

The sweet curd cheese filling here has the flavour of a cheesecake and the texture of a soufflé. A simple cherry sauce, with its hint of kirsch, adds a touch of glamour. This makes 2 small strudels and each will serve 6.

1 Preheat the oven to 180°C/350°F/gas 4. Make the Strudel Dough following the method on page 281, but don't stretch it yet; if using filo unwrap it but keep it covered with clingfilm to prevent it from drying out.

2 To make the filling, toast the almonds in the oven for 7–10 minutes. Cool, then grind to a coarse powder. Stir in 2 tablespoons of the sugar. Turn the oven to 190°C/375°F/gas 5.

3 Soak the sultanas in the rum. Beat the egg yolks with the rest of the sugar, the butter and lemon zest with an electric mixer until thoroughly combined and very smooth. Stir in the flour and curd cheese. Leave to stand for 20 minutes. Whisk the whites until stiff, then fold into the yolk mixture in 3 batches.

4 Stretch the strudel dough, if using, then trim it, on the cloth, into 2 long strips roughly 40 × 80cm. If using filo, arrange 4 sheets, slightly overlapping, on a lightly floured cloth to make a strip about 48 × 80cm; arrange the other 4 sheets in a similar strip next to the first. Brush the strudel or filo lightly with melted butter.

5 Divide the almond mixture in half. Spoon half of one portion onto a pastry strip, 8cm in from one short side, to make a band about 8cm wide and stretching to within 3cm of the edge. Scatter the rest of the portion over the rest of the strip. Repeat with the other strip of pastry and second portion of almond mixture.

6 Divide the cheese mixture in half and spoon one portion onto each almond band. Scatter the sultanas on top of the cheese. Fold the flap of pastry over the filling, then roll up each strudel loosely, using the cloth to help and tucking in the ends. Roll onto the baking sheets and make sure the ends are tucked in. Brush with melted butter, then bake for 30–35 minutes until golden brown and crisp.

7 Dust the warm strudels with icing sugar (we used a doily to create the pattern here; see page 148 for directions). Cut into thick slices and serve with the hot cherry sauce.

Spiced Apple Croustade

SERVES 8

1 quantity Strudel Dough (see page 281), made but not stretched, OR about 360g filo pastry (8 sheets, 25.5 x 48cm), thawed if frozen
about 100g unsalted butter, melted
icing sugar, for dusting

FOR THE FILLING
4 large Bramley apples
50g unsalted butter
½ teaspoon ground cinnamon
2 tablespoons honey
100g demerara sugar

1 x 23cm springclip tin; a baking sheet

Here's a pretty pudding that's perfect for Sunday lunch – a sticky, caramelized apple mixture encased in delicate leaves of strudel or filo pastry. Enjoy warm with crème fraîche.

1 If using Strudel Dough, make it following the method on page 281, but don't stretch it yet. Peel, core and thickly slice the apples. Melt the butter in a large heavy pan, add the apples and cook gently, shaking the pan from time to time (rather than stirring), until tender. Add the cinnamon, honey and half the demerara sugar, and gently stir in – try to keep a few larger pieces of apple. Turn up the heat and cook, stirring as little as possible, until the mixture is soft, thick and starting to caramelize. Remove the pan from the heat and leave to cool.

2 When ready to assemble the pie, preheat the oven to 190°C/375°F/gas 5. Stretch the strudel dough now, if using; or if using filo, unwrap it but keep it covered with clingfilm to prevent it from drying out.

3 Using kitchen scissors, cut the stretched strudel dough into 8 sheets about 20 × 40cm; save all the torn sections and scraps for the topping and use the large sections to assemble the pie. You will need 6 sheets of strudel or filo for the base: brush one sheet with a little melted butter, then arrange in the tin so it covers the base and drapes over one side. Sprinkle with a little of the remaining demerara sugar. Brush another sheet with butter and arrange at a right angle to the first sheet. Sprinkle with demerara sugar. Continue in this way with 4 more sheets sprinkled with sugar, so the base has 6 pastry layers and the sides of the tin are completely covered with pastry.

4 Spoon the cooled filling into the pastry case. Fold over the overhanging flaps of pastry, brushing them with butter (and sprinkling with any remaining sugar) as you go, to cover the filling. Trim off any thick, unsightly or dry edges with kitchen scissors. Brush the remaining 2 sheets of pastry with butter, then tear into strips. Crumple up each piece, rather like a chiffon scarf, and carefully arrange on top in a big pile to look like a frilly hat. Sprinkle and dab with any remaining butter, then set the tin on the baking sheet. Bake for 25–30 minutes until a good golden brown and crisp.

5 Remove from the oven and leave to cool for 10 minutes, then carefully unclip the side of the tin. Dust the croustade with icing sugar before serving. Best eaten the same day.

Sour Cherry Strudel

SERVES 8

1 quantity Strudel Dough (see page 281) made with 2 tablespoons mild olive oil instead of butter, not stretched, OR about 360g filo pastry (8 sheets, each 25.5 x 48cm), thawed if frozen)
about 90g unsalted butter, melted
40g flaked almonds
40g walnut halves or roasted pecans
icing sugar, for dusting

FOR THE FILLING

50g dried sour cherries
30g raisins
1 ½ tablespoons brandy
1 tablespoon vegetable oil
70g fresh brioche crumbs
1 large Bramley apple
3 large Granny Smith apples
finely grated zest of ½ unwaxed lemon plus 1 teaspoon juice
110g light brown muscovado sugar
½ teaspoon ground cinnamon
good pinch each of ground cloves and grated nutmeg
85g pecan nuts or walnuts, chopped

1 baking sheet, lined with baking paper

1 Soak the cherries and raisins in the brandy for at least an hour, or overnight.

2 Make the Strudel Dough following the method on page 281, but don't stretch it yet; if using filo, unwrap it but keep it covered with clingfilm to prevent it from drying out. Preheat the oven to 200°C/400°F/gas 6.

3 Heat the oil in a frying pan and fry the brioche crumbs, stirring, for 3 minutes until golden brown; cool. Peel, core and thinly slice all the apples. Put into a large bowl and mix in the lemon zest and juice, the sugar,

The combination of cooking and eating apples gives this strudel a wonderfully flavoured and textured filling.

all the spices and the soaked fruit mixture. Mix thoroughly.

4 If using strudel dough, stretch it now and trim to a square with 80cm sides; assemble the filo sheets, overlapping, to make a square of the same size. Sprinkle with some of the melted butter and use your hand to delicately brush the butter so it covers every bit of the dough. Scatter the brioche crumbs evenly over the buttered surface.

5 About 8cm in from one side of the dough, spoon the chopped nuts in a band about 70cm long, leaving a gap at each end. Drain the apple filling thoroughly, then pile on top of the nuts. Fold over the flap of dough to cover the filling, then roll up the strudel with the help of the cloth (see page 282). Gently tip it seam side down onto the baking sheet and shape into a crescent to fit.

6 Make sure the ends are thoroughly tucked in – use kitchen scissors to cut away any thick excess pastry at each end of the roll first if necessary. Brush with melted butter, then bake for 25 minutes. Brush lightly with the last of the melted butter and scatter the flaked almonds and pecan or walnut halves over the top. Bake for a further 5 minutes until the strudel is golden brown and crisp.

7 Transfer to a serving platter and cool slightly. Dust with icing sugar and serve.

Sticky Toffee Puddings

MAKES 8

160g stoned chopped dates, preferably Medjool
½ teaspoon bicarbonate of soda
300ml boiling water
175g unsalted butter, softened
175g dark brown muscovado sugar
1 large free-range egg, at room temperature, beaten
175g self-raising flour
1 teaspoon baking powder

FOR THE SAUCE

100g unsalted butter
100g dark brown muscovado sugar
1 tablespoon dark rum
100ml double cream
2 tablespoons syrup from a jar of stem ginger in syrup (optional)

8 x 200ml ramekins, well greased; a baking sheet

Very light individual sponge puddings, these are quick to make and bake, with a rich but not oversweet toffee sauce. Perfect for Sunday lunch!

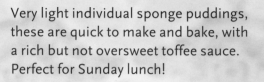

1 Preheat the oven to 180°C/350°F/gas 4. Put the chopped dates and bicarbonate of soda into a heatproof bowl and pour over the boiling water. Stir well, then leave to cool to lukewarm – about 20 minutes.

2 Meanwhile, beat the soft butter with the sugar until light and fluffy. Gradually add the egg, beating well after each addition. Sift the flour with the baking powder, then gently fold into the mixture in 3 batches using a large metal spoon. Stir in the dates and their liquid to make a very thick batter-like mixture.

3 Spoon into the prepared ramekins (they should be no more than two-thirds full, to allow space for the mixture to rise in the oven). Set the ramekins on the baking sheet and bake for about 20 minutes until firm when pressed in the centre.

4 Meanwhile, melt the butter with the sugar and rum over low heat, then bring to the boil. Remove from the heat and whisk in the cream and ginger syrup (if using). Pour into a heatproof serving jug.

5 Leave the puddings to cool on a wire rack for 5 minutes, then carefully turn out onto serving plates. Serve hot with the sauce.

JUDGE'S TECHNICAL CHALLENGE

Mary's Queen of Puddings

SERVES

600ml full-fat milk
25g unsalted butter
finely grated zest of 1 lemon
225g caster sugar
3 large free-range eggs, at room
    temperature, separated
75g fresh white breadcrumbs

FOR THE JAM
200g mixed summer fruits
    (raspberries, blueberries,
    blackcurrants and redcurrants)
    OR 500g frozen mixed berries
200g caster sugar, or to taste

1 x 1.4 litre capacity shallow ovenproof
    dish, buttered; a roasting tin; a piping
    bag fitted with a plain or star tube
    (or a disposable piping bag with
    the tip snipped off)

1 To make the custard base, very gently warm the milk in a small pan. Add the butter, lemon zest and 50g of the sugar and stir until the butter has melted and the sugar dissolved. Lightly whisk the egg yolks in a large heatproof mixing bowl, then gradually whisk in the warm milk mixture.

2 Sprinkle the breadcrumbs over the base of the buttered dish. Pour over the custard. Leave to stand for about 15 minutes so the breadcrumbs can absorb the liquid. Meanwhile, preheat the oven to 160°C/ 325°F/gas 3.

An old favourite revisited with a new twist – home-made soft fruit jam. If you prefer, you can use a good raspberry jam. There are 3 key elements to get right here: custard, jam and meringue and to get top marks with Mary and Paul the 3 must remain separate.

3 Carefully set the dish in the roasting tin and pour enough hot water into the tin to come halfway up the side of the dish. Bake for 25–30 minutes until the custard base is firm and set. Remove from the oven and lift the dish from the roasting tin. Leave to cool for 15 minutes. Leave the oven on, but reduce the temperature to 150°C/300°F/gas 2.

4 While the custard base is cooling, make the jam. Put the mixed fruits into a pan and warm over low heat until they have softened and released their juices. Add the sugar and continue to cook gently, stirring occasionally, for about 3 minutes until you have a jam-like consistency. (If using frozen berries, they will release more liquid, so will take longer to cook to a jam-like consistency.)

5 Put the egg whites into a large bowl and whisk with a hand-held electric mixer on full speed until stiff. Whisk in the remaining sugar a teaspoon at a time, still on full speed, to make a very stiff and glossy meringue. Spoon the meringue into the piping bag fitted with the plain or star tube.

6 Spread 4–5 tablespoons of the fruit jam over the custard base, then pipe the meringue on top to cover the jam completely. Bake for 25–30 minutes until the meringue is pale golden and crisp. Serve immediately, with a jug of pouring cream.

PETER

November Pudding

115g unsalted butter, softened
115g caster sugar
2 large free-range eggs, beaten
1 tablespoon milk
115g self-raising flour
1 ½ teaspoons ground cinnamon
50g mixed soft-dried apricots
    (chopped) and cranberries
    (whole)
1 small Bramley apple (about 200g),
    peeled and cored
50g walnut pieces
4 tablespoons maple syrup, plus
    extra for serving

1 ovenproof pudding basin,
    900ml to 1 litre capacity, greased

Elegant comfort food for cold days, this is a light cinnamon sponge pudding rich with fruit and nuts and flavoured with maple syrup. Serve with a jug of warm maple syrup plus some double cream or custard (see page 299) for a real treat.

1 Preheat the oven to 180°C/350°F/gas 4. Put the soft butter and sugar into a mixing bowl and beat with a wooden spoon or an electric mixer until light and creamy. Gradually add the eggs, beating well after each addition. Stir in the milk. Sift the flour and cinnamon into the bowl and fold in with a large metal spoon. Fold in the apricots and cranberries. Chop the apple into pieces roughly the size of your little fingernail and fold in.

2 Put the walnuts into the base of the pudding basin and spoon the maple syrup on top of them. Carefully spoon the sponge mixture into the basin. Gently tap the basin on the worktop to dislodge any pockets of air.

3 Bake for 45 minutes to 1 hour until a skewer inserted into the centre of the sponge comes out clean. If the sponge is getting too brown towards the end of the cooking time, cover with a sheet of baking paper or foil.

4 Loosen the sponge by running a round-bladed knife around the inside of the basin, then invert the sponge onto a serving plate. Serve hot with more maple syrup. Any leftover pudding can be gently warmed in a microwave before serving.

TIP
To add to the nutty flavour, use a light brown self-raising flour, milled for pastry and cakes (not the heavier wholemeal flour used for bread-making).

Paul's Rum Babas

MAKES 4

220g strong white bread flour
1 x 7g sachet fast-action dried yeast
50g caster sugar
½ teaspoon salt
2 medium free-range eggs,
   at room temperature
70ml milk, at room temperature
100g unsalted butter, softened

FOR THE SYRUP
250g caster sugar
3–4 tablespoons dark rum, to taste

TO FINISH
250ml double cream
100g icing sugar
1 vanilla pod, split open
seasonal fruit

4 x 12cm fluted rum baba moulds;
   a baking sheet

This was the first Technical Challenge of series 3 and a real test of the bakers' skills. Made with a very rich yeasted dough, these sweet rum-infused little cakes are irresistible served with whipped cream and fresh fruit.

1 Put the flour into a large bowl. Add the yeast, sugar and salt in piles on separate sides of the bowl so they are not touching (the yeast can be killed by the salt), then stir with a spoon until everything is evenly mixed.

2 Beat the eggs with the milk; add three-quarters to the flour mix and stir. Work in the rest of the egg mixture, then knead for about 10 minutes until smooth and glossy. Work in the soft butter, a little at a time, kneading until completely amalgamated and the dough is silky and stretchy. Cover the bowl with clingfilm and leave the dough to rise at room temperature for 1 hour until doubled in size.

3 Meanwhile, butter the moulds generously, then coat with a little caster sugar – this will help you remove the fragile babas once they are cooked.

4 Punch down (knock back) the risen dough to deflate; it should have a piping consistency. Either pipe or carefully spoon the dough into the prepared moulds, filling them evenly. Leave at room temperature until the dough has risen to cover the raised centre of the moulds. Be careful not to over-prove, otherwise you'll get a 'muffin top' around the edges of the moulds. Towards the end of the rising, preheat the oven to 180°C/350°F/gas 4.

5 Set the moulds on the baking sheet, then bake for 20–25 minutes until golden brown and firm to the touch. Meanwhile, make the syrup. Put the sugar, rum and 200ml water in a medium pan. Stir over medium heat until the sugar has dissolved, then bring to a rolling boil. Remove from the heat.

6 Leave the cooked babas to cool for a couple of minutes before carefully turning out into a shallow dish. Reheat the syrup if necessary, then pour half of it over the babas. Once all the syrup has been absorbed, carefully turn the babas over and pour the rest of syrup over them. Leave to cool.

7 Whip the double cream with the icing sugar and the seeds scraped from the vanilla pod until it is firm enough to be piped. Pipe or dollop on top of each baba, add some seasonal fruit and serve.

Warm Blackberry Torte

SERVES 8

150g unsalted butter, softened
150g caster sugar
150g ground almonds
150g self-raising flour
1 teaspoon ground cinnamon
1 large free-range egg, at room
    temperature, beaten
3 drops of almond extract (optional)
2 tablespoons crème fraîche
300g fresh blackberries
2 tablespoons flaked almonds

TO FINISH
icing sugar
ground cinnamon

1 x 23cm springclip tin, well greased
    and the base lined with baking paper

1 Preheat the oven to 180°C/350°F/gas 4. Put the soft butter, caster sugar, ground almonds, flour, cinnamon, egg and almond extract, if using, into a large mixing bowl. Beat with a wooden spoon or an electric mixer until thoroughly combined to make a fairly stiff cake mixture.

2 Spoon half of the mixture into another bowl and reserve for the topping. Mix the crème fraîche into the remaining mixture, then transfer to the prepared tin and spread evenly. Scatter the blackberries over the top, making sure they are evenly distributed.

This simple yet totally more-ish dessert is a cross between a rich sponge cake and a juicy fruit crumble with a crunchy topping. It's great served with crème fraiche, but is even more comforting with cinnamon ice cream or custard (see opposite).

3 To make the topping, pinch off pea-sized pieces of the reserved cake mixture and dot over the fruit so it is almost entirely covered. Scatter the flaked almonds over the top. Bake for 50–60 minutes until a good golden brown and just firm to the touch. If the top is browning too quickly during baking, cover with a sheet of baking paper or foil.

4 Remove from the oven and run a round-bladed knife around the inside of the tin to loosen the cake, then carefully unclip the tin side. Set the torte on a serving platter and dust with sifted icing sugar followed by a sprinkling of cinnamon. Serve warm. Any leftovers can be served at room temperature as a cake, or gently reheated (7–10 minutes in a 160°C/325°F/gas 3 oven).

Little Plum Crumbles

SERVES 75ml port
75ml orange juice
2 ½ tablespoons light brown
   muscovado sugar
2 star anise
1kg just-ripe plums
175g amaretti
2 tablespoons toasted flaked almonds

FOR THE CUSTARD
300ml creamy milk (preferably
   Jersey or Guernsey)
1 vanilla pod, split lengthways
3 large free-range egg yolks,
   at room temperature
2 tablespoons caster sugar,
   plus extra for sprinkling

1 baking dish; 6 heatproof tumblers

1 Preheat the oven to 190°C/375°F/gas 5. Put the port, orange juice, sugar and star anise into a small pan and heat gently to dissolve the sugar. Simmer for 3 minutes, then remove from the heat and set aside while preparing the fruit.

2 Cut the plums in half and remove the stones; cut large fruit into quarters. Spread in the baking dish. Discard the star anise and pour the port mixture over the fruit. Bake for 20–25 minutes until the plums are soft but not falling apart. Remove from the oven and leave to cool until warm (or allow to cool completely).

Here is a delicious confection of juicy plums, crunchy amaretti and custard layered in tumblers, to make when you want some posh comfort food.

3 Meanwhile, make the custard. Put the milk into a medium pan, preferably non-stick. With the tip of a small knife, scrape a few of the seeds from the vanilla pod into the milk, then add the pod too. Bring the milk just to the boil, then remove from the heat, cover and leave to infuse for 15 minutes.

4 Put the yolks and sugar into a heatproof bowl and beat well with a wooden spoon for a minute until smooth and light in colour. Remove the vanilla pod from the milk, then pour the hot milk onto the yolks in a thin steady stream, stirring constantly. Tip the mixture back into the pan and stir constantly over medium heat until the custard thickens just enough to coat the back of the wooden spoon. Don't let the mixture come anywhere near boiling or the eggs will scramble. Pour the custard into a jug, sprinkle a little extra sugar onto the surface to prevent a skin from forming and keep warm.

5 Lightly break up the amaretti so there's a mixture of large fragments and smaller crumbs. Divide half the amaretti among the tumblers and add half the plums. Repeat the layers. Divide the custard among the tumblers, then finish with a sprinkling of toasted flaked almonds and serve.

Mary's Toffee Apple & Pecan Pudding

SERVES 6

FOR THE TOFFEE SAUCE
300ml double cream
75g butter, softened
100g light brown muscovado sugar
1 teaspoon vanilla extract
75g pecan nuts, roughly chopped

FOR THE SPONGE
125g butter, softened
125g light brown muscovado sugar
2 large free-range eggs, beaten
125g self-raising flour
250g Bramley apples, peeled and diced

1 x 1 litre pudding basin, well buttered,
    a jam jar lid, a large saucepan

A good recipe to have at hand, at any time of year, this is a quickly made, light baked sponge pudding. What makes it special is how you use the toffee pecan sauce!

1 To make the toffee sauce, measure all the ingredients, except the nuts, into a saucepan. Stir over the heat until melted, then boil for 2 minutes. Set aside to cool.

2 To make the sponge, measure the butter and sugar into a bowl and beat with a hand-held electric mixer until pale and fluffy. Add half of the beaten eggs and beat well, then add the remaining eggs plus a heaped tablespoon of flour. Beat until smooth. Using a metal spoon, fold in the remaining flour until combined. Fold in the apples.

3 Spoon half the toffee sauce into the pudding basin and scatter over half the pecans, then leave to cool. Spoon the apple sponge into the basin and level the surface. Cut a disc of baking paper to neatly fit the top of the sponge. Cut a square of foil to make a lid for the basin, butter it and fold a pleat along the centre. Top the sponge with the baking paper circle and cover the top of the basin with the foil lid and fold under the edges to seal. Cut a 21cm wide strip of foil (it needs to be long enough to hang over the edges of the saucepan when the pudding is in position, see step 4). Folded the strip 3 times to create a 7cm-wide strip of foil and position a jam jar lid in the centre. Set the basin on the jam jar lid.

4 Put the foil, jam jar lid and pudding basin into a large saucepan, so that the foil ends hang over the edge of the saucepan. Pour boiling water into the saucepan so that it reaches half way up the sides of the basin. Cover the saucepan and bring to the boil. Reduce the heat to a simmer and leave to cook for 2 ½ hours or until the sponge is golden, risen and springy to touch (lift the foil and baking paper lid to check this).

5 Remove the foil lid and baking paper. Loosen the sides of the pudding from the basin and invert it onto a serving plate with a lip. Heat the remaining toffee sauce in a pan. Spoon a little over the sponge and serve the rest alongside.

The Basics

CONVERSION TABLES

Weight

Metric	Imperial		Metric	Imperial		Metric	Imperial		Metric	Imperial
25g	1oz		200g	7oz		425g	15oz		800g	1lb 12oz
50g	2oz		225g	8oz		450g	1lb		850g	1lb 14oz
75g	2½oz		250g	9oz		500g	1lb 2oz		900g	2lb
85g	3oz		280g	10oz		550g	1lb 4oz		950g	2lb 2oz
100g	4oz		300g	11oz		600g	1lb 5oz		1kg	2lb 4oz
125g	4½oz		350g	12oz		650g	1lb 7oz			
140g	5oz		375g	13oz		700g	1lb 9oz			
175g	6oz		400g	14oz		750g	1lb 10oz			

Volume

Metric	Imperial		Metric	Imperial		Metric	Imperial		Metric	Imperial
30ml	1fl oz		150ml	½ pint		300ml	½ pint		500ml	18fl oz
50ml	2fl oz		175ml	6fl oz		350ml	12fl oz		600ml	1 pint
75ml	2½fl oz		200ml	7fl oz		400ml	14fl oz		700ml	1 ¼ pints
100ml	3½fl oz		225ml	8fl oz		425ml	¾ pint		850ml	1 ½ pints
125ml	4fl oz		250ml	9fl oz		450ml	16fl oz		1 litre	1 ¾ pints

Linear

Metric	Imperial		Metric	Imperial		Metric	Imperial		Metric	Imperial
2.5cm	1 in		7.5cm	3 in		13cm	5 in		20cm	8 in
3cm	1¼ in		8cm	3¼ in		14cm	5½ in		22cm	8½ in
4cm	1½ in		9cm	3½ in		15cm	6 in		23cm	9 in
5cm	2 in		9.5cm	3¾ in		16cm	6¼ in		24cm	9½ in
5.5cm	2¼ in		10cm	4 in		17cm	6½ in		25cm	10 in
6cm	2½ in		11cm	4¼ in		18cm	7in			
7cm	2¾ in		12cm	4½ in		19cm	7½ in			

Spoon Measures

Metric	Imperial
5ml	1tsp
10ml	2tsp
15ml	1tbsp
30ml	2tbsp
45ml	3tbsp
60ml	4tbsp
75ml	5tbsp

COOK'S NOTES

For fan-assisted ovens, set the temperature 20°C lower than stated in the recipes.

All teaspoons and tablespoons are level unless otherwise stated.

Some recipes contain raw or partially cooked eggs. Pregnant women, the elderly, babies and toddlers and people who are unwell should avoid these recipes.

Accuracy is essential when baking. Weigh all ingredients, use accurate scales and a kitchen timer and the correct equipment. Oven temperatures vary so practice makes perfect. An oven thermometer is useful.

ICINGS & FILLINGS

Butter Icing

A simple but useful icing for filling and topping cupcakes and sponges.
Makes enough to decorate 24 fairy cakes or 12 larger cupcakes, or to fill and top a 20cm sponge cake
125g unsalted butter, softened
400g icing sugar
3–4 tablespoons milk
To flavour
1 teaspoon vanilla extract OR 3 tablespoons cocoa powder

Put the soft butter into a mixing bowl and beat with a wooden spoon or an electric mixer until paler in colour and very creamy. Sift the icing sugar into the bowl. Add the milk and the vanilla or cocoa powder, depending on whether you want a vanilla or chocolate icing. Beat (on low speed if using an electric mixer) until very smooth and thick.

Buttercream

This is richer, lighter and creamier than simple Butter Icing, but slightly trickier to make. For the best results use a sugar thermometer.
Makes enough to decorate 24 fairy cakes or 12 larger cupcakes, or to fill and top a 20cm sponge cake
85g caster sugar
2 large free-range egg yolks
150g unsalted butter, very soft but not runny
To flavour
1 teaspoon vanilla extract OR 75g dark chocolate (70% cocoa solids), melted (see page 308) and cooled

1 Put the sugar and 4 tablespoons water into a small heavy-based pan and heat gently, without boiling, until the sugar dissolves. Bring to the boil and boil until the temperature reaches 110°C/225°F on a sugar thermometer. This will take about 5 minutes. Don't let the syrup start to caramelize.
2 Meanwhile, put the egg yolks into a heatproof bowl and mix briefly. Stand the bowl on a damp cloth to keep it from slipping. Pour the hot sugar syrup into the bowl in a thin, steady stream, whisking constantly with an electric mixer. Keep whisking until the mixture becomes very thick and mousse-like, pale in colour and completely cold.
3 Gradually whisk in the soft butter followed by the vanilla or chocolate. Spoon or pipe the buttercream onto the cakes. In warm weather, chill the decorated cakes just until the icing is firm.

Chantilly Cream

This sweetened whipped cream can be piped as a decoration or filling or served piled in a bowl. For the best results chill both your mixing bowl and whisk beforehand.
Makes about 350g
250ml whipping cream, very well chilled
2 tablespoons icing sugar, sifted
1 teaspoon vanilla extract

Whip the cream with the sugar and vanilla until just stiff enough to hold a peak. Use immediately or cover tightly and chill for up to an hour.

Crème Pâtissière

Also known as pastry cream, this thick and rich sweet vanilla egg custard mixture is used to fill all manner of desserts and pastries. Cornflour prevents the cooked egg mixture from separating and gives a velvety-smooth finish, and whipped cream adds lightness. Flavour is added with vanilla extract, but you could substitute finely grated lemon or orange zest and/or a dash of fruit liqueur, or replace some of the milk with strong coffee to taste.
Makes about 500ml
250ml creamy milk
1 vanilla pod, split open OR finely grated zest of 1 medium unwaxed orange or lemon and/or 1 teaspoon liqueur (or to taste)
3 large free-range egg yolks, at room temperature
50g caster sugar
1 ½ tablespoons cornflour
150ml double or whipping cream, well chilled

1 Heat the milk with the split vanilla pod, or the zest, in a medium pan. Remove from the heat and leave to infuse for 10 minutes. If using a vanilla pod remove it and use the tip of a knife to scrape a few seeds out of the pod back into the milk (the pod can be rinsed, dried and used again or used to make vanilla sugar).

2 Set a heatproof bowl on a damp cloth (to stop it wobbling), add the egg yolks, sugar and cornflour and whisk for a couple of minutes until smooth, light and thick. Whisk in the hot milk, then tip the whole lot back into the pan. Set over medium heat and whisk constantly until the mixture boils and thickens to make a smooth custard – take care the mixture doesn't scorch on the base of the pan. Transfer to a clean bowl and press a piece of clingfilm or dampened greaseproof paper onto the surface to prevent a skin from forming. Cool, then chill thoroughly.

3 Whip the cream until it holds a soft peak. Stir the custard until smooth and stir in the liqueur, if using. Fold in the whipped cream. Use the crème pâtissière immediately or cover tightly and keep chilled for up to 4 hours.

Ganache

A rich, smooth chocolate and cream mixture, ganache is used for making truffles as well as fillings and coverings for cakes and pastries. White chocolate ganache doesn't firm up as well as dark chocolate, so if you need a white ganache that sets well replace a small quantity of the cream with butter (use 80ml whipping cream with 20g unsalted butter).
Makes 200g
100g dark chocolate (70% cocoa solids) OR
    good-quality white chocolate
100ml whipping cream

1 Finely chop the chocolate into even-sized pieces and put into a heatproof bowl. Heat the cream (or cream and butter if using white chocolate) until hot but not boiling, then pour in a slow, steady stream over the chopped chocolate. Leave to stand for a couple of minutes, then stir gently until melted and smooth and glossy.

2 Leave to cool and thicken slightly, then stir gently – don't overbeat or the mixture will separate. To cover a cake, you can pour the still liquid ganache over it. To use as a spread or filling or if piping,

leave the ganache to thicken until firm enough to hold its shape. You can add powdered praline at this point. If the ganache gets too firm, it can be gently warmed in a bowl set over a pan of warm water; do not overheat or the mixture will seize up.

Glacé Icing

100g icing sugar
about 2 ½ teaspoons orange juice or water

Sift the icing sugar into a bowl and stir in enough juice to make a smooth, thick icing that can be piped. For a runny icing work in more liquid a few drops at a time. The icing can be coloured.
NOTE
For larger quantities, increase the sugar and liquid proportionally: for 150g sugar use about 3 ¾ teaspoons liquid; for 200g sugar use about 5 teaspoons liquid; for 250g sugar use about 6 ¼ teaspoons (or 2 tablespoons) liquid.

Lemon Curd

Useful for filling cakes and pastries, as well as for flavouring the Marbled Lemon Squares on page 99.
Makes about 560g
125g unsalted butter, diced
225g caster sugar
finely grated zest and juice of 3 medium
    unwaxed lemons
3 large free-range eggs, at room temperature, beaten

1 Put the butter, sugar and lemon zest and juice into a heatproof bowl. Set over a pan of just simmering water (don't let the base of the bowl touch the water) and stir gently with a wooden spoon until the mixture is completely melted and smooth.

2 Remove the bowl from the pan and strain the eggs into the mixture. Stir well, then set the bowl over the pan of simmering water again and stir constantly until the mixture becomes thick and opaque. Take your time – don't be tempted to turn up the heat because the eggs will scramble if the mixture gets anywhere near boiling. The lemon curd is ready when you can draw a finger through the mixture on the wooden spoon and make a clear path.

3 Immediately lift the bowl from the pan and transfer the lemon curd into a clean bowl or screw-topped jar. When cold, cover tightly and chill. The lemon curd can be kept in the fridge for up to 2 weeks.

Royal Icing

This bright white icing, made from icing sugar and egg whites, is used to cover celebration cakes and for decoration. It can be piped or used for 'flooding' and run-outs as well as spreading. When using to cover a cake mix in ½ teaspoon glycerine: the icing will set firm but not rock-hard.

Makes enough to cover a 20.5cm round deep cake
2–3 large, very fresh free-range egg whites,
    at room temperature
few drops of lemon juice
½ teaspoon glycerine (optional – see above)
500–600g icing sugar, sifted

1 Put 2 of the egg whites, the lemon juice and glycerine, if using, in a large bowl and beat with a wooden spoon until thoroughly combined. Gradually beat in the icing sugar to make an icing that is completely smooth. For coating and piping the icing should be fairly thick and leave a solid trail. Icing for run-outs and flooding should be slightly softer, so beat in the extra egg white a tablespoon at a time until you have a consistency that is pourable but still thick enough to coat the back of the spoon. (The icing must be free of air bubbles, which could ruin the final appearance. If your icing does have a lot of bubbles simply press a piece of clingfilm onto the surface and leave at room temperature overnight.)
2 Use immediately, or press clingfilm onto the surface of the icing, tightly cover the bowl and keep in the fridge for up to week.
3 Royal Icing can be coloured or tinted using edible food colouring, which is available in many colours and even shimmery tones. Add a tiny amount of colouring using a cocktail stick and mix in well before adding more – some colours darken as they set. If you are trying to match a colour scheme, always do a trial on a small cake or biscuit first.
NOTE
If you are avoiding eating raw eggs you can make the icing using ready-made Royal Icing sugar.

SAUCES

Beurre Blanc

Here's a quickly made buttery sauce to serve with a savoury strudel or with steamed vegetables. A tablespoon of finely chopped fresh herbs stirred in just before serving makes it extra nice.
Serves 6
40g shallots, finely chopped
2 tablespoons white wine vinegar
2 tablespoons dry white wine
200g unsalted butter, chilled and diced
squeeze of lemon juice
salt and pepper
1 tablespoon chopped fresh herbs (optional)

Put the shallots, vinegar and white wine in a small heavy pan and simmer to reduce to 1 tablespoon of liquid. Whisk in 2 tablespoons cold water, then gradually whisk in the butter, moving the pan on and off the heat until the sauce becomes thick and creamy (the sauce must not get too hot or the butter will melt and separate). Season to taste with lemon juice, salt and pepper. Stir in the herbs, if using, and serve immediately.

Bitter Chocolate Sauce

Serves 6
100g dark chocolate (70% cocoa solids),
    broken or chopped up
1 tablespoon instant coffee powder or granules,
    dissolved in 100ml boiling water
1 tablespoon caster sugar, or to taste

Put the chocolate in a small heavy-based pan and add the coffee liquid and sugar. Warm gently over the lowest possible heat, stirring frequently, until smooth and melted. Taste – the sauce should be bittersweet or it won't contrast with the sweetness of meringues or other dessert, but add more sugar if you prefer. Keep warm until ready to serve.

Black Cherry Sauce

Serves 6

1 x 390g jar black cherries in light syrup with kirsch
  (250g drained weight)
2 teaspoons cornflour

Tip the contents of the jar into a small pan. Remove 2 tablespoons of the juice to a small heatproof bowl and mix to a smooth paste with the cornflour. Heat the cherries and the rest of the juice until almost boiling, then add a little of the hot juice to the cornflour mix, stirring well. Pour into the pan and stir until the mixture boils and thickens. Serve warm.

DECORATIONS

Chocolate

Melting chocolate

Chop or break up the chocolate into even-sized pieces that will melt at the same rate. Put it into a heatproof bowl and set over a pan of steaming hot but not boiling water – don't let the base of the bowl touch the water. As the chocolate starts to soften, stir it gently so it melts evenly. It is ready to use as melted chocolate as soon as it is liquid and smooth, around 30°C/86°F – if the chocolate overheats and reaches 50°C/122°F it will seize up and become grainy and hard. It will then be unusable.

White chocolate melts at a lower temperature than dark chocolate and easily seizes up into a solid mass if it gets too hot. It also keeps its shape even when the middle of each chunk has melted, so remove the bowl from the hot water just before the chocolate looks totally softened.

Tempering chocolate

Tempering – melting and then cooling to specific temperatures – makes chocolate shiny and very smooth and even. Use tempered chocolate when you want a professional finish for a covering or coating, an icing or decoration, or chocolate curls. It's hard to temper a small quantity of chocolate – 250g is about the minimum, and any leftover chocolate can be reset in small containers for another time (just heat gently to melt). Use good-quality dark chocolate with around 70 per cent cocoa solids. You will need a digital sugar thermometer.

First melt the chocolate (see above). To temper it, slightly turn up the heat under the pan of water until the temperature of the chocolate reaches 45°C/113°F on the sugar thermometer, constantly stirring the chocolate so it heats evenly. As soon as the required temperature is reached, remove the bowl from the pan and quickly cool it by setting it in a larger bowl of quite cool but not icy water (take care not to let the water get into the chocolate bowl). Gently stir until the temperature falls to 27°C/80°F. Now reheat the chocolate by setting the bowl over the pan of steaming water again and stirring until the chocolate reaches 29–30°C/84–86°F. When the chocolate gets up to temperature, remove the bowl from the heat and use.

Chocolate decorations

The simplest and quickest chocolate decorations are those bought ready-made, and there is a huge variety available. Take care handling and storing chocolate decorations – obviously they melt easily and pick up finger marks.

You can be as extravagant as you like, depending on the occasion. Chocolate buttons, drops, fingers, sprinkles and shavings are great for children's cakes. Chocolate truffles will give a sophisticated touch to an adult's chocolate birthday cake. For more special occasions, cigarellos (which can be bought in a variety of colours) look very good around the sides of a deep cake.

You can buy ready-made chocolate flowers in an assortment of colours and sizes from specialist bakeware suppliers, as well as moulded chocolate shapes, including numbers and a variety of greetings.

Alternatively, you can create your own chocolate decorations with ready-made modelling chocolate (made from chocolate and glucose). It comes in a bar, which can be warmed and moulded by hand or pressed into silicone moulds to create different shapes, such as leaves, Christmas trees, teddy bears, shoes, handbags and bows. The list is endless!

For a chocolate rose, first make a small cone, about 2.5cm high and 2cm base, from modelling chocolate, then press out small balls to petal shapes and wrap them around the cone, on alternate sides, so they overlap. Gradually make larger petals – you will need a total of 9 – and curve the top edges outwards so they resemble open blooms. Use a small, sharp knife to trim off the thick cone to leave a small neat base. Set the rose (on its base) on a flat surface and leave to firm up before using as a decoration.

Home-made decorations look impressive yet they are fairly quick and easy to make, and you don't need fancy equipment. You can even make your own modelling chocolate by mixing melted chocolate with glucose to create flowers, ribbons and bows (see page 46 for the method).

Chocolate shavings and curls
Chocolate shavings and curls can be made in 2 ways. The easiest is to hold a bar of chocolate in a piece of kitchen paper and either grate (using the coarse hole side of a cheese grater) or shave (using a vegetable peeler) the chocolate onto a tray lined with baking paper. You could also set the bar of chocolate on the worktop so the flat underside of the bar is uppermost and scrape off curls with a melon-ball cutter.

For a more professional finish, use tempered chocolate. Pour it onto a clean marble slab and, working quickly before it sets, use a metal spatula to spread it out fairly thinly – about 2–3mm. Keep working the chocolate with the spatula, gathering it and spreading it out again, until it sets and looks matt and dull instead of shiny. To make curls, hold a large sharp knife at a 45-degree angle away from you and shave off the chocolate thinly into curls.

Piping, acetate and transfers
Piped decorations (as used on Mary's Fraisier; see page 52) can be made from melted dark, milk or white chocolate. Spoon the chocolate into a disposable piping bag and turn up the tip, then leave for a couple of minutes so the chocolate can firm up – you want it to hold a shape. To pipe letters or a shape, draw an outline on the underside of a sheet of baking paper, or on acetate. Set the sheet on a flat surface or baking tray. Snip the tip off the bag and pipe over the outline. Leave to set, then peel away the paper or acetate.

Alternatively, pipe free-hand patterns like stars, flowers or writing, or swirls and zig-zags. For curved shapes, drape the paper or acetate over a rolling pin while the chocolate is setting.

Melted chocolate can also be spread onto strips of acetate (or over sheets of chocolate transfers; see below) and wrapped around the sides of a cake as a finishing touch. Cut a strip of acetate (or transfer-printed acetate) as wide as the cake is high, and long enough to wrap around it. Set the strip on a very clean worktop and spread with melted chocolate (you'll need 75g for a cake about 21cm diameter), making sure the chocolate evenly covers the entire strip. Immediately lift up the strip and wrap it around the cake, then leave it to set. If the strip is slightly too big, it can be trimmed with kitchen scissors before the chocolate sets. Once the chocolate is hard, peel away the strip of acetate to leave a neat chocolate 'collar' on the cake.

Chocolate transfer sheets (transfer-printed acetate), which come in a variety of patterns and colours, give instant impact. They can be used to decorate anything that has a smooth, sticky surface that they can be pressed and transferred on to, including biscuits with a flat surface (such as Lebuchen Lollipops and gingerbread stars; see below). Transfers can be cut into small discs or strips and painted with melted chocolate, then used to decorate biscuits and cakes as well as used to make a cake 'collar' (see above).

To stick a chocolate transfer to either Lebkuchen Lollipops (see page 85) or un-iced Iced Stars (see page 78), cut the chocolate transfer to fit the flat surface of each biscuit (for the stars, use the cookie cutter as a template). Working on one biscuit at a time, use a pastry brush to spread melted chocolate over the flat surface, then press the transfer onto the melted chocolate, shiny acetate side up (be careful not to touch the transfer itself or it might smudge or melt). Very gently smooth the chocolate transfer over the melted chocolate – if you are too rough you might make a hole in the transfer. Leave to set completely before carefully peeling away the acetate. Eat within 24 hours of coating in chocolate.

For a dramatic cake topping, try making a chocolate wave: spread melted chocolate evenly onto strips of baking paper or acetate, then quickly drape the strips over 2 rolling pins, tins of food or jam jars. Leave to set before carefully peeling the chocolate off the paper or acetate. Break into large random shapes (handling the chocolate as little as possible), or keep the wave shapes whole, and set onto your cake.

Edible Flowers

The most beautiful way to decorate a special cake or dessert is with edible flowers. You need to take care, though – not all flowers are edible, of course, and you must be sure they have not been sprayed with pesticides or other nasties (don't pick from the sides of roads, for example). If you can grow your own flowers to match a colour scheme, go for these: primroses, violets, pansies, marigolds, carnations, cornflowers, nasturtiums and roses. Don't overlook flowering herbs: chives, basil, thyme and lavender plus courgette and squash blossoms.

Food Colouring

Glacé icing, royal icing, sugar paste, fondant icing, butter icing and buttercream can all be tinted to match a particular colour scheme using edible food colouring. For glacé icing, royal icing, butter icing and buttercream, liquid food colourings work well and they are easy to use, making them ideal for beginners. Add liquid food colouring a drop at a time, stirring thoroughly after each drop is added, until you achieve the right intensity of colour.

Food colouring in gel and paste form has a thicker consistency and a more concentrated colour, so will not dilute icing in the way that liquid food colouring does. This means they are better for tinting sugar paste and fondant icing. To use, add a tiny amount of colouring gel or paste – dip a cocktail stick in the pot – and knead until the sugar paste or icing is evenly coloured before adding more.

Most food colourings are gluten-free and suitable for vegetarians, but do check the labels carefully before purchasing because many might contain traces of nuts. If you are purchasing online, be aware that legislation varies in the EU and the USA, so check the origin of the food colouring and make sure it is marked as 'edible' or 'for consumption' and 'for everyday use'. Some E-numbers used in edible colourings have raised health concerns (e.g. E122 possibly causing hyperactivity in children), so be sure the colours you are using are suitable for the occasion.

Natural extracts are available, which can both flavour and colour bakes (blackcurrant and radish create red dye, carrot makes orange, etc.). We found that these natural colours faded as some of the bakes in this book cooked, but do experiment with these yourself and find the best colourings for you.

With all types of food colouring, some colours fade when exposed to bright light, so it's worth making a small test batch if you are baking for a big occasion.

Metallic Leaf, Lustre & Paint

Edible gold or silver leaf looks very dramatic against a dark chocolate background. You can buy it in tiny containers in larger supermarkets for under £5 (a little goes a long way as it's thinner even than tissue). It needs to be handled carefully because it easily disintegrates, so use the tip of a small knife to transfer small segments to the cake or dessert (it will stick better if the icing is still slightly soft or damp).

Fine gold leaf powder or lustre can be brushed onto a decoration like a chocolate leaf (see page 275) or onto a dark chocolate biscuit or cake (see Aztec Cookies on page 96) using a small, dry paintbrush. You can create gold paint by mixing a couple of drops of vodka with a similar quantity of edible gold powder and then paint this onto dried piping on biscuits or cakes using a small brush. There are pre-mixed edible metallic gold paints available to buy online.

As with edible food colouring, do check the labels carefully for allergy warnings and to ensure that metallic decorations are EU-compliant and for everyday consumption.

Shimmer Sprays & Glitters

Edible shimmer sprays, in small aerosol cans, come in many colours. They will add a misty metallic gloss to large areas of a cake – for example, a gold shimmer spray would work particularly well on Chocolate Truffle Cake (see page 32) – and you can also use them to create stencilled patterns on biscuits (such as the Iced Stars on page 78) and over smooth-iced cakes. But use shimmer sprays with care and a light hand – it's all too easy to over-do the effect!

Edible glitter (and metallic shaped sprinkles) looks wonderful scattered over biscuits, cakes, pastries and tarts and comes in an amazing array of colours. Do take care to ensure that you have bought glitter (or metallic sprinkles) that is clearly labelled 'edible' or that carries similar wording that makes it clear that it is non-toxic and suitable for consumption. American and EU rules on edible glitters vary. Some food glitters are marked 'for food contact' or 'for restricted use in food' and are intended for decoration purposes only, not for consumption, so always read the labels carefully before using. Also check that the spray/glitter is suitably for your purposes: for everyday consumption, suitable for vegetarians, is gluten-free/dairy-free and nut-free and is EU- and FSA- (Food Standards Agency) compliant.

Praline

Praline is simply caramelized nuts. Once cold it can be broken into chunks for a decoration; chopped or crushed; or ground (in a food-processor) to a fine powder and added to butter icing, buttercream, ganache, whipped cream or ice cream.

Makes 200g
100g caster sugar
100g whole blanched almonds or hazelnuts,
    or a combination

Put the sugar and nuts into a medium-sized heavy-based pan and set over fairly low heat. Stir occasionally with a metal spoon until the sugar starts to melt. When all the sugar has melted turn up the heat to medium and cook until the mixture starts to colour, then stir gently until it turns a good chestnut-brown colour. Immediately pour onto a well-oiled baking sheet and leave to cool and set. Break up into chunks and store in a screw-topped jar for up to a month.
TIP
For a stronger flavour use unblanched nuts – that is, those with their papery brown skins still on.

Sugar Paste

Ready-made sugar paste shapes and decorations are fun, usually inexpensive and come in a vast range of styles – there's something special for every occasion you could think of, and many you haven't.

Alternatively, you can make your own simple sugar paste decorations. Blocks of ready-to-roll sugar paste or fondant icing can be bought white or ready-tinted in any number of colours. Lightly dust the worktop with a little icing sugar, then roll out the sugar paste or icing about 2mm thick – you can use your usual (spotlessly clean) rolling pin or a special white cake-decorating pin. Stamp out shapes using the cutters you've chosen; the paste can also be embossed using an embossing tool. Lightly brush a little warmed apricot jam over the top of the biscuits or cakes to be decorated, then gently set the cut-out shapes in place. Save the scraps, re-roll and use for smaller decorations. You can finish by piping on top of the sugar paste shapes with royal icing. Leave to firm up and set before moving or serving.

Stencils

A simple doily makes a really beautiful stencil template for a pattern of icing sugar, cocoa powder or flour (we've used this on bread, pies and strudels in the book). You can use the same technique on iced cakes. Another idea is to use a doily with an edible shimmer spray to decorate biscuits, such as gingerbread Iced Stars (see page 78).

You can make your own stencils using thin card (a cereal packet works well) with a simple cut-out design such as a Christmas tree, a large star or several smaller stars. Draw around biscuit cutters or a traced picture, then cut out the shape or shapes with a craft knife or sharp scissors. Alternatively, use more elaborate thin plastic and card stencils, which are available from specialist cake-decorating shops and coffee suppliers (these stencils are used for making patterns on cappuccino). After use, wipe or brush the stencil carefully and store flat.

Before you use the stencil to decorate, it's worth practising first on a sheet of paper. Then make sure the surface to be decorated is firm and dry, and that there are no open windows, fans or gusts of wind. And try not to sneeze!

Set the stencil gently in place and dust over sifted icing sugar or cocoa powder, or powder lustres or shimmer spray, depending on the underneath colour – you want to make sure there's a good contrast. Cocoa powder mixed with edible gold dust looks really effective on darker surfaces.

TECHNIQUES & TIPS

To 'blind' bake a pastry case

Preheat the oven. Line the pastry case with a sheet of crumpled greaseproof paper and fill with baking beans (ceramic or dried). Bake for 12–15 minutes until the pastry is firm. Carefully remove the paper and beans, then return the tin to the oven and bake for a further 5–7 minutes until the pastry is thoroughly cooked and starting to colour. Pastry containing sugar should be watched carefully as it can burn on the edges before the base is cooked. If this happens reduce the oven temperature slightly.

Blanching pistachios

For brilliant green pistachios, blanch them before chopping: put the nuts into a small pan with enough water to cover and bring to the boil, then drain in a sieve. When cool enough to handle, slip off the papery skins. Leave to dry on kitchen paper before chopping.

To line a flan tin

Roll out the pastry on a lightly floured worktop to a circle about 7cm larger than your tin. Roll up the pastry around the rolling pin and lift it over the tin, then unroll the pastry slowly so it gently drapes over the tin. With floured fingers gently press the pastry onto the base and sides of the tin, pressing out any pockets of air. Roll the pin over the top of the tin to cut off the excess pastry (if there are any holes in the pastry case, use this excess to patch them). Use your thumbs to ease the pastry just slightly higher than the rim of the tin, to allow for shrinkage; curve your forefinger inside this new rim and gently press the pastry over your finger so it curves slightly inwards, to make it easier to unmould after baking. Prick the base well with a fork, then chill the case for 20 minutes.

Piping equipment

Piping and flooding equipment is readily available and easy to use. Trial and error will help you decide which equipment you prefer.

To pipe icing, you can use standard reusable piping bags or small disposable piping bags, either plastic or made from greaseproof paper (see below), with or without piping tubes. If you aren't using a piping tube, snip an aperture of the right size off the end of the disposable bag.

For flood work you can use piping bags, or you may find it easier to use squeezy bottles from cake-decorating shops. You can also simply spoon a very little icing onto the centre of a biscuit or other item to be flooded and gently spread it out until it fills the space (add just a drop of water to the icing if it is hard to spread).

Making a paper piping bag

Cut out a 23 x 35cm rectangle of greaseproof paper. Fold it in half diagonally and cut through the fold to give 2 pieces. Take one piece and roll the corner of one short side inwards over to the right-angled corner to make a cone with a fine point. Hold the cone tightly with one hand and wrap the other long point of the triangle around and behind the cone. Fold this point in to secure all the ends. For fine writing and icing fill the cone with about 3 tablespoons of icing, then fold the top over and snip off the tip. If you want to use a piping tube, snip off just enough of the tip so the tube fits snugly, then fill the bag with icing and fold over the top.

Filling a piping bag

Put the piping bag in a pint glass or tall mug and fold the top of the bag over the glass/mug rim (the glass/mug will support the piping bag, making it easier to fill). Spoon the icing into the bag, filling it about two-thirds full. Unfold the bag from the glass. Twist the top of the bag to push the icing down to the tube end of the bag, getting rid of any air pockets, then twist the top again to compact the icing. To test the flow speed of the icing and the shape, squeeze a little out onto a plate. Wipe the tube clean.

Home-made puff pastry

What makes puff pastry so flaky is how the butter is rolled into the flour and water dough to make literally hundreds and hundreds of layers. The lightness is the result of the water in the dough turning to steam during baking and puffing up the fragile layers.

A few tips: Stick to the chilling times between each 2 'turns' so the dough has time to relax. Don't let the butter get warm and start to ooze out of the dough, or it will be hard to handle and end up greasy and heavy. Before folding the dough use a dry pastry brush to remove excess flour – this will stop the pastry becoming dry.

It's difficult to make puff pastry in small quantities, but once the dough has had 4 'turns' it can be kept in the fridge for 4 days or frozen; complete the last 2 'turns' when you want to use the dough. If you have any pastry trimmings, stack them on top of each other to re-roll; don't knead them together as for shortcrust pastry.

Makes about 750g
300g plain flour
½ teaspoon salt
300g unsalted butter, cold but not rock-hard
1 teaspoon lemon juice
about 140ml icy water

1 Put the flour and salt into a food-processor and 'pulse' a few times just to combine and aerate the flour. Cut 50g of the butter into small pieces and add to the bowl, then process until the mixture looks like fine crumbs. Mix the lemon juice with the icy water and add through the feed tube, with the machine running, to make a ball of slightly moist dough. (Alternatively, make the dough by rubbing the butter into the flour, then stirring in the water mixture with a round-bladed knife.) Turn out onto a lightly floured worktop, shape into a ball and cut a deep cross in the top. Wrap and chill for 15 minutes.
2 Sprinkle a little flour on the remaining piece of butter, then place it between 2 sheets of clingfilm. Pound it with a rolling pin until half its original thickness. Remove the film and fold the butter in half, then cover with film and pound again. Keep doing this until the butter is pliable but still very cold. Beat it into a square with sides about 13cm.
3 Put the ball of dough on a floured worktop and roll out in 4 directions to make 4 flaps with a thick square in the centre. Set the butter square, lightly dusted with flour, in the centre and fold the flaps of dough over to enclose it. Gently press the seams with the rolling pin to seal the butter in. Turn the dough upside down and lightly press with the rolling pin to flatten it – don't squeeze out the butter.

4 Gently roll out the dough away from you into a rectangle about 54 x 18cm. Then fold the dough in 3 like a business letter: fold the bottom third up to cover the centre third, then fold the top third down to cover the other 2 layers and make a neat square. Lightly press the open edges with the rolling pin to seal. This is your first 'turn'.
5 Lift up the dough and give it a quarter turn anti-clockwise so the folded rounded edges are to the left and right. Roll out the dough away from you into a rectangle and fold it in 3 again, just as before. This is your second 'turn'.
6 Wrap and chill the dough for 15 minutes, then give it 2 more 'turns'. Wrap and chill again. Before using, give the dough 2 more 'turns' to make a total of 6.

MAKING A CELEBRATION CAKE

The Chocolate Truffle Cake on page 32 can be scaled up or down, and 2 or 3 cakes can be filled and covered with ganache to make a stacked cake (see page 34).

Round deep tin:	16cm	20cm	24cm
For the sponge			
Dark chocolate	85g	170g	260g
Unsalted butter	60g	125g	185g
Large eggs, room temp	3	6	9
Caster sugar	75g	150g	225g
Vanilla extract	½ tsp	1 tsp	1 ½ tsp
Self-raising flour	75g	150g	225g
Baking time, about	50 mins	60 mins	70 mins
For the ganache filling			
Whipping cream	50ml	100ml	150ml
Dark chocolate	50g	100g	150g
For the ganache covering			
Whipping cream	80ml	150ml	225ml
Dark chocolate	80g	150g	225g
For a firmer white chocolate ganache covering			
Whipping cream	60ml	120ml	160ml
Unsalted butter	20g	35g	65g
White chocolate	80g	150g	225g

Winter Woodland Cottage Templates

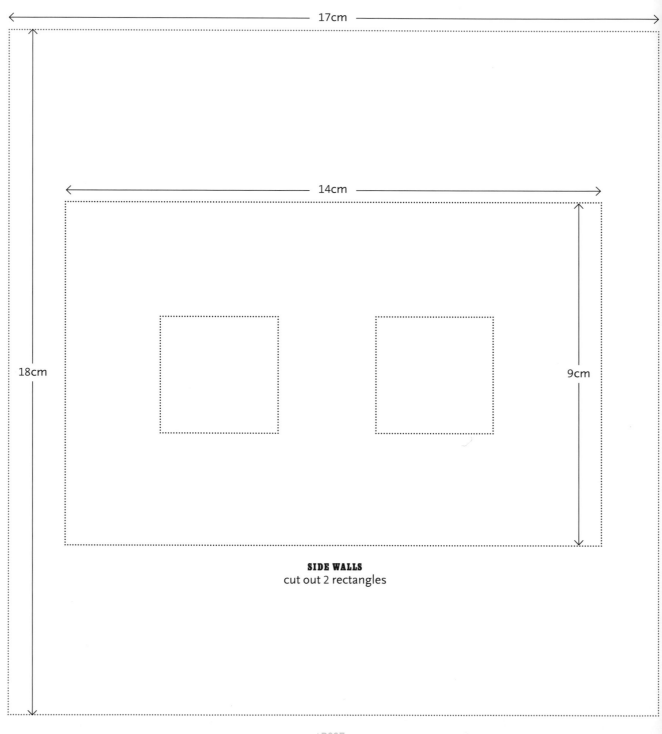

17cm

14cm

18cm

9cm

SIDE WALLS
cut out 2 rectangles

ROOF
cut out 2 rectangles

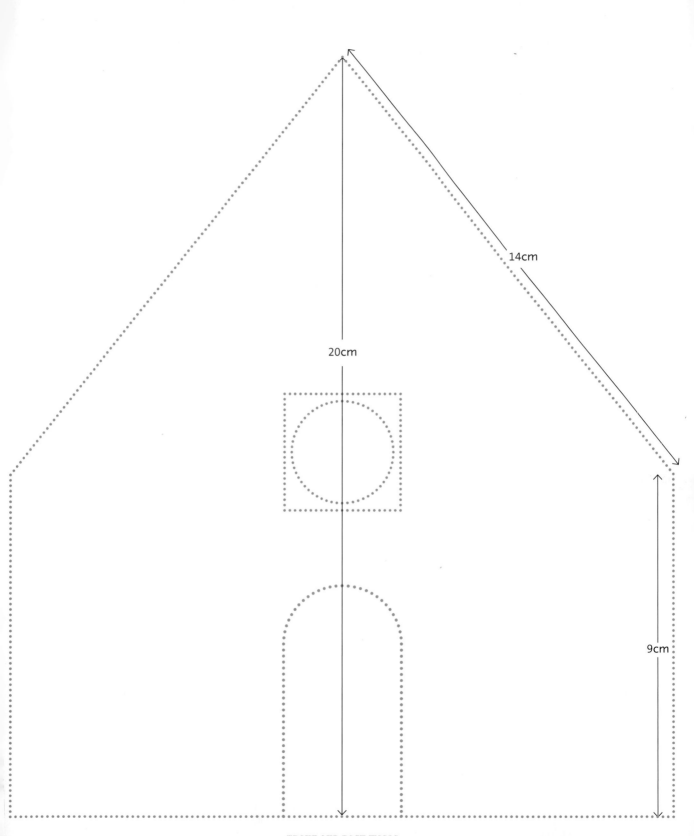

20cm

14cm

9cm

FRONT AND BACK WALLS
cut out 2 of this shape but only cut the door in 1 piece

INDEX

BBC Books and Love Productions would like to thank the following people for their invaluable contribution to this beautiful book: Linda Collister, who has tirelessly written, tested and perfected the recipes in this book; Norma MacMillan for her patient and methodical editing to ensure this book is as easy to follow as possible; Lucy Knox for her creative input; Smith & Gilmour for the stunning design; Dan Jones and Kim Morphew for beautiful photography and mouth-watering bakes, and to Polly Webb-Wilson for the thoughtfully chosen props. Thanks also to Poppy and Sophie for their help at the shoot.

Thank you to all the friendly and helpful Love Productions crew, including Letty Kavanagh, Amanda Westwood, Kieran Smith, Tallulah Radula-Scott, Flora Gooding, Samantha Beddoes, Harriet James, Eleanor Perryman, Faenia Moore and Nina Richards.

Thanks for Mary Berry and Paul Hollywood for contributing their Technical Challenge and Signature Bake recipes and to the amateur bakers of Series 3: Cathryn, Brendan, Danny, James, John, Manisha, Natasha, Peter, Ryan, Sarah-Jane, Stuart and Victoria.

Cakes, biscuits and teatime treats from your favourite show – now in your pocket!

LEARN HOW TO ACHIEVE BAKING PERFECTION

- Download the Great British Bake Off app now and get 50 amazing recipes.

- Clearly laid out recipes let you flick between introduction, ingredients and steps – plus you can create a shopping basket and share with friends at the touch of a button!

- Fully customisable search means you will always find a great recipe.

- You can also activate our revolutionary Touch-Free mode – perfect for when your hands are a little dirty in the kitchen.

- Take a photo and share your baking successes with friends via facebook, twitter or email.

Now available in the iTunes app store

Find out more at www.bakeoffbook.co.uk/app